DICTIONARY OF
KEY WORDS IN
PSYCHOLOGY

DICTIONARY OF KEY WORDS IN PSYCHOLOGY

Frank J. Bruno, Ph.D.

Routledge & Kegan Paul
London and New York

First published in 1986

First published as paperback 1987
by Routledge & Kegan Paul Ltd

11 New Fetter Lane, London EC4P 4EE

Published in the USA by

Routledge and Kegan Paul Inc.

in association with Methuen Inc.

29 West 35th Street, New York NY10001

Set in Times, 10 on 11 pt
by Inforum Ltd, Portsmouth
and printed in Great Britain
by Billing and Sons Ltd,
Worcester

Library of Congress Cataloguing in Publication Data

Bruno, Frank Joe, 1930—
    Dictionary of key words in psychology.

    Bibliography: p.
    Includes indexes.
    1. Psychology—Dictionaries.   I Title.
BF31.B78   1985   150'.321   85—2277
ISBN 0—7102—0190—7
        0—7102—1394—8 (pb)

To my parents

Contents

Preface

The other day I overheard one person say to another, 'I don't blame myself. My id made me do it.' That was all I caught of the conversation. But I couldn't help wondering: (1) What it was that the id made the person do, and (2) Was the individual using the term *id* with any degree of accuracy?

The aim of this book is to expand your psychological vocabulary. This aim needs only slight defense during a time period that has been called, among other things, 'the age of psychology', and 'the era of psychobabble.' The popular success of psychology is everywhere evident. Psychology books on all aspects of the art of living regularly make best-seller lists. The authors of these books are interviewed with frequency on talk shows. Our magazines and the feature sections of newspapers favor articles with a psychological slant. Psychology is, if not the most popular, certainly one of the most popular courses on college campuses. We use psychological terms to explain not only the behavior of others, but to explain our own behavior to ourselves. For example, when you reflect, you may find yourself musing to yourself, 'I was being too defensive in my conversation with John. I've got to stop acting that way and start being more assertive.' You may or not be aware that the term *defensive* was lifted out of Freudian psychology, and refers to Freud's concept of ego defense mechanisms. And the use of the term *assertive* was in all likelihood inspired by its recent association with assertiveness training.

Of words and concepts

The book does not seek to present an exhaustive catalog of psychological terms, but a selective list of key terms – terms that are used with very high levels of frequency. These key terms represent the foundation stones upon which psychology builds its house. They are the terms that appear over and over again in the

PREFACE

standard introductory textbooks, in the popular publications, and in conversation. If you know these key terms, and use them correctly, you will be better equipped than most people to understand and use the language of psychology.

One of the principal assumptions of this book is that a term itself is just the tip of an iceberg. The term represents a point of entry into a *concept*, a set of meanings. It is really these meanings that we want to reach for. Accordingly, each important term in the book is presented in tripartite form: (1) definition, (2) example, and (3) connections.

The *definition* sets forth the principal meaning or meanings of the word in abstract form. Each definition is brief, accurate, and to-the-point.

The *example* brings the abstract definition of the term down-to-earth, makes it real. Without examples, terms tend to float off into a nebulous and remote stratospheric realm. Each example is chosen to give the word in question as much solid dimension as possible. I try to give examples that have a ready appeal in terms of familiar experiences. The regular use of examples in the book is one of its recommendations.

The sections headed *Connections* seek to set each term within a larger framework, pointing out associations and links with other aspects of psychological thought. Such connections may include variously the story behind a word, similarities of the word with parallel concepts, the root meaning of a word, anecdotal material, or other items of relevance. The connections help to expand the meaning of the word under discussion. In the early 1930s the influential theorist Edward L. Thorndike said, 'Learning is connecting. The mind is man's connection-system.' Thorndike was known to have a very mechanistic view of the mind, and most of us aren't going to be willing to go all of the way with Thorndike. But we can go half of the way, and agree that even if connections are not all-important they are of substantial importance. It is with this observation in mind that I would assert that the *Connections* sections for each term make up one of the more valuable and unique features of the book.

Additional features

In addition to the characteristics already described, the book has these additional features:

1 *A topical index.* The topical index is arranged according to standard subjects in general psychology such as learning, motiva-

tion, perception, personality, abnormal behaviour, and therapy. Within each category, words are listed alpahbetically with corresponding page numbers. This makes it possible readily to look up sets of related words.

2   *A brief sketch of major personalities.* The basic biographical facts about those individuals who have been the makers and shakers of psychology are given. The book provides a handy reference to such people as Sigmund Freud, Ivan Pavlov, John Watson, Carl Jung, Alfred Adler, William James, Wilhelm Wundt, Carl Rogers, and others. The major theoretical viewpoint of these thinkers is identified, as is one or more of their major publications.

3   *A name index.* The name index toward the back of the book includes the major personalities as well as other people referred to in the book.

4   *A subject index.* The subject index immediately following the name index not only lists all of the key words defined in *Dictionary of Key Words in Psychology*, but also other important terms used in the *Connections* sections. This substantially expands the scope of the book.

Concluding remarks
The eighteenth-century Irish political philosopher and author Edmund Burke commented, 'A very great part of the mischiefs that vex this world arises from words.' I take Burke's statement to mean that it is the *misuse* of words that causes problems. The present work seeks to be a partial antidote to the vexation that Burke spoke of by providing a guide to the clear and accurate use of key psychological terms.

Well, I've had my say. Now it's time for the words of psychology to speak for themselves. I hope you find the book enjoyable and instructive.

Frank J. Bruno

A

ABNORMAL BEHAVIOR

Definition
Abnormal behavior is behavior that deviates significantly from a cultural norm or a group standard. When the word *abnormal* is used in a negative or pejorative sense it refers to behavior that is *maladaptive*, behavior that is self-defeating. Such behavior is usually distressing to the individual or to others.

Example
Martin is a twenty-three-year-old patient in a mental hospital. Martin's psychiatrist has made the diagnosis that Martin is suffering from a *schizophrenic disorder*, a kind of psychotic disorder (see entry) characterized by disordered thinking. Martin believes that this behavior, including his thoughts, are being controlled by aliens from the planet Saturn. He says they are planning to promote him to one of the gods of the Solar System and then sacrifice him. He refuses much of the food that is prepared in the hospital because he thinks it may be poisoned. From time to time he hears a voice that tells him, 'You are the Alpha of the universe and all beings are your enemies!'

Connections
Martin's schizophrenic disorder is just one of the many kinds of mental disorders. A whole spectrum of such disorders has been classified and described, including mental retardation, multiple personality, neurotic behavior, organic mental disorders, personality disorders, and phobic disorders (see entries).

The first question that comes to mind when we observe abnormal behavior is: *Why?* We seek explanations. Many explanations exist, some satisfactory, some unsatisfactory. Demon possession, for example, is an explanation of abnormal behavior that is unsatisfactory to most psychiatrists and clinical psychologists.

1

ABREACTION

A general explanation of much abnormal behavior is that conflicts in one's emotional life are principal causes. This is the line of explanation favored by psychoanalysis (see entry).

Another general explanation of abnormal behavior is in terms of adverse learning experiences. This is the approach favored by behaviorism (see entry).

It is also possible to look at genetic factors, biochemistry, vitamin deficiencies, food additives, and interpersonal relations in our search for explanations of abnormal behavior. It is clear that no single explanation exists. For a spectrum of disorders we need a spectrum of explanations.

ABREACTION

Definition
Abreaction is the discharge or release of emotional tension associated with a repressed idea, conflict, or memory. The term often implies the 'reliving' or vivid recall of a painful emotional experience.

Example
When Paul was three years old his father slapped him across the front of his face so hard that he gave Paul a bloody nose. When Paul cried, his father said, 'Shut up or I'll give you a black eye to go with the bloody nose!' In psychoanalysis, thirty-year-old Paul recalls the long-forgotten incident. It has been apparently blocked or repressed from conscious memory for many years. Now Paul 'relives' the incident and cries again. He even tells his therapist that his nose feels swollen. The emotional release associated with the recall of the memory (i.e. the abreaction) helps Paul to connect with a whole set of attitudes concerning his authoritarian father.

Connections
The concept of abreaction is associated primarily with psychoanalysis. The first psychoanalytic case history was the case of Anna O. conducted not by Sigmund Freud, but by Joseph Breuer. Anna had a number of repressed conflicts about her feelings toward her deceased father who she had cared for during his dying days. When Anna brought out her blocked feelings she often found temporary relief from her neurotic symptoms (e.g.

difficulty in swallowing). She herself referred to Breuer's treatment as 'chimney sweeping.'

Freud gives Breuer credit for conducting the first psychoanalysis, and the concept of abreaction played an important part in Freud's early formulations. (Incidentally, Anna O's real name is now known. It is Bertha Pappenheim, and she is famous in her own right as a founding figure of social work with unwed mothers in Germany.)

Although, as already indicated, the concept of abreaction is associated primarily with psychoanalysis, the idea of relief by emotional release is certainly not unique to psychoanalysis. It is not at all unusual to hear such common-sense advice as, 'Let yourself go. Have a good cry. You'll feel better.' This kind of advice provides an example of the possible value of an abreactive process in daily living. If there is anything that is unique about abreaction as it is thought of in psychoanalysis, it is the idea that repressed material – material that seems 'cold' and forgotten – still contains a strong emotional charge.

ACHIEVEMENT MOTIVE

Definition
The achievement motive is the motive within the person to successfully complete a task, attain a goal, or reach a given standard of excellence.

Example
Oliver, age twenty-four, is an employee of a large manufacturing corporation. He has set himself the goal of being a vice-president in charge of one sales division by the time he is thirty years old. To attain this end he is working toward a master's degree in business administration, is punctual, misses work very rarely, dresses the way the firm expects him to dress, and so forth. Even behavior outside of the day-to-day business of the firm revolves around his achievement motive. Unmarried, he seeks a wife who will 'fit in' with the organization and be approved of by his superiors.

Connections
One of the primary investigators into the nature of the achievement motive has been David McClelland. McClelland and his coworkers discovered that a high level of achievement motivation

is not the same thing as a high *need to avoid failure*. Persons with a high need to achieve tend to take *moderate* risks. They really want to achieve their objectives. On the other hand, people with a high need to avoid failure often suffer from low self-esteem. They can't stand to fail. So they will either take no risk to achieve a goal or a great risk. It is easy to understand why they take no risk. They are playing it safe. But why will they take a substantial risk? They are still playing it safe, psychologically safe. If they do not succeed, they can easily rationalize that the conditions were too difficult, that 'the System' was against them, that 'it's who you know' and so forth.

It has been pointed out that different societies exhibit varying degrees of achievement motivation among their members. For example, the middle class in the United States traditionally exhibits a high level of achievement motivation. It admires the go-getter, the ambitious person. On the other hand, the poor people of many underdeveloped countries exhibit low levels of what we are calling achievement motivation. Persons who see yawning gaps between their present status and lofty goals may give up before they start.

It appears that the achievement motive is quite complex, combining biological tendencies toward mastery with learned values.

ADLER, ALFRED
(1870–1937)

Alfred Adler occupies an important place in the history of psychotherapy. He, Sigmund Freud, and Carl Jung are often referred to as the Big Three, the principal founders of depth psychology. Adler was one of Freud's associates in the early days of psychoanalysis, but had a falling out with Freud and started his own school of psychotherapy called *individual psychology*. Individual psychology, in contrast to psychoanalysis, emphasized the importance of the conscious will and the ability of the individual to take charge of his or her own destiny.

Adler was a physician, a specialist in ophthamology before he developed a psychiatric practice. It was from his work with eye patients that Adler formulated the concept of *compensation*. He noted that some of his patients with eye problems often became avid readers, placing excessive importance on the faculty of vision.

Adler was greatly influenced by the philosopher Friedrich Nietzche's writings on the subject of the *will to power*, an inborn urge, according to Nietzche, toward mastery, competence, and superiority over others. Adler became convinced that the will to power was certainly as important as the sex drive in human affairs. The frustration of the will to power produces an *inferiority complex*, a feeling of inadequacy, that resides at the core of many neurotic disorders. This was one of the several theoretical points over which Adler and Freud disagreed. Adler felt that Freud made too much out of the sex drive. And Freud felt that Adler had inflated the importance of the will to power.

Toward the latter part of his life Adler defined a concept he called the *creative self*. The creative self is the power within each of us to take a stand against the external forces that shape our personalities. It is the ability of the person to create, to some extent, his or her own personality. Adler said, in essence, that we are not pawns of fate, that we do not need to play the role of victims in the game of life. These views on Adler's part are related to ideas found in existentialism (see entry), and make Adler a forerunner of humanistic psychology (see entry).

Two of Adler's books are *Practice and Theory of Individual Psychology* (1927) and *What Life Should Mean to You* (1932).

AFFECTIONAL DRIVE

Definition
The affectional drive is thought of as an inborn tendency in one organism to desire contact, either on a physical or emotional basis, with another organism.

Example
Robby is a nine-month-old infant. He smiles when his parents enter the bedroom, making eye contact. He holds out his arms, indicating he would like to be picked up. He appears to enjoy being bounced, hugged and rocked by his mother and father. When he is alone too long he cries for his parents and they say, 'He just wants attention.' These behaviors on Robby's part are all possible manifestations of the affectional drive.

Connections
Harry Harlow made extensive investigations into the nature of the affectional drive. He placed rhesus monkeys in social isolation

at birth. Subsequently these monkeys were given the opportunity to spend time on *mother surrogates*, dummies resembling monkey mothers. Say that monkey 22 was consistently fed by a milk bottle attached to a mother surrogate with a wire body. A second mother surrogate in the same cage gives no milk, but it is covered with sponge rubber and terrycloth, giving contact comfort when it is hugged.

Say that a fearful stimulus is introduced into the monkey's cage. It is a little toy soldier beating on a drum, and the infant has never seen it before. Monkey 22 lets out a shriek and it runs to one of its 'mothers.' Which one will it run to? One hypothesis is that it will run to the wire mother because it 'loves' the wire mother out of association with being fed. A second hypothesis is that the affectional drive is independent of the hunger drive and the infant will run to the mother surrogate giving the most contact comfort. Monkey 22, like most similar subjects, in fact runs to the terrycloth mother, suggesting the independent status of the affectional drive.

The existence of the affectional drive has been demonstrated to a convincing degree in monkeys. And most people would say that common sense suggests it also exists in infants and young children. But what about adults? Do we too have an active affectional drive? It seems quite likely that we do. It sometimes takes less obvious form in adults than it does in infants and children. More than one psychologist has suggested that the need for recognition – the need to attain a certain status, earn degrees, enjoy applause, and so forth – are all expressions of the affectional drive.

AGGRESSIVE BEHAVIOR

Definition
Aggressive behavior takes place when one organism makes a hostile attack, physical or verbal, upon another organism or thing.

Example
A husband and wife are bickering, exchanging insults. They are indulging in name calling. He is saying things such as, 'You bitch!' And she is saying things such as, 'You jerk!' Both of them are displaying verbal aggression. As the argument escalates, he

loses his temper and slaps her hard across the face. He has now displayed physical aggression.

Connections
Aggressive behavior is so common that it is easy to infer that there is an inborn behavioral tendency to exhibit aggressive behavior, that it is one of the biological drives. Variations of this view have been expressed by researchers of animal behavior such as Konrad Lorenz. Freud also believed that aggressive behavior has a strong inborn basis and postulated a *death instinct*, a primitive urge toward destruction of others as well as self-destruction.

More optimistic thinkers indicate that aggressive behavior is not completely inborn, although it may be the result of an inborn mechanism. The *frustration-aggression* hypothesis advanced by Neal Miller and John Dollard suggests that when an organism is blocked in attaining a goal this frustration invokes a natural aggressive response. The link between frustration and aggression is such that finding ways to reduce the level of frustration in a person's life should have the effect of reducing the amount of aggression expressed.

Even more optimistic is the view of aggressive behavior expressed by B. F. Skinner. He asserts that aggressive behavior is maintained by its *reinforcers* (see entry) or behavioral payoffs. Skinner expresses the hope that we can engineer a world in which human beings get very little out of being aggressive. He suggests that a person will be aggressive primarily because of what he or she gets out of it.

Another way of looking at aggressive behavior is to explain it in terms of *observational learning*, learning by watching a model display behavior. Children who have aggressive parents or siblings are likely to copy some of their behavior. The research of Albert Bandura and his associates suggests that watching models display aggressive acts on television may in some cases induce the observer to imitate the viewed behavior. This seems to be truer of pre-schoolers and emotionally disturbed individuals than it does of emotionally mature adults.

AMBIGUOUS STIMULUS

Definition
An ambiguous stimulus is one that can be perceived in two or

AMBIGUOUS STIMULUS

more ways. Its meaning is vague or uncertain.

Example
You and a companion are looking at an oddly shaped cloud. You venture the opinion that the cloud looks very much like an elephant. Your companion disagrees, asserting that the cloud looks very much like a battleship. The cloud itself is an ambiguous stimulus because it is open to a number of perceived organizations.

Connections
Ambiguous stimuli have been used in many contexts in psychology. For example, the famous Rorschach or inkblot test uses ambiguous stimuli (see entry). Another example is provided by research in social psychology. There is an effect known as the *autokinetic effect*. A stationary pinpoint of light is displayed in a very dark room. Because of the spontaneous movement of the eyeballs the light itself will be perceived to move. If a subject is told the light is moving, it will be interpreted as real motion. Because there is no actual motion, and because the motion of the eyeballs is random, the perceived motion of the light is ambiguous. Say that you are the subject in the room, and a friend is brought in. Little do you suspect that the friend has been instructed by an experimenter to engage in deception. The friend is to say that he or she sees the light moving counterclockwise in a circle with a one foot diameter. This suggestion from your friend will exert a great influence on your perception. You too will 'see' the motion described. The significance of a finding such as this is that many situations in life are ambiguous. We are not sure how to act when we are new on a job, when we are at a party with an unfamiliar group of people, and so forth. In such ambiguous situations we take our cues from the opinions and actions of others, and may develop our attitude toward the situation largely on this basis.

An idea that has been advanced is that people are *intolerant of ambiguity*, meaning it frustrates them and makes them anxious. Thus we seek ways to resolve ambiguity, to structure a stimulus and give it meaning.

AMBIVALENCE

Definition
Ambivalence refers to a motivational conflict such that one is simultaneously attracted to and repelled by the same goal.

Example
In the novel *Anna Karenina* by Leo Tolstoy, Anna, a married woman, finds herself attracted to the handsome bachelor Count Vronsky. Being married, she feels guilty about her attraction and struggles against the process of falling in love. Although she is strongly motivated to seek out the Count, she at the same time is 'repelled' by him in the sense that a sexual affair will spell disaster in her personal life. While she is going through the attraction-repulsion phase of her struggle she is in a state of ambivalence. (If you are familiar with the novel, you know she overcomes her ambivalence and eventually has an affair with Count Vronsky. And the novel has a tragic ending.)

Connections
A term sometimes used to characterize ambivalence is *approach-avoidance* conflict. Approach-avoidance conflicts were studied in some detail by Kurt Lewin, both a social and a Gestalt psychologist. Lewin proposed that each of us lives in a *psychological world*, a personal world created by our own thoughts and feelings. This world is a kind of inner landscape or territory in which we move about. Within this inner space there are goals and *valences*, directional trends of a plus or minus variety. These valences are caused by our own motives and desires. (For example, it is Anna herself who creates the conflict that ends in tragedy. The conflict has no 'real' or objective status.) Looking at the word *valence* as Lewin used it helps us to see its meaning in the word *ambivalence*. A person who is ambivalent is affected by two valences.

Ambivalence is a common problem for human beings. Sometimes the problem is rather trivial. You can't decide if a greeting card is quite right or not. There are things about it you like and there are things you don't like. Sometimes the problem is significant. You can't decide on a vocation. A particular one appeals to you, but you also see its drawbacks.

Recently the term *decideophobia* was coined to describe the behavior of persons who suffer from an inability to make choices, who suffer from chronic ambivalence.

AMNESIA

Definition
The basic meaning of amnesia is simply loss of memory. The use of the word by a clinical psychologist or a psychiatrist usually implies a pathological loss of memory involving a fairly extensive area of experience. The causes of amnesia can be emotional, organic, or a combination of both.

Example
Psychogenic amnesia, amnesia due to emotional causes, has formed the basis for many novels and melodramas. Albert has a furious argument with his wife and comes close to murdering her one night in a fit of rage. Horrified at himself, he runs out of his house. The next day he finds himself wandering in the city with no recollection of the argument, who he is (he does not have his wallet or identification on his person), or why he is where he is. As time passes, he recalls that he is an auto mechanic, and gains employment. Interestingly enough, he has not forgotten how to do his work, suggesting that the amnesia is selective – he is blocking out his identity because it is emotionally painful. As far-fetched as Albert's case appears to be, psychogenic amnesia of the type described does in fact take place.

Connections
The kind of amnesia described in the example, psychogenic amnesia, should be contrasted with *organic amnesia*, amnesia due to brain damage. Brain damage itself can have more than one cause. A severe blow to the head or a stroke are common causes. Somewhat less obvious is brain damage due to *Alzheimer's disease*, a disease involving deterioration of the brain's neurons.

Freud wrote about *infantile amnesia*, the lack of memory most of us have for the early years of life. He contended that this kind of amnesia is due to more than simple forgetting, hypothesizing instead that it is caused by repression (see entry). We block out the early memories because of emotional conflicts associated with them. Freud's hypothesis is, of course, debatable.

ANTHROPOMORPHISM

Definition
Anthropomorphism is the tendency to assign humanlike qualities to plants, animals, or nonliving objects.

Example
Noella, a child of three, accidentally breaks the arm on one of her favorite dolls. In tears, she asks her mother, 'Does the dolly's arm hurt?' The tendency on Noella's part to project human feelings such as pain into the doll represents anthropomorphic thinking on her part.

Connections
Although anthropomorphism is often associated with an early cognitive developmental stage known as *preoperational thought* (see *cognitive development*), it would be a mistake to identify it only with the ideas of children. Adults are also prone to use anthropomorphic thinking. The famous novel *The Call of the Wild* by Jack London is essentially an exercise in anthropomorphism. The protagonist is a dog named Buck. He thinks and feels in human terms. His behavior is explained with human motives. For all practical purposes he is simply a human being in a dogskin.

Primitive people use anthropomorphism to explain many of the phenomena they encounter in their surroundings. For example, a volcano's eruption may be explained by saying that the spirit of the volcano is angry.

There is a long-standing debate in psychology as to whether or not it is appropriate to explain at least some animal behavior in anthropomorphic terms. Ivan Pavlov felt it was an error. The behavior of a dog, for example, must be explained in physiological terms without the human experimenter trying to imagine what it must be like to be a dog. On the other hand, the Gestalt psychologists, particularly Wolfgang Köhler, argued that much animal behavior can be understood in the same terms that we use to explain our own behavior. He conducted experiments designed to show that apes demonstrate learning by insight (see entry).

ANXIETY

Definition
Anxiety is a state of heightened emotional arousal containing a feeling of apprehension or dread. Like fear, the subject feels threatened. Unlike fear, the subject often perceives the source of the threat in vague or poorly defined terms.

Example
Walcott is driving his car down a country road. It is a sunny day and the weather is pleasant. Abruptly, for no apparent reason, he feels that in some strange way the day is beginning to close in on him. Very quickly he feels that something awful is about to happen, but he doesn't know what. It is as if a black cloud of danger is over the car, following him. His heart begins to pound, his chest feels tight, he begins to tremble, and he feels faint. He doesn't know if he's about to have a blowout, a collision, a heart attack, or if some other terrible event is about to occur. He has to pull over to the side of the road, and some time passes before he regains a portion of his composure.

Connections
The example given above fits into a class of anxiety labeled by Freud *neurotic anxiety*, anxiety caused by mental or emotional conflicts, not objective circumstances. Without knowing something about Walcott's personal history or life situation we can only speculate as to what triggered his anxiety attack. However, long-standing doubts about sexual desires and/or aggressive tendencies provide convenient examples of the kinds of factors sometimes linked to neurotic anxiety.

Realistic anxiety has about the same meaning as fear. In realistic anxiety the feeling that one is threatened has a clear source. Say that you have been asked to give a short speech. The anxiety you feel before you give the talk is directly linked to the possibility that your audience will be bored or laugh at you. The potential loss of self-esteem is the threat that makes you anxious.

A very interesting form of anxiety, one that merits study and understanding, is the kind of anxiety described by the Danish philosopher, Sören Kierkegaard. Kierkegaard spoke of a general anxiety about the conditions of life itself, now labeled *ontological anxiety*. Ontological anxiety is reflected in questions such as: 'Where am I going?' 'Who am I?' 'What am I to do with my life?' 'Is death the end of everything?' A certain amount of concern over such questions is part and parcel of the human condition, and neither neurotic nor abnormal.

The poet William Wordsworth described anxiety well with these lines:

My apprehensions come in crowds;
I dread the rustling of the grass;
The very shadows of the clouds
Have power to shake me as they pass . . .

APTITUDE

Definition
An aptitude is the ability to profit readily from instruction, training, or experience in a defined area of performance.

Example
The famous violinist Yehudi Menuhin began his musical studies when he was four years old. By the time he was eight years old he had developed remarkable playing ability, and was giving concerts soon after. It would, of course, be possible to say. 'He was a genius.' If the word *genius* makes you flinch and seems a bit grandiose, it would be possible to say that Menuhin displayed unusual or remarkable aptitude for playing the violin.

Connections
The root of aptitude is *apt*, which is a word in itself having such meaning as *inclined, lively*, and *quick to learn*.

We often speak of persons who are born athletes, born writers, born actors, and so forth. The use of the word 'born' suggests that aptitudes are intrinsic to a particular person, not acquired. This is a debatable point. It can be argued that high-quality nurturing in infancy and early childhood can create aptitudes in certain areas. Nonetheless, the popular way of thinking of aptitudes is in terms of inborn propensities.

Whether or not an aptitude is inborn or acquired is not as important from a practical point of view as the fact that we can conceptualize it as existing in the person at a given time. We take the person where he or she is, and are curious about what we can predict from the individual's aptitudes. As a result, various kinds of standardized aptitude tests have arisen designed to give information useful in vocational guidance. Schools, military organizations, corporations, and so forth all commonly employ aptitude tests in placement and guidance of personnel. To some this is inhuman 'brain probing.' To others it is the efficient and effective use of human beings.

AQUINAS, THOMAS
(1225–1274)

Thomas Aquinas, a Roman Catholic saint, is the author of *Summa Theologica*, or *The Sum of Theology*, a book that integrates the teachings of the philosopher Aristotle (see entry) with the doctrines of early Christianity. In part because of the *Summa Theologica* Aquinas was canonized in 1323, and became Saint Thomas Aquinas.

Although he was a philosopher and a theologian, Aquinas had a great impact on psychological ideas because of his emphasis on the importance of the doctrine of *free will*. According to Aquinas, every human being is possessed of an immortal soul, and this soul is not of the natural world. It is a sojourner in the physical world, but does not belong to the world as such. Therefore, it is *not* in fact subject to natural law, nor is it constrained by cause and effect. If this is so, our conviction that we can freely will our own behavior, that we can make real choices as human beings, is real. Assuming that free will is a reality, it is at once awful and wonderful. It is awful because a tremendous burden falls on our shoulders. We have ultimate responsibility for every action. It is wonderful because we are not robots or things. (See *will*.)

The doctrine of free will has had a great influence on existentialism and humanistic psychology (see entries).

ARCHETYPE

Definition
As formulated by Carl Jung, an archetype is an inborn image or impression held in common by all people. The archetype is said to reside in the collective unconscious mind in contrast to the personal unconscious mind, and is the equivalent of the concept of instinct in animals.

Example
Jung said that the collective unconscious mind contains numer-

ous archetypes such as the Hero, the Great Earth Mother, the Wise Old Man, the Evil One, the Trickster, the Animus (the male personality) and the Anima (the female personality), and others. Evidence in favor of the archetypes appears in the study of myths, legends, religions, dreams, fairy tales, and other narratives of humankind. The same basic archetypes or images appear over and over again even though they may differ in detail or name. Jung's logic is that the archetypes are expressions of universal psychological needs. For a specific example, let's take the archetype of the Hero. He appears in various tales as Sir Galahad, the Lone Ranger, Superman, Agent 007, Luke Skywalker, and so forth. Although he has many names, he is the same basic personality. He is good, trustworthy, helpful to females in distress, brave, and a man of action. When a human being feels victimized or trapped, the need to be rescued activates the archetype of the Hero.

Connections
Jung's concept of the archetypes of the collective unconscious is similar to the ancient doctrine of innate ideas. Plato (427–347 BC) taught that we have an inborn knowledge of the Good, the Beautiful, and the True. In various forms, the doctrine of innate ideas has often made an appearance in the history of philosophy and psychology.

A much-debated concept, the doctrine of innate ideas has also often been rejected. The philosopher John Locke (1632–1704) said that the mind at birth is a *tabula rasa* or a blank slate. It is experience that writes upon the slate and eventually fills the mind with ideas. The father of behaviorism, John B. Watson, also rejected the doctrine of innate ideas, categorically denying the existence of instincts or anything like them in human beings.

The possibility that innate factors or inborn trends (not necessarily ideas as such) may play an important part in determining the behavior of organisms has been given new vitality by the research of the sociobiologists (see entry).

ARISTOTLE
(384–322 BC)

Aristotle worked and lived in ancient Greece, and is considered a founding father of *empiricism*, the point of view that all knowledge is derived from sensory impressions (see entry). One of his claims to fame is that he was a tutor of Alexander the Great. Aristotle's teachings about natural science was incorporated into St Thomas Aquinas' classic work *Summa Theologica* (i.e. *The Sum of Theology*) in the thirteenth century.

Aristotle's views on psychology have been very influential, and have colored much of our thinking about human behavior down through the ages. His teachings have had a great impact on Western assumptions about learning and motivation.

Aristotle said that the mind at birth has no inborn ideas, that it is like a blank tablet. Although this view is also associated with the English philosopher John Locke (see entry), Aristotle was the forerunner. Aristotle said that ideas are acquired by the principle of *contiguity*, the fact that some ideas become associated with each other because they touch in space and time (see entry). Thus learning plays an all-important part in the mind's ability to think with ideas.

One of Aristotle's principal teachings was that we take action because of pleasure and pain. We seek objects that give us pleasure, and we avoid objects that inflict pain. This view is known as *hedonism*, and resides at the base of Freud's concept of the id (see entry). It is also implicit to a large extent in the concept of reinforcement (see entry).

ASSERTIVENESS

Definition
Assertiveness is a behavioral trait characterized by positive social behavior designed to defend a right or gain a goal.

Example
Turner orders a steak in a restaurant. He had asked that the meat be cooked medium well. When the steak arrives it is quite rare. If Turner was a passive person, he would hesitate to complain, eat the steak, and suffer in silence. If he were an aggressive person, he would call the waitress back to his table and ask, 'What kind of a restaurant is this? Why isn't this steak medium well as I asked? Doesn't your chef know anything about cooking?' Being an assertive person, Turner calls the waitress back to his table and says, 'This steak is underdone. Please take it back to the kitchen and see to it that it is cooked medium well. Thank you.'

Connections
Assertive behavior should be visualized as having a location on a continuum. At the extreme left is located passive behavior. At the extreme right is located aggressive behavior. Assertive behavior is located in the middle, and is considered the 'just right' or optimal response to a frustrating social situation.

Robert E. Alberti and Michael L. Emmons, pioneers in research on assertive behavior, argue that people who are rather consistently passive in their dealings with others will tend to feel in the long-run hurt and anxious. They realize that they are being used and abused. And this may lead to depression. To be overly inhibited in one's dealings with others is thus a tactical error.

A certain percentage of people are not only socialized, they are oversocialized. They tend to be excessively polite, agreeable, and overly concerned about the feelings of others. For such persons courses in *assertiveness training* have arisen. In an assertiveness training course the nonassertive person observes a model manifesting assertive behavior in a role-playing situation. Than the nonassertive person is encouraged to imitate the model's behavior. Usually the assertiveness training takes place in a small group setting with much reinforcement from the trainer and members of the group for small steps in the assertive direction.

ATTENTION

Definition
Attention is the capacity of the organism to respond selectively to a stimulus or small set of stimuli from a larger set of stimuli impinging on its receptor organs.

Example
Let's say that seven-year-old Steven is watching a cartoon on television. It is Saturday morning, and it is raining outside. But at this moment Steven isn't aware of the rain. His mother calls him from another room to come and hang up his clothes, and he doesn't hear her. What is going on? Steven's behavior is perfectly normal. He finds the cartoon at the moment so interesting that he is giving it most of his attention. Consequently, he has shut out other stimuli such as the sound of the rain or his mother's voice.

His mother comes into the room where Steven is watching television and says loudly, 'Steven! Didn't you hear me? I called

ATTENTION

you!' Now Steven looks up at her, and indeed says in all innocence, 'No.' If his mother is understanding, she will be aware that it is quite possible that Steven did not hear her. The fact that he hears her now demonstrates she was able to shift his attention from the cartoon to her by increasing the intensity of stimuli competing with the cartoon. In other words, she came in to the room and spoke more loudly.

Connections
Wilhelm Wundt, father of the school of psychology known as structuralism, was one of the first psychologists to study attention. As a result of his investigations, he concluded that attention has a focus and a field. It will be helpful to imagine a flashlight shining on a wall in a dark room. Whatever is illuminated at the bright center of the beam is like material at the center of attention. Things more dimly illuminated are, however, still within the field of attention. Thus when you are reading an interesting novel, the action and dialogue may be in the focus of the attention. The turning of pages and the way you fit into the chair are also in your attention, but only in its field. They are dimmer than your awareness of the story line.

William James made a distinction between voluntary and involuntary attention. Voluntary attention is willed. That is, you decide to pay attention to something. You may say to yourself, 'I must pay attention to this textbook.' And then you may find your attention drifting away from the book after a few minutes. Voluntary attention can be given, but it requires effort. On the other hand, involuntary attention is freely and spontaneously given. A friend says, 'Let me tell you this new joke I heard.' And you pay attention to your friend's narrative without the slightest conscious effort. James would say this is because you have a high level of intrinsic interest in what your friend is telling you, and perhaps not much intrinsic interest in some textbooks.

One of the master principles governing involuntary attention is motivation. If you are on a long drive and you are hungry, you will notice restaurant signs. If you are thirsty, you will notice water fountains. If you feel like being amused, you will pay attention to a joke. The second master principle governing involuntary attention is change of stimulation. We automatically notice novel stimuli. The ringing of a telephone bell provides a ready example. The contrast of the bell with the silence a few moments before captures almost anyone's attention. An important point to bring out here, however, is that it is not the presence of a stimulus or the increase in the level of stimulation that is necessarily attention-getting. A sudden *decrease* in stimulation is also perceived as having momentary novelty. If the power fails, and all of the lights suddenly go off in a room, the event is almost certainly guaranteed to elicit your attention. A rather amusing version of this is the fact that if a person is sleeping in front of a television set, he or she will often wake up when someone else turns off the set. And people sleeping in a moving vehicle often wake up when the vehicle stops. So it is fairly clear that it is actually the *change* of stimulation that commands one's attention.

ATTITUDE

Definition
An attitude is a more or less stable predisposition to react in either a positive or a negative manner to given categories of persons or objects.

Example
Assume that Lance has a negative attitude toward authority figures. In college he tells friends that you cannot trust the professors to give you a fair deal. When he is in the armed forces he constantly gripes that the officers are stupid. As an employee he confides to coworkers that his immediate supervisor is a dumb dictator.

Connections
The word *attitude* is used in contexts other than psychology. And its use in another context gives us deeper insight into its meaning. In aeronautics, for example, the attitude of an airplane is its *tilt* with reference to the horizon. The airplane can have a positive or a negative tilt, suggesting that it is either ascending or descending. Of course it can also have no tilt, or attitude, suggesting it is on a level course. The concept of a tilt in aeronautics can be easily carried over to psychology. A fruitful way of looking at attitudes is to think of them as the tilt – positive, negative, or neutral – with which one approaches aspects of the world.

An attitude is usually said to have three attributes. These are cognitive, emotional, and behavioral. The *cognitive* attribute refers to the conscious beliefs that the individual has toward the object of the attitude. Lance presumably believes that authority figures are untrustworthy, stupid, dictatorial, and so forth. The *emotional* attribute refers to the pleasant or unpleasant feelings induced when the attitude is activated. We would predict that in the presence of authority figures Lance might feel angry and hostile. The *behavioral* attribute refers to actual actions taken in response to the attitude. Mark gripes to friends about bosses, supervisors, etc. He also avoids them whenever possible. He seldom gives them a friendly greeting or a smile. His behavior is to a large degree predictable from his attitude.

ATTRIBUTION

Definition
An *attribution* in social psychology refers to our tendency to perceive motives, traits, intentions, and abilities in other people based on our observations of their behavior. In other words it is a more or less automatic tendency to seek explanations for the actions of others.

Example
You are a student in a public speaking class. Anya, another student, is called upon to give an impromptu talk. She walks to the front of the room and faces the class. You notice a slight tremble in her hands, a flush on her face, and a quaver in her voice. You think, 'She's nervous.' You have made an attribution. Her nervous state is used by you to explain her behavior.

Connections
It is very important to realize that an attribution is not a fact, although it may seem to be. In the example given above it is possible that your attribution is incorrect. Say that you talk to Anya after class and comment, 'You seemed a bit nervous about giving the talk.'

Anya answers, 'I wasn't nervous at all. I have a touch of the flu, but I felt I couldn't afford to miss the class.'

It is possible based on the perceiver's personality to assign all sorts of incorrect motives to the behavior of other people. For example, a person with paranoid tendencies will see other people as untrustworthy or crooked. If such a person is accidentally short-changed by a cashier, he or she will think, 'This person wants to cheat me.' The attribution obviously has little to do with reality and a lot to do with the perceiver's fantasies.

AUTHENTIC PERSON

Definition
An authentic person is one who lives in a genuine or honest manner. The authenticity is expressed on two levels: (1) the person is unusually free of self-deception, and (2) the person avoids presenting a false front to others.

Example
Myra is a thirty-three-year-old attorney in a private legal practice. She is married and the mother of two children. People who get to know her are impressed by her easy, straight-forward manner. She seems remarkably free of pretensions and artificial mannerisms. She has a general reputation as a person who doesn't brag, who speaks the truth, and is totally unwilling to participate in any shady transactions. Her dealings with her husband and children also reflect her authenticity. She treats them as persons, with love and respect, not as things to be manipulated. When she makes a mistake she avoids making excuses or blaming others, but tends to take responsibility for the mistake.

Connections
The concept of the authentic person arises to a large extent from the philosophy of existentialism (see entry). Thinkers such as Sören Kierkegaard stressed the importance of living life in terms of one's own standards, not the standards of others. He valued the individual who was truly an individual, not excessively adapted to the group in the way that an ant is adapted to an ant colony. The father of Gestalt therapy, Frederick 'Fritz' Perls, used to speak of 'being real' or 'not being a phony.'

Freedom from self-deception is basically the same idea as avoiding defense mechanisms (see entry). The person who avoids self-deception is not prone to rationalize, project, or otherwise distort information arising from the evidence of one's senses.

Applying the concept of authenticity to human relationships, the work of the theologian Martin Buber is frequently cited. He indicated that too often our relationships are of an *I-it* variety, in which we realize that we are persons, but fail to grasp fully that the other individual is a real person too. When a relationship is authentic it can be called *I-thou*. In an I-thou relationship the subject perceives that he or she is a person to be treated with

21

respect, but that the other individual is a person too.

Shakespeare expressed the concept of authenticity well in *Hamlet*: 'To thine own self be true. And it must follow, as the night the day, thou canst not then be false to any man.'

AUTHORITARIAN PERSONALITY

Definition
A person with an authoritarian personality tends to exhibit the following traits: blind obedience to higher authority, dependence on rigid rules, the expectation of unquestioning loyalty from underlings, hostility to members of outgroups, and admiration of powerful persons.

Example
Byron is a career military officer, an army major with twelve years of service. His superiors think of him as a loyal and dependable officer, if a bit unimaginative. Men he commands perceive him as inflexible and too dependent on written regulations. He holds frequent inspections, is quick to punish infractions of any kind, holds frequent drills, and in general is seen as a very predictable martinet. Byron also exhibits his authoritarian personality at home. His wife and children take orders. He insists on having an extremely neat and orderly home. He lays down the law and expects no contradictions.

Connections
In 1950 T.W. Adorno, Else Frenkel-Brunswik, Daniel Levinson, and Nevitt Sanford wrote a book entitled *The Authoritarian Personality*. The book is considered a classic investigation into both the descriptive and explanatory aspects of the behavior of persons such as Byron. The authors suggest that authoritarianism in one's personality is a way of coping with hostility: it is possible to repress it toward superiors and vent it on those perceived as inferiors. The authors hypothesize that an authoritarian personality is most likely to develop in an individual who was overcontrolled and excessively obedient as a child.

Although it is easy to speculate that the armed forces and the police force tend to attract those with an authoritarian personality, it should be noted that any organization with a tightly defined hierarchy of rank meets some of the psychological and emotional needs of the authoritarian personality. For example, some large corporations have very well-defined status ladders and detailed books of regulations. People low on the status ladder are expected to display substantial deference to leader figures, etc: The concept of the 'organization person' is very similar to the concept of the authoritarian personality.

Authoritarian personalities enjoy neither having too much latitude in their own lives nor granting it to others.

AVOIDANCE LEARNING

Definition
Avoidance learning takes place when an organism acquires the ability to use a given cue or signal to avoid contact with a noxious stimulus.

Example
When Gary was eight years old he was bitten by a dog. He is twelve years old now and remembers how painful it was to be bitten. Recently he was walking and heard a dog barking from behind a fence. He immediately quickened his pace and crossed over to the other side of the street, putting as much distance between the dog and himself as possible.

Connections
The essence of avoidance learning is found in Mark Twain's humorous anecdote about a cat that sat on a hot stove and burned itself. Twain pointed out that the cat was thereafter fearful of hot stoves. More than that, it was also fearful of cold stoves! The stove had become a cue or signal signifying to the animal that it was in danger of being burned.

A substantial amount of research has gone into studying the acquisition and extinction (see entry) of avoidance learning. The reason for this is that in behavioral psychology avoidance is taken to be the basic model for neurotic behavior. Behavior therapists see many, if not most, phobias and anxiety disorders as strategies by which the person avoids contact with threatening situations. If the learned avoidance behavior is no longer functional, or maladaptive, it is to the person's advantage to be rid of it. However, in view of the fact that the individual tends to shun the noxious stimulus little or no extinction takes place under ordinary conditions. Desensitization therapy (see entry) is particularly useful in helping people get rid of useless fears.

B

BEHAVIOR

Definition
Behavior is anything an organism does, any of its actions.
Responses to stimuli, motor or glandular, are considered to be
kinds of behavior.

Example
You turn a page of this book.

Connections
Behavior is usually complex, seldom simple in actual situations.
In the example given above, a seemingly simple one, it should be
noted that you are reading the book, not simply turning its pages.
Reading is also behavior. The way you sit as you read, the eye
movements you make, and so forth, all represent discrete behaviors.

Even a seemingly simple action usually consists of a set of
smaller behaviors. Let's say that for an example of behavior we
give: drinking a glass of water. It is obvious that the glass must be
obtained, the faucet turned on, and a series of swallows must be
made.

Behavior is the subject matter of psychology (see entry). It is
the object of the discipline's study, and it is the source of its data.
Therefore a clear understanding of the word *behavior* is essential. The definition and example given above would seem to be
conclusive. However, of late some psychologists have suggested
that the meaning of the word *behavior* be expanded somewhat.

In the past the unadorned word *behavior* was consistently
taken to refer to *observable* behavior. It can be argued, however,
that *unobservable* or *covert* mental and emotional processes are
behavior too. In brief, one can assert that thoughts and feelings
are kinds of behavior. And a number of contemporary psychologists have taken this approach.

24

We now find psychologists in divided camps on the use of the word *behavior*. There are those who prefer to limit its meaning to observable actions. And there are those who insist on including covert events. From a practical point of view, the thing to do is to always include the adjective *covert* before the word *behavior* if one wants to speak of thoughts and feelings as kinds of behavior. Otherwise communication is muddled.

BEHAVIOR THERAPY

Definition
Behavior therapy is a treatment approach based upon conditioning principles. It makes an assault on maladaptive behavior patterns by looking on them as learned and subject to modification or extinction.

Example
Tyson, an adult in his mid-forties, suffers from emphysema, a lung condition characterized by difficulty in breathing. The condition is greatly aggravated by the fact that Tyson is a heavy smoker. His physician has told him to stop smoking several times, but Tyson has been unable to do so. The physician refers Tyson to a behavior therapist.

The behavior therapist does not take the approach that Tyson's inability to stop smoking on his own is either a failure of will power or the expression of a self-destructive tendency. Instead, he assumes that the behavior is learned and is sustained by several reinforcing factors. First, Tyson derives quite a bit of immediate gratification, a small amount of momentary pleasure, out of each cigarette he smokes. Second, smoking a cigarette makes him feel relaxed. And he is a somewhat tense and anxious person. Third, it gives him something to do with his hands when he is talking on the telephone. His vocation requires that he spend a lot of time at his desk talking on the telephone to clients.

In several discussions with Tyson, the therapist helps him find ways to cope with each of the reinforcing factors identified. First, Tyson is asked to suck on a piece of hard sugar-free candy each time he craves a cigarette. This gives him a substitute action that is also pleasurable. Second, the therapist teaches Tyson some self-relaxation techniques. Third, the therapist suggests that Tyson doodle instead of smoke when he is talking on the telephone. The practical and direct approach of the behavior therapist is designed to bring about the ultimate extinction of Tyson's cigarette smoking habit by taking away much of its reinforcing value.

Connections
It is possible to divide behavior therapy into three general kinds: assertiveness training, behavior modification, and desensitization. You will find entries in the book for both assertiveness training and desensitization. Behavior modification is included in this discussion, and is the kind of behavior therapy used by Tyson's therapist. *Behavior modification* may be defined as a therapeutic approach in which a systematic attempt is made to alter or shape learned behavior patterns by utilizing the principles of operant conditioning (see entry). A key characteristic of behavior modification is the attention paid to the importance of reinforcers.

Behavior therapy, unlike psychoanalysis, makes no assumption about an unconscious mental life. A person's maladaptive behavior is not seen as a symptom of a repressed emotional problem. Instead, the problem is seen as the behavior itself. The conviction of behavior therapists is that they can modify and extinguish undesirable habits without a lengthy exploration of childhood or months of soul-searching.

Some of the roots from which behavior therapy draws its nurture are the work of Ivan Pavlov on classical conditioning, the research of Edward L. Thorndike on trial-and-error learning, the inspirational writings of John Watson on behaviorism, and the experiments of B. F. Skinner on operant conditioning (see entries).

BEHAVIORAL GENETICS

Definition
Behavioral genetics is the study of how an organism's underlying genetic structure plays a role in determining traits, talents, or predispositions.

Example
A small percentage of males are born with an extra Y chromosome as part of their genetic structure. The Y chromosome determines that the individual's gender will be male. Thus most males have one female chromosome (X) and one male chromo-

some (Y). The conventional pattern is usually coded XY. (A female's conventional pattern is coded XX.) Males with an extra Y chromosome are coded XYY. There is evidence suggesting that individuals belonging to this group tend to be somewhat more impulsive and aggressive than males in general. If this is so, it is possible that the increased agressiveness is linked to the high levels of testosterone production association with two Y chromosomes. (Data from other studies indicate that testosterone, male hormone, production is linked to aggressiveness.)

Connections
The philosophers Aristotle and John Locke said that the mind at birth is a blank slate. John Watson, the father of behaviorism, said that infants are born without instincts, just a few reflexes. There has been a strong line of thought tending to downplay or discredit the possible importance of inborn factors in behavior. Behavioral genetics is opposed to the general direction taken by such thinkers as Aristotle, Locke, and Watson. The emphasis in behavioral genetics is not on learning or the acquisition of behavior, but on the *nature* of the organism.

There has been a rebirth of interest in the idea that intrinsic factors, such as genetics, play substantial causative roles in behavior. Old ideas such as 'madness runs in the blood' are reappearing in modern dress. Some researchers suggest that there is a predisposition in some people to develop a schizophrenic reaction given stress or emotional conflict of a certain magnitude. The key word here is *predisposition*. This predisposition is presumably inherited, part of one's genetic structure. A sophisticated position, however, does not go so far as to say that the genetic structure is the simple cause of a schizophrenic reaction. The cause is the *interaction*, or interplay, of the predisposition and, for examples, stress. However, the predisposition is like loaded dice, and it is easy for the roll of fate to go against the individual.

BEHAVIORISM

Definition
Behaviorism is the doctrine that behavior can be explained, predicted, and controlled without reference to the concept of consciousness. (This is the original meaning of behaviorism, not to be confused with neobehaviorism discussed below.)

27

Example
You are a parent and your infant is crying. Perhaps you comment to your spouse, 'I think Alice wants to eat. She hasn't had anything for three hours.' What explains Alice's crying? You have really offered two explanations. The first one refers to the infant's consciousness: she *wants* to eat. The second one refers to a stimulus situation: three hours of food deprivation. A radical behaviorist would say that stating what Alice wants explains nothing. The wanting is not the cause of anything. The wanting exists, if it exists at all, because Alice has not had anything to eat for a given time period. It makes more sense to say that she is crying because of food deprivation than it does to say that she is crying because she wants food. The concept of consciousness, and in turn a mental life, has been bypassed.

Connections
The father of behaviorism is John Watson. His book *Psychology From the Standpoint of a Behaviorist* appeared in 1919 and greatly excited many psychologists, particularly younger ones. Watson was a radical behaviorist, meaning he wanted to study only the objective and observable aspects of behavior. His approach led to what is known as *S–R psychology*, a psychology that takes as its major concepts the *stimulus* and the *response*.

There is a contemporary approach that may be called *neobehaviorism*. Neobehaviorism, like radical behaviorism, agrees that the subject matter of psychology is behavior, not the mind or consciousness. However, it asserts that *cognitions*, thought processes, are properly included in the class behavior. It is true that the thinking process can be classified as a kind of behavior, but such a classification presents the problem of *private* events versus *public* events. A thought is a private event and observable only by the subject that has the thought. Drinking a glass of water is a potentially public event in the sense that it allows observation by two or more persons. By admitting private events into the class behavior the neobehaviorists have in effect steered psychology back in a direction from which Watson sought to depart.

BINET, ALFRED
(1857–1910)

Alfred Binet's first calling was the law, and he did not begin his career in psychology until he was thirty-seven years of age.

Working in France, Binet's claim to fame is that he is the father of the modern intelligence test. His initial efforts were aimed at demonstrating that children of the slums were not mentally retarded as was commonly believed in the latter part of the nineteenth century.

Binet found that it is futile to attempt to assess intelligence by measuring physical attributes. The size of the cranium, the strength of one's grip, and so forth have little relationship to intelligence. Thus he rejected the *biometric method* advocated by Sir Francis Galton (see entry). Instead, Binet pioneered a *performance method* in which intelligence was assessed in terms of tasks requiring comprehension, arithmetical ability, vocabulary skills, and so forth.

The concept of a *mental age*, an average ability expected of an individual, particularly a child, at a given chronological age was introduced by Binet. This led eventually to the concept of *intelligence quotient* (see entry).

Binet's work inspired Lewis Terman at Stanford in the United States, giving birth to the Stanford-Binet Intelligence Scale (see entry).

BIOFEEDBACK TRAINING

Definition
Biofeedback training is a conditioning procedure by which one gains voluntary control of autonomic responses such as heart rate, brain wave patterns, blood flow in the cardiovascular system, and muscle tension.

Example
Walter, a forty-four-year-old businessman, suffers from high blood pressure. The cause of the high blood pressure in his case is said to be 'functional' – meaning that no specific organic cause can be identified. Instead of prescribing antihypertensive medication, Walter's physician, as an alternate treatment, refers Walter to a biofeedback training clinic. Walter visits the clinic twice a week for ten weeks and participates in a series of sessions in which an electronic device gives him a moment-to-moment blood pressure reading. Walter is instructed to find some internal way – through thoughts or images – to influence the blood pressure reading. At first Walter's efforts have no visible effect. But little-by-little he begins to find through an internal process of

trial-and-error that voluntary control over his blood pressure is possible.

Connections
Although biofeedback training is a relatively recent development in contemporary psychology, its roots go back to familiar psychological principles. A term in use for years has been *knowledge of results*. It is argued that without knowledge of results leaning is very difficult. For example, it would be very hard to learn how to type without a ribbon in the typewriter. You would be in the dark – not knowing whether you were hitting the right or wrong keys. A similar state has existed for years with regard to voluntary control of autonomic functions such as heart rate. Learning self-control of such functions without biofeedback equipment is like trying to learn to type without a ribbon. It can be done to a certain extent, of course. Yogis have been doing it for centuries. But the training is very long and difficult without the aid of the modern devices.

It is also possible to look upon biofeedback training as a kind of operant conditioning. The operant responses are the covert thoughts and images produced by the subject. The reinforcer is the positive display given by the biofeedback equipment. A set of positive reinforcers shapes the internal responses in such a way that desirable ones appear at a higher rate.

BIOLOGICAL DRIVES

Definition
The biological drives are a set of inborn energizers of behavior reflecting tissue needs and physiological processes.

Example
Hunger is one of the biological drives. If you have eaten recently and feel quite satisfied, you will not look for food. If you have eaten a few hours ago, you may feel moderately hungry, and start exhibiting behaviors that will bring you into eventual contact with food. If you have not eaten for a whole day, your efforts will have more energy and persistence. This illustrates that, within practical limits, a biological drive is activated by deprivation.

Connections
What is meant when it is said that a biological drive is an

energizer of behavior? The logic is that a biological drive acts for a human being in somewhat the same way that a battery acts for a mechanical toy: it makes it *move*. The biological drives make us move. They obviously exist only in a living organism. And they are often assumed to be the basic foundation stones upon which all behavior is built.

Freud's concept of the id (see entry) is very similar to the concept of biological drives. Freud included hunger, thirst, and sex in the id. In his later theorizing he added aggressiveness. This addition makes the scope of the id somewhat larger than the scope of the biological drives. Aggressive behaviour does not directly meet a tissue need or reflect a physiological process.

Although the concept of the biological drives would seem to be a simple one, it presents some challenges. Pain is usually classified as a biological drive. However, the drive does not meet a tissue need as such; its aim is tissue *protection*. Sleep too is classified as a biological drive. But it is difficult to tie it directly to tissue needs. There is no known substance in the blood – such as a hormone – that is obviously connected to sleep. The biological drives in fact escape highly precisely definition. And, although they are inborn, they are greatly affected by learning. Hunger, perhaps the most obvious of the biological drives, interacts with emotional states and cultural norms.

BODILY DIMENSION

Definition
The three bodily dimensions proposed by William H. Sheldon, a psychologist and physician, are: endomorphy, mesomorphy, and ectomorphy. *Endomorphy* predisposes an individual to have a soft, flabby body. *Mesomorphy* predisposes an individual to have a hard, muscular body. *Ectomorphy* predisposes an individual to have a slim, frail body.

Example
Prudence, three years old, is an unusually plump and placid child. Her mother says, 'She's been a butterball since she's been born.' Prudence's aunt, who has studied a little psychology, comments, 'Her soft fleshy body and good nature suggest that Prudence is a constitutional endomorph.' (This draws a baleful stare from Prudence's mother.)

Connections

Sheldon did his research with the assistance of S. S. Stevens, a noted Harvard psychometricist. The cooperative work of these two men is not to be quickly discounted. However, it should be noted that attempts to repeat Sheldon's observations have met with limited success.

Essentially, based on the measurements of the physiques of male subjects, Sheldon concluded that the human body varies on the three basic dimensions defined above. All of us exhibit all three dimensions, so it is better to think of individuals as having a profile based on a low or high score on each dimension. This profile for the individual Sheldon called the *somatotype*. (*Soma* is the Greek word for body.)

The interest of psychologists in Sheldon's work resides in his proposal that the bodily dimensions have something to do with temperament. *Viscerotonia* goes with endomorphy, and refers to a temperament that is placid and fun-loving. *Somatotonia* goes with mesomorphy, and refers to a temperament that is assertive and action-oriented. *Cerebrotonia* goes with ectomorphy, and refers to a temperament that is inhibited and reclusive. Sheldon collected data to support his proposal. Again, efforts to repeat his findings have led to only partial support for his approach.

BRAIN

Definition

The brain of a human being is a complex nervous system structure located in the skull. It is assumed to be the seat of the higher thought processes such as memory and reason.

Example

Richard, a steelworker, suffered an industrial accident that destroyed a portion of an area of his brain known as *Wernicke's center*, located in the vicinity of the auditory cortex. Formerly quite bright and effective as a person, he is now unable to understand spoken language – a deficit associated with injuries to Wernicke's center.

Connections

It took humankind quite a while to figure out the purpose of the brain. Aristotle, for example, thought that the brain existed to cool the flowing blood – a kind of bilogical radiator. He thought that the heart was the seat of consciousness. This made a kind of odd sense. Soldiers pierced through the heart in battle by a spear lose consciousness. Aristotle's keen powers of observation sometimes led him astray.

Many silly theories have been associated with the brain. During the nineteenth century, *phrenology* was a popular pseudoscience asserting that bumps on the head revealed one's intelligence and character. This was based on the notion that brain growth in certain areas would push out the skull. For example, a person with a lot of will power would logically have more brain mass in the will power region. The only trouble is that there is no specific brain region dedicated to will power.

The brain weighs about three pounds and is approximately 18 inches (45 cm) in circumference. Into this relatively small volume are packed an incredible 30 billion neurons (see entry).

BYSTANDER APATHY

Definition
Bystander apathy is a phenomenon of social behavior in which an observer shows little or no interest in helping a person in trouble.

Example
Bart is on his way to work and is going down an escalator to catch a subway train. On the crowded loading platform a man clutches at his chest, begins to gasp, and falls to the floor just as the train arrives. Bart is tempted to offer assistance to the fallen stranger, but he is late for work. There are plenty of other people available to render aid. So, with a touch of guilt, Bart boards the train and leaves the scene.

Connections
Why does the bystander apathy effect take place? It is perhaps a bit too glib to explain it by saying that people today are cold and alienated. Research conducted by social psychologists John M. Darley and Bibb Latané suggests the tendency of bystander apathy to make an appearance increases when there are many observers present. Say that twenty-five people are on the loading platform in the above example. Bart is obviously one out of twenty-five, and consequently carries only four per cent of the responsibility burden. This burden is not great enough to bring Bart to the threshold of action.

BYSTANDER APATHY

Imagine that someone seems to have been suddenly taken ill or be having a heart attack in a place with only Bart or one other observer present. Bart would feel all or one-half of the responsibility burden, and would almost certainly act to aid the stricken individual.

The value that we should avoid the tendency to bystander apathy is an ancient one. It is expressed, for example, in the centuries-old tale of the Good Samaritan who helps a stranger in distress on the road.

Connections
The single most influential theory of cognitive development is the one that was formulated by Jean Piaget (see entry), a highly influential Swiss scientist who worked for many years in France. According to Piaget, the four stages of cognitive development are: (1) Sensorimotor (0–2 years), (2) Preoperational (2–7 years), (3) Concrete operations (7–11 years), and (4) Formal operations (7–11 years).

During the *sensorimotor stage* infants exhibit a lively curiosity about the world. Their behavior is dominated by responses to stimulation. Motor habits form the foundation upon which thought will be built.

The thinking of children during the *preoperational stage* is anthropomorphic, magical, and egocentric. Mr Wind, in the example, reflects an *anthropomorphic explanation*, meaning one in which the explanation is derived from human-like qualities. Children during this stage believe that events can take place by magic, and fairy tales often have a great deal of appeal. *Egocentric thinking* is thinking in which children feel that they are at the middle of all events, that everything in the world revolves around them. Egocentric thinking makes it difficult for them to see any point of view other than their own.

During the stage of *concrete operations* the thinking of children is literal and down-to-earth. They can understand that $8 + 11 = 19$, but an abstract formulation such as an algebraic equation is beyond their grasp.

During the stage of *formal operations* the thinking of children moves toward the adult level. They become capable of highly abstract thought, can make inferences, and can even think about thinking. The highest mental abilities of human beings are associated with this stage.

COGNITIVE DISSONANCE

Definition
Cognitive dissonance takes place when two consciously held ideas are mutually antagonistic.

Example
Steven has just received his weekly paycheck. He is tempted to get into a poker game, thinking, 'I really want to play this weekend. I feel lucky.' Steven was raised by parents who taught

him that gambling is sinful. So he also thinks, 'It's a sin to gamble.' Idea 1 is, 'I want to gamble.' Ideas 2 is, 'Gambling is sinful.' Assuming that both ideas have some weight for Steven, he is in a state of cognitive dissonance.

Connections
The concept of cognitive dissonance is usually traced to the social psychologist Leon Festinger. Festinger pointed out that cognitive dissonance acts as a motivating force in human affairs: we do what we can to reduce dissonance. There is more than one way to reduce dissonance. Let's return to the example of Steven. First, Steven can alter the course of his behavior. He can avoid the poker game, making his behavior congruent with his moral training. Second, Steven can change one of the two conflicting ideas, making it match the remaining one. He can think, 'My parents were wrong. Gambling's no sin. I trust my lucky feeling.' Or he can think, 'Gambling *is* a sin. My lucky feeling is just wishful thinking.' Third, he can add a rationalizing idea. He can think, 'Gambling's not a sin when you play with good friends.'

COMPARATIVE PSYCHOLOGY

Definition
Comparative psychology is the study of the similarities and differences in the behavior exhibited by contrasting species of organisms.

Example
Harry Harlow, well-known for his research on primate behavior, deprived infant rhesus monkeys of their biological mothers and raised the infants in social isolation. The deprived animals displayed developmental deficits and behavior reminiscent of autistic children. It is an easy step to suggest that human infants deprived of high-quality social stimulation are likely to display similar kinds of developmental deficits.

Connections
It is a grand tradition in psychology to do experiments with animals and in turn to make inferences about human behavior from the results of the animal research. (The inference may not always be made by the original researcher.) Thus Pavlov's experiments with dogs have led to the general observation that

human beings are also subject to many of the phenomena of classical conditioning. B. F. Skinner's experiments with rats and pigeons present a model for human learning emphasizing the importance of reinforcement. Experiments on insight learning in apes conducted by Wolfgang Köhler, one of the founders of Gestalt psychology, suggested to him that both people and animals sometimes learn by sudden forward leaps of understanding.

The principal problem with comparative psychology is that obviously human beings have important differences from 'lower' species, and a strict comparison is not completely valid. A principal physiological difference between human beings and other organisms is that we have, in proportional terms, a larger cortex than they do. Our capacity to think, reflect, and speak often makes a substantial difference in our behavior. And this greatly limits the generalizations that can be made from animal research. This is not to say that speculative generalizations and interesting hypotheses are inappropriate. However, they should be qualified and made with caution.

COMPENSATION

Definition
Compensation is an ego defense mechanism characterized by behavior designed to counterbalance a real or imagined inadequacy.

Example
Clifton is below average in height. He is subjected to nicknames such as 'Shorty,' and 'Runt.' In order to feel taller he wears lifts in his shoes. More importantly, he becomes a very ambitious and successful executive. He thus demonstrates that he is a 'big man' too. His importance as an executive serves to ameliorate some of the feelings of low self-esteem associated with his height.

Connections
The principal formulator of the concept of compensation as we presently understand it was Alfred Adler, one of the leading figures in the early history of psychotherapy. Adler hypothesized that an *inferiority complex*, a set of related negative ideas, arises when an individual is frustrated in attaining an important personal goal. One way to reduce the emotional suffering arising from

the inferiority complex is to engage in compensating behavior. Although compensation is essentially defensive, it has its positive side. Adler said that it is the ability to turn a minus into a plus.

COMPLEX MOTIVES

Definition
Complex motives are those which are made up of two principal factors: (1) inborn drives and (2) learned drives.

Example
Sexual desire is a complex motive. Its foundation is an inborn sexual drive, a biological drive, controlled to some extent by specific hormones. In addition, the expression of sexual desire is greatly affected by learned, or acquired, drives associated with a given culture and one's particular developmental experiences. Thus the basic biological drive that we think of as the sex drive can express itself in a variety of ways. (See the entry on sexual variance.)

Connections
It is possible to draw up an imposing list of complex motives. These include achievement motivation, affiliation, autonomy, dominance, exhibition, nurturance, and aggression. The level of various complex motives in a particular individual can be assessed by a psychological test called the Thematic Apperception Test, a test pioneered by personality investigator Harry A. Murray. (See *Thematic Apperception Test*.)

The concept of the complex motives teaches us that we should not oversimplify our explanations of human behavior. It is difficult, if not impossible, to reduce the *why* of behavior to a small set of inborn drives. And we don't have to wait for adulthood to see the emergence of complex motives. By the time children are preschoolers they are already exhibiting behavior composed of a combination of inborn and learned factors. Saying that there is a set of complex motives important in determining human behavior is another way of saying that we ourselves are complex.

CONCEPT FORMATION

Definition
Concept formation is the learning process by which we create cognitive, or mental, classes.

Example
Tommy, age three, is acquiring the concept *dog*. At first he thinks of a dog as a 'thing' that has fur and a tail. He thus mistakenly confuses a cat with a dog. His parents tell him that a cat meows and a dog barks. Now Tommy thinks of a dog as a 'thing' that has fur, a tail, and barks. As he adds defining characteristics, he becomes better at discriminating dogs from other organisms. He reaches a point at which most of us would say that Tommy 'knows' what a dog is.

Connections
The kind of concept Tommy is forming in the example is called a *conjunctive concept*, one in which two or more defining attributes are joined to form the concept. Two other important kinds of concepts are disjunctive concepts and relational concepts. *Disjunctive concepts* are of the either/or variety. It is *either* a pen *or* a pencil *or* a typewriter, etc. *Relational concepts* create some sort of ranking or ordinal scaling among objects of perception. Phrases such as 'less than,' 'more than,' 'bigger than,' 'smaller than,' 'shorter than,' and 'taller than' can all be used to create relational concepts. The statement, 'John is taller than Harry' assumes a relational concept involving differing levels of height.

Pioneering research in concept formation was conducted by Jerome Bruner, long associated with Harvard University, and his coworkers Jacqueline J. Goodnow and George A. Austin. In their highly influential book *A Study of Thinking* (1956) they report many findings of interest about concept formation. Among their findings is the tendency of human beings to use *cognitive strategies*, consciously applied plans and hypotheses, to reduce the time taken to form a concept. An important point is that concept formation is an active and forward-looking process in human beings, not a passive one.

CONSCIOUSNESS

Definition
Consciousness is the awareness of both the external world and one's own existence.

Example
You are in a garden and a bird lands on the branch of a tree. Suddenly you are conscious of the bird's existence. The motion of the bird as it lands and its chirp are both events that command your attention. The processes of *attention*, your *perception* of the bird as an object in your field of vision, and your *cognition* that the bird is indeed a bird are all aspects of the general phenomenon that we call consciousness.

Connections
The concept of consciousness has had a controversial history in this century. For most of the history of philosophy and psychology the idea that we are conscious was simply taken for granted. Then in the 1910s the father of behaviorism, John Watson, proposed that the concept of consciousness is useless for psychology. It is subjective and consequently not open to the public observation of two or more independent observers, a basic requirement of the scientific method. Also, consciousness does not explain anything. To say that a person does or does not do something because he or she is using a conscious process such as thinking or decision-making begs the question of the *why* of behavior. According to Watson the *why* of behavior can always be traced back to the learning history of the organism. Therefore the concept of consciousness is just excess baggage as far as an explanation is concerned. Watson's views were highly influential and led to a substantial downgrading of the importance of consciousness as an explanatory construct in psychology.

In more recent times the pendulum has swung back from the extreme of Watson's radical behaviorism. Today there is a conviction that consciousness is important, that phenomena associated with it merit serious study.

When used in association with human beings the word *consciousness* often implies consciousness of consciousness. We are not only conscious. We are conscious that we are conscious, or self-conscious. It is often taken for granted that we possess this kind of consciousness to a much higher degree than any other organism. This point has been made, for example, by the philosopher Jean-Paul Sartre.

CONSTITUTIONAL TRAITS

Definition
Constitutional traits are behavioral tendencies that are essentially inborn.

Example
Maxine, age seven, is described by her father as a shy child. He says that even when she was an infant she displayed obvious signs indicating a reserved and withdrawn temperament. The father also asserts that his older daughter, Mildred, age ten, is a venturesome child. Even as an infant she displayed a certain quality of confidence and high social responsiveness. The father of these two girls is expressing in essence the constitutional traits hypothesis. He believes that important aspects of personality are inborn.

Connections
The status of constitutional traits is open to debate. Such famous behaviorists as John Watson and B. F. Skinner discount the importance of constitutional traits.

On the other hand, more than one prominent psychologist or researcher has argued in favor of the existence of constitutional traits. William H. Sheldon argued that behavioral traits are associated with body type (see entry on bodily dimension). Raymond B. Cattel, author of a standardized test titled *The Sixteen Personality Factor Inventory*, asserts that some traits of personality are inborn. Carl Jung introduced the introversion-extroversion dimension into psychology and hypothesized that it is largely inborn.

Folklore tends to agree with the concept of constitutional traits. Parents often speak of children that are 'just born that way.' Maxine and Mildred's father is a member of a large company.

CONTIGUITY

Definition
Contiguity exists when two objects or events touch, or are close together, in time and space. There is a tendency to associate such objects or events.

Example
A common association to the word *thunder* is the word *lightning*. This is because the hearing of thunder and the seeing of lightning are contiguous in experience.

Connections
The philosopher Aristotle (382–322 BC) is credited with formulating the principle of contiguity as a law of association. And it has become established as a basic principle of learning. The importance of contiguity can be demonstrated in many ways. When a rat is learning to press a lever to obtain a pellet of food the presentation of the food must follow very closely in time after the pressing of the lever or no learning will take place. Aristotle would have said that there must be a contiguity between the animal's action and the presence of food for the animal to associate its action with the reward (i.e. reinforcer, in conditioning terms).

CONTROL GROUP

Definition
A control group is a group of subjects used in an experiment to provide a contrast observation to the behavior of the experimental group, the primary group under study.

Example
An experimental psychologist hypothesizes that the taking of examinations with a background of soft classical music will enhance examination performance. Student subjects are randomly assigned to one of two conditions: (1) taking an examination with music playing and (2) taking an examination without music playing. The group that hears the music is designated the experimental group because it is expected that the effects of music playing will affect their performance in a positive way. The group that does not hear the music is designated the control group. Its sole function in the experiment is to provide a contrast observation, as indicated above. The control group is treated in every respect the same way as the experimental group, with the exception of the experimental manipulation.

Connections
A control group is always important in an experiment because

the changes that may occur in an experimental group must be compared with some standard or criterion. In drug research a control group is useful to provide a measure of the placebo effect (see entry). The control group will receive an inert pill every time the experimental group receives a pill containing the drug under study. The control group often shows a certain amount of improvement due to the placebo effect, and a measure of this improvement must be subtracted from the measured improvement of the experimental group in order for the results of the research to be meaningful.

CORRELATION

Definition
A correlation exists when two variables change in such a way that measures on one variable are to some degree predictable from measures on the other variable.

Example
Let a first variable be intelligence test scores. Let a second variable be grades of school-age children. Assume that we take a large sample, perhaps a thousand children. We need two measures on each child: an intelligence test score and a semester grade. The thousand sets of scores are plotted on a graph with one variable (for example, the intelligence test scores) represented on the abscissa, or horizontal line, of the graph and the second variable (for example, the semester grades) represented on the ordinate, or vertical line. A plot of the paired data points will show a definite tendency for the two variables to go together. Children with higher intelligence test scores will, on the whole, display higher grades in school than children with lower intelligence test scores. The correlation will not be perfect. Individuals will depart from the group trend. But the trend itself will be quite distinct. And it is the magnitude of this trend that represents the importance or unimportance of the correlation.

Connections
The father of the concept of correlation is Sir Francis Galton (1822–1911), a researcher very much interested in measuring human traits. One of Galton's early projects was a study in which he correlated the eminence of sons with the eminence of their fathers. He found, as might be expected, that eminence of

fathers and sons tends to go together. Eminent sons tend to have eminent fathers and vice versa. Galton took this as evidence for the importance of heredity as a determining factor in behavior. A critic of Galton's research is likely to point out that the sons of eminent fathers have more opportunities for achievement, more avenues toward success are open to them, than the sons of less highly placed fathers. Thus Galton's work on eminence sheds little light on the importance of heredity.

Galton enlisted the aid of a mathematician, Karl Pearson, to help him quantify the concept of correlation. Pearson developed a statistical test called the *correlation coefficient*, a measure of the magnitude of the relationship between two variables. You will find the correlation coefficient, and the formula for it, described in every standard introductory statistics textbook. It has many uses in research and the standardization of psychological tests. So the collaborative work of Galton and Pearson was quite fruitful.

COUNTERCONDITIONING

Definition
Counterconditioning is a process combining conditioning and extinction. It involves (1) the presentation of a conditioned stimulus capable of eliciting an unwanted response and (2) the simultaneous presentation of a stimulus capable of evoking a response antagonistic to the unwanted one.

Example
A classic case of counterconditioning was reported in the 1920s by Mary Cover Jones. Peter, age three, was afraid of white rabbits. Peter was offered crackers and milk while a white rabbit was in his presence a safe distance away. Over a period of days the white rabbit was moved closer and closer to Peter until his fear of the rabbit was extinguished. The white rabbit was the conditioned stimulus and fear was the unwanted response. Food, capable of evoking a relaxation response, was the counterconditioning stimulus.

Connections
Counterconditioning is often used in daily living. We send flowers to the sick. It is assumed that flowers make us cheerful and that this mood is antagonistic to the depression associated

with illness. Perhaps a child dislikes eating peas. Assume that the child favors melted cheese. The understanding parent may allow the child to cover the despised peas with melted cheese. This is a counterconditioning paradigm, and gradually the child may lose his or her dislike of peas.

Desensitization therapy (see entry), often used to treat anxiety disorders, utilizes the counterconditioning process. Anxiety is extinguished by evoking an antagonistic relaxation response. Although in desensitization therapy the relaxation response is evoked by verbal suggestion instead of crackers and milk, the process is at root the same as the one used to help Peter overcome his fear of the white rabbit.

CREATIVE THINKING

Definition
Creative thinking is thinking characterized by the ability to give up unnecessary assumptions and to generate original ideas.

Example
Prior to the first actual powered flight of an airplane most people assumed that a flying machine would have to flap its wings much like a bird. This was an unnecessary assumption. Pioneers such as the Wright brothers, and others, saw that the wings might remain stationary. The forward thrust might be supplied by a propellor. In view of the fact that no creature in nature flies with a stationary wing and a propellor the combination of the two into a single object constituted an original idea.

Connections
Sometimes the question is asked: What is the difference between intelligence and creativity? It is possible to answer, 'It takes intelligence to learn to fly an airplane, but it took creativity to invent one.' Intelligence (see entry) relies to a large extent on *convergent thinking*, an approach to problem-solving in which there is only one best answer. Creativity relies primarily on *divergent thinking*, thinking in which there may be several adequate answers to a problem.

Although it is correct that divergent thinking is at the core of creative thinking, high-quality creative work is a happy blend of both convergent and divergent thinking. The two kinds of thinking are not necessarily opposed. The invention of the airplane did not by any means reject all conventional wisdom about flight and the construction of lightweight frames. On the contrary, much standard knowledge was required to build the first airplane. The Gestalt psychologist Max Wertheimer coined the apt phrase *productive thinking* to describe thinking that really gets somewhere useful. Random and often chaotic divergent thinking may be crudely creative, but it is not productive.

The application of creative thinking is not limited to fields such as science and the arts. Creative thinking is useful in any arena of life.

CURIOSITY BEHAVIOR

Definition
Curiosity behavior is behavior characterized by exploratory or stimulus-seeking responses to either novel or complex stimuli.

Example
Connie, age four, is given a choice of playing with two different toys. Toy A is familiar, a toy she has played with several times. Toy B is unfamiliar and is thus perceived by Connie as a novel stimulus. If she selects toy B over toy A, we are likely to explain the choice by saying, 'She is curious about toy B.'

Connections
Curiosity behavior is common, and we are not at all surprised by Connie's behavior in the above example. So common is curiosity behavior that there is a general hypothesis in psychology that such behavior has an inborn basis. Curiosity is classified as one of the general drives (see entry).

A deeper understanding of curiosity behavior can be gained by examining the attributes of the stimuli that control it. Novelty and complexity were identified in the definition. A stimulus is *novel* if it is new or different. Something that has never been seen before, such as toy B for Connie, qualifies as a novel stimulus. We may also speak of novel places. The urge to travel to faraway places, a wanderlust, may be understood in terms of the curiosity motive.

The complexity of an object depends upon the changes of stimulation it presents. A jig-saw puzzle with forty pieces is not as complex as one with two hundred pieces. The hobbyist who has lost all interest in puzzles with forty pieces might be curious about one with two hundred pieces (or even more). To feel challenged by a puzzle or a problem that is complex is a facet of curiosity behavior.

It is important to note that a stimulus can be too novel or too complex in terms of one's own level of experience. A timid person will not be curious enough about a novel place to travel too far from home. A preschooler will be interested in a jig-saw puzzle with a few pieces, but not one with several hundred. There is an optimal level of novelty and/or complexity capable of eliciting the curiosity behavior of a given individual.

D

DEATH INSTINCT

Definition
As formulated by Freud, the death instinct is an inborn tendency to seek the destruction of both other organisms and oneself.

Example
Eliot is an elderly man in poor health. He eats incorrectly, takes no exercise, and in general avoids following his physician's advice. Eliot's life has been disappointing to him in many ways and he appears to be chronically depressed. His physician tells the family that Eliot seems to almost be wishing for death. A Freudian interpretation would suggest that self-destructive behavior can be an expression of the death instinct. The death instinct cooperates with Eliot's age, failing health, and depression to hasten his departure from life.

Connections
Freud's concept of the death instinct was developed in his later theorizing. Initially Freud held that there were a set of inborn instincts, or drives, associated with the id (see entry). The life instincts were given the collective name *Eros*. Eventually Freud became convinced that there was another instinct, just one, pitted by the personality against the life instincts. This was the death instinct. He called it *Thanatos* after the Greek god of death. In youth the death instinct is usually weak. If it does express itself, it takes the form of doing damage to others. Freud was greatly depressed by World War I and believed it to be a mass neurosis in which the death instinct had been unleashed upon the world.

The example of the elderly Eliot was used for Thanatos because Freud felt that it is the death instinct that brings about our final collapse as organisms. We are, so to speak, programmed to die. Although Freud's formulation of the death instinct is regarded by many psychologists as fanciful and poetic, recent research in biology suggests that the hypothesis of an inborn timetable for aging and dying is one that merits exploration.

DEFENSE MECHANISMS

Definition
Defense mechanisms are unconscious strategies by which the ego protects itself against the harsher aspects of reality.

Example
During his young manhood Count Leo Tolstoy, author of *War and Peace* and *Anna Karenina*, lived a life of debauchery. After the age of fifty he looked with increasing disgust, guilt, and shame upon his earlier behavior. He became very saintly, gave freedom to some of the serfs on his estates, and made a great effort to lead an exemplary life. It can be hypothesized that he was employing a defense mechanism called *undoing*, a mechanism characterized by behavior designed to atone for past misdeeds.

Connections
A number of defense mechanisms can be identified including compensation, fantasy, narcissism, rationalization, reaction formation, regression, and repression (see entries).

The concept of ego defense found its first formal presentation in the writings of Freud. Subsequently, Anna Freud, Freud's daughter, enriched and developed more adequately details of the various defense mechanisms.

In a very general sense defense mechanisms can be understood as devices for self-deception. They help us to tell lies to ourselves. The purpose of these lies is to enhance self-esteem when any form of information threatens to lower it.

Defense mechanisms are considered to be a form of normal behavior. They are quite common. They can become neurotic or maladaptive if they are used excessively and interfere with effective functioning in life.

DELUSION

Definition
A delusion is a fixed false idea resistant to change even if objective information is provided contrary to the idea.

Example
Angelina is a mental patient suffering from a psychotic disorder (see entry). She is convinced that she can fly about the hospital ward from bed to bed. As she hops off of one bed and onto another she declares, 'See, I can fly! I can fly! My name is Angelina and that means angel and angels can fly!' No one else, including other patients, perceives Angelina as capable of flying. The objective fact that she is unable to fly does not destroy Angelina's delusion.

Connections
Although there is a tendency to associate delusions primarily with psychotic disorders, they can occur in cases of brain disorders and among drug abusers. It is possible to have delusions about almost anything – the nature of the world, other people, or oneself. One might have the delusion that gravity is an evil plot, that air is really thin water, that the sun is a giant match, and so forth. Persons suffering from paranoia have delusions of persecution. They often think that others are going to trap, punish, or poison them. It is possible to have the delusion that one has incredible strength, uncanny sensory ability, unbelievable intelligence, and so forth.

It is possible to raise a philosophical question about delusions. When a psychiatrist, clinical psychologist, or other mental health professional says that a person has delusions a critic can say, 'Why should the mental health professional be the person to define reality for another? What is reality anyway?' The statement that the patient has delusions is based on the assumption that the professional has a better grasp of reality than does the patient. In view of the fact that more than one philosopher (e.g. Immanuel Kant) has pointed out that there are serious problems in defining the nature of things, about all we can go on is a perceptual consensus. It seems practical to say that if only Angelina is convinced she can fly, then her idea is a delusion.

DEOXYRIBONUCLEIC ACID (DNA)

Definition
Deoxyribonucleic acid (DNA) is a large organic molecule with a double helix structure. DNA molecules are the building blocks from which genes are made.

Example
The search for a specific DNA molecule starts at the level of the chromosome. Every human cell has in its nucleus 23 pairs of chromosomes. Each chromosome has approximately twenty thousand genes. Each gene will be made up of many strands of DNA. The double helix structure of DNA contributes to its most remarkable property, the ability to replicate itself. This property makes possible both the sexual and asexual reproduction of living cells without the loss of genetic information.

Connections
Closely related to DNA is another organic molecule, *ribonucleic acid* (RNA). RNA, like DNA, is found in the nucleus of a cell. One of the duties of RNA is to provide information for a cell's synthesis of chemicals. Both DNA and RNA can be looked upon as instruction codes for cells.

The general importance of DNA and RNA for behavioral science is substantial. The study of the structure of DNA contributes to a deeper understanding of behavioral genetics (see entry). The study of the structure of RNA, particularly in neurons, helps us understand more about the action of neurotransmitters (see entry).

The Nobel Prize for physiology and medicine was awarded in 1962 to James Watson, Francis Crick, and Maurice Wilkins for their work in ascertaining the molecular structure of DNA.

DEPTH PERCEPTION

Definition
Depth perception is the ability to experience one's visual field, including the objects in it, in three spatial dimensions.

Example
You are driving an automobile. You can estimate that a distance of approximately one hundred feet separates your automobile

from the one in front of you. As you look down the road some objects appear close to you and others appear far away. And the objects of perception – other automobiles, trucks, people, buildings, and so forth – appear to be rounded and solid. Length, width, and height are associated without effort with everything you see.

Connections

The experience of depth perception is so commonplace that we fail to wonder about it. But philosophers and psychologists have pondered more than one question about depth perception. How is it possible for us to experience depth – three dimensions – when we work with a retina that is essentially a curved two-dimensional plane? Is depth an inborn idea or is it a concept acquired by experience?

The first question is answered in terms of *cues* to depth perception, aspects of the visual field that assist us. There are two cue categories: (1) Retinal disparity and (2) monocular cues. *Retinal disparity* is a cue used by both eyes working together. Disparity itself is due to the fact that the eyes are located slightly apart in the head. This gives us two slightly different images of the same scene, and a rich look at it. However, depth perception with only one working eye is possible. Thus retinal disparity is important only in that it augments or enhances depth perception.

Monocular cues are cues that can be used by a single eye. *Linear perspective*, the tendency of parallel lines to appear to converge and vanish at the horizon, is an example of such a cue. *Interposition*, the tendency of one object to block out another object, is another example of a monocular cue. And *shadows* provide a third example.

The second question posed was: is depth an inborn idea or is it a concept acquired by experience? Philosophers such as Plato and Kant thought that depth is an inborn idea. The philosopher George Berkeley suggested that depth is a concept acquired by experience. Contemporary research suggests that neither answer is adequate. Infant human beings only a few months old can reach for an object fairly accurately, revealing depth perception. Infant kittens and chickens behave in such a way that we can infer they have depth perception shortly after birth. What seems to be inborn is not the idea of depth, but a brain and nervous system capable of experiencing depth given the appropriate visual cues. Learning augments this innate information processing ability.

DESCARTES, RENÉ
(1596–1650)

René Descartes was a French soldier of fortune, a mathematician, and a philosopher. The Roman Catholic church of the seventeenth century was at some odds with the teachings of natural philosophers who suggested that the body worked much like a machine. This suggested to some that perhaps the mind, like the body, obeyed natural law.

Descartes 'solved' this problem, and reasserted the teachings of Aquinas (see entry) on the importance of free will by asserting that although it is true that the body does in fact operate much like a machine, the mind belongs to the soul and is not constrained by cause and effect. This is the doctrine of *dualism*, the teaching that the body and the mind are distinctly different substances (see entry).

Descartes postulated a corollary doctrine known as *interactionism*, meaning that the body and the mind do in fact, to some extent, influence each other. He speculated that the point of interaction is the *pineal gland*, a tiny endocrine gland located in the head. This doctrine is imbedded to some extent in the term *psychosomatic illness*, literally a mind-body illness (see entry).

One of Descartes' most famous proclamations was '*Cogito ergo sum*,' meaning, 'I think, therefore I am.' Because of his emphasis on the primacy of thought, it may be said that Descartes foreshadowed the eventual emergence of the importance of *cognition* in psychology (see *cognition, cognitive development, cognitive dissonance*, and *consciousness*).

DESENSITIZATION THERAPY

Definition
Desensitization therapy is a form of psychotherapy in which a patient learns to extinguish unwanted emotional responses to certain classes of stimuli. This is accomplished through a process of repeated exposure to these stimuli either in life or in fantasy.

Example
Desensitization therapy is of particular value in the treatment of phobic disorders (see entry). Assume that William has an irrational fear of snakes. His vocation takes him into many outdoor

situations and his imagination works overtime. He is highly motivated to get rid of his snake phobia.

William's psychotherapist first gives William a set of relaxation exercises. After William is deeply relaxed he is taken on a guided fantasy by the therapist designed to invoke a moderate level of anxiety. The guided fantasy includes the presence of snakes. Perhaps in a first fantasy William looks at snakes in a zoo. The deep relaxation has a counterconditioning effect (see entry) on the anxiety, and a certain amount of extinction of the unwanted fear response to snakes will occur. On subsequent sessions the fantasies will involve closer contact with snakes until at last William can handle snakes in fantasy. It is possible in many cases to take the therapy one step farther and have the subject handle snakes in reality.

Connections
Almost any kind of phobia responds to desensitization therapy. However, the value of desensitization therapy is not limited to phobias. It can be used to treat any unwanted emotional reaction. For example, desensitization therapy is useful in the treatment of depression if it can be ascertained what conditioned stimuli trigger depressive responses in the individual.

Desensitization therapy was pioneered by the psychiatrist Joseph Wolpe when he found himself increasingly disenchanted with classical psychoanalysis as a form of treatment for conditions involving chronic anxiety.

DISCRIMINATIVE STIMULUS

Definition
In operant conditioning a discriminative stimulus is one to which an organism learns a response in order to obtain a reinforcer.

Example
A pigeon is placed in an operant conditioning apparatus, or Skinner box. The pigeon is trained to peck at a lighted disc in order to obtain a reinforcer in the form of food. When the light is off pecking at the disc will not bring forth the reinforcer. The lighted disc itself is the discriminative stimulus. It provides information to the organism that allows a discrimination between when pecking will be reinforced and when it will not.

Connections
The discriminative stimulus in operating conditioning is the equivalent of the conditioned stimulus in classical conditioning (see entry). Both classes of stimuli, through learning, come to command quite a bit of the behavior of organisms. The conditioned stimulus elicits much reflexive behavior mediated by the autonomic nervous system. The discriminative stimulus sets the stage for much 'voluntary' behavior mediated by the somatic nervous system. The word *voluntary* is in quotation marks in the prior sentence to indicate it is being used in a qualified manner. B. F. Skinner suggests that much of what we like to think of as voluntary behavior is in actuality controlled by discriminative stimuli and the reinforcers associated with them.

It is not only pigeons and experimental animals that respond to discriminative stimuli. In everyday life situations there are many discriminative stimuli. Here are a few examples: a traffic signal, a school bell, a factory whistle, an 'open' sign in a shop door, a change of pitch in another person's voice, and a parent's smile.

DISPLACEMENT OF AGGRESSION

Definition
Displacement of aggression takes place when aggressive behavior, either verbal or physical, is shifted from an original source of frustration to a substitute one.

Example
Cyrus has a bad day at work. He is criticized by his employer at every turn. In the presence of his employer he is submissive, saying, 'Yes sir. I'll try to do better sir.' When he comes home he is in a terrible mood. Later in the evening he gives his six-year-old daughter a severe tongue lashing for a minor infraction of a household rule.

Connections
The concept of displacement of aggression has its roots in psychoanalytical thinking. A general idea in psychoanalysis is that the personality can build up an emotional charge as a result of the blockage of a drive or impulse. And the eventual target of this charge can be quite different than its natural one. The concept of sublimation (see entry) in psychoanalysis is another example of this principle.

The example of Cyrus giving his daughter a tongue lashing is a mild example of displacement of aggression. In severe cases an innocent person can be beaten or even killed. The word *scapegoat* is applied to the victims of displaced aggression.

DISTRIBUTION OF PRACTICE

Definition
Distribution of practice is a condition of learning characterized by the taking of rest periods, or breaks, between trials. The concept derives meaning by contrasting it with *massed practice*, a condition of learning in which no rest periods are taken between trials.

Example
Two groups of human subjects, Group A and Group B, are given an opportunity to learn a perceptual-motor skill. An example of such a skill is playing a computer game requiring subjects to hit spaceship targets by simultaneously manipulating a joystick and pressing a button. A subject's score on each trial is the number of hits he or she makes. Group A receives ten learning trials with distribution of practice. Group B receives ten learning trials with massed practice. Assuming that subjects have been randomly assigned to the two conditions in order to cancel out individual differences, almost invariably the learning curve for Group A will be superior to the learning curve for Group B.

Connections
The value of distributed practice for learning can hardly be exaggerated. A great many learning experiments indicate that it is an important contributing factor to effective learning. However, it should be noted that the value of distributed practice is somewhat greater for perceptual-motor learning than it is for verbal learning.

Why do breaks facilitate learning? One hypothesis advanced by the learning theorist Clark L. Hull is that a learning trial causes the build-up of a slight amount of specific fatigue for a given response. Hull called his fatigue factor *reactive inhibition*. Breaks between trials allow for the spontaneous dissipation of reactive inhibition. It is also possible to advance a cognitive hypothesis associated with the phenomenon of attention. This second hypothesis suggests that massed practice makes a subject bored and less attentive to whatever it is he or she needs to learn. A break restores some of the novelty or freshness to the learning task, allowing a subject to pay more spontaneous attention to the task. Both hypotheses appear to have some merit.

DOUBLE BIND

Definition
A double bind takes place in the communication process when one individual is given two logically contradictory statements by another person.

Example
Eight-year-old Tammy's mother tells her, 'I expect you to get straight *As* in school.' When Tammy is studying, her mother says, 'Why don't you spend more time outside playing like the other kids? You look too pale.' The messages contain a double bind in that Tammy doesn't feel she can both get straight *As* and also spend more time playing outside. If both behaviors on Tammy's part are required to maintain her mother's affection, Tammy feels that she is in a no-win situation.

Connections
The concept of the double bind was articulated in detail by the anthropologist Gregory Bateson. He believed that a history of double binding in childhood was an important factor in the development of psychotic disorders. The argument runs that some parents are chronic double binders, creating emotionally impossible situations for their children. Bateson's view is shared by the British psychiatrist R. D. Laing who also points to a history of double binding among persons suffering from psychotic disorders.

A parallel idea to the double bind can be discovered in the work of Pavlov on conditioning with dogs. He presented dogs with a difficult discrimination between a circle and an ellipse. Formerly the dogs had been trained to salivate upon seeing a circle and to inhibit their salivation upon seeing an ellipse. When presented with an oval stimulus somewhere between a full circle and a narrow ellipse, the dogs for all practical purposes were put into a double bind (although Pavlov did not call it that). Dogs in this situation develop what Pavlov termed an *experimental neurosis*. They froth at the mouth, can't concentrate on stimuli being presented, snap at the trainer, and seem to 'go crazy.' Pavlov's classic work on experimental neurosis lends additional credence to Bateson's hypothesis that double bind messages may play a significant role in the development of psychotic disorders.

DREAM

Definition
A dream is a series of thoughts and images taking place while one is sleeping.

Example
Harvey, a thirty-three-year-old accountant, dreams he is a gladiator in the ancient Roman Colosseum. He kills an opponent in combat. He awakens from the dream in a state of excitement. There is a lingering feeling of fear. A moment ago he was in danger of losing his life! There is also a sense of satisfaction associated with his success in a fight to the death. Harvey smiles and thinks to himself, 'It seemed real.'

Connections
There have been many attempts to explain the meaning of dreams. One of the most famous is Freud's dream theory. Freud said that a dream is the expression of a forbidden wish in life. The dream exists on two levels: the manifest content and the latent content. The *manifest content* is the actual thoughts and images of the dream, the surface of the dream. The *latent content* is the meaning of the dream and contains the forbidden wish. The manifest content is a disguise for the forbidden wish, a kind of censorship imposed by the ego.

Harvey's dream is fairly transparent in Freudian terms. The manifest content of his dream makes him a killer under permissible conditions. The latent content is a repressed wish to inflict harm or injury against some other person in his life, perhaps someone who is frustrating him and toward whom he has built up hostility. The identity of this person is masked in the dream because the knowledge is too threatening to Harvey's ego.

There are, of course, other explanations of the meaning of dreams than Freud's. Carl Jung hypothesized that dreams can express any concern or preoccupation of the personality, not just forbidden wishes. Thus one's hopes and fears may appear in dreams in undisguised form. Jung believed that dreams follow the principle that a picture is worth a thousand words. Dreams are a showing by the total self to the ego of important themes in one's life.

Frederick Perls, the father of Gestalt therapy, said that the elements in a dream are alienated parts of the self. Each image or figure represents a fragmented part of one's personality. The aim of dream interpretation in Perls' version of psychotherapy is to make contact with these fragmented elements and to incorporate them once again into the total personality, thus making the personality into a proper Gestalt, or organized whole. (See the entry on Gestalt psychology.)

When we are dreaming we are usually in a state known as rapid-eye-movement or REM sleep (see entry).

William Dement, a leading dream researcher, said, 'Dreaming permits each and every one of us to be quietly and safely insane every night of our lives.'

DUALISM

Definition
Dualism is the point of view that mind and matter are two entirely different entities.

Example
One of the most well-known early exponents of dualism was the philosopher Plato (427–347 BC). He taught that the mind is an aspect of the immortal soul. It is, during life, *in* the body, but not *of* the body. After death it is released from the body and travels to a higher plane of existence. The body is both in the world and of the world. It is, so to speak, made of clay. The mind's quality of existence is much finer than the body's.

Connections
The philosopher René Descartes (1596–1650) preserved and advanced Plato's point of view when he proposed that although the mind and body are different they *interact*, meaning they have an effect on each other. Descartes chose as the point of interaction the *pineal gland*, a tiny gland located in the head.

The influence of men such as Plato and Descartes was so great that leading psychologists have often felt that it is necessary to take a position on what is called the mind-body problem. The *mind-body problem* may be stated as follows: Are the mind and the body two entirely different entities? If so, do they interact? Or are they incapable of influencing each other?

Wilhelm Wundt, the highly influential father of structuralism (see entry), took a position on the mind-body problem known as *psychophysical parallelism*. This position agrees that the mind and the body are different entities, but they have no cause and effect influence on each other. They *seem* to have such an effect because they march in lock-step. However, just as soldier A does not cause soldier B to march, nor does soldier B cause soldier A to march, so the mind and the body travel a parallel course during one's sojourn on Earth without either one actually affecting the other.

John Watson, the father of behaviorism, was an opponent of structuralism and Wundt's whole way of thinking. Watson suggested that the mind-body problem is a false problem. We need only assert that what we call the mind is in fact the activity of the brain and nervous system (body), and we have no problem. There is only one basic entity according to Watson. And that entity is the body.

The mind-body problem has not been solved to everyone's satisfaction by the authority of famous thinkers. The problem continues to be discussed.

E

ECLECTICISM

Definition
Eclecticism is the point of view that it is prudent to see the value in concepts drawn from two or more systems of thought, or schools of psychology. In addition, one who adopts eclecticism will not be quick to arbitrarily reject a finding or a principle simply because it does not fit in well with long-established assumptions.

Example
Walter G., Ph.D., is a forty-two-year-old clinical psychologist in private practice. He was first attracted to psychology by an interest in psychoanalysis. For several years he accepted certain basic assumptions of psychoanalysis, such as unconscious motivation (see entry), without question. He thought of them as truth. In his university training he was exposed to behavior therapy (see entry), and learned that many behavior therapists reject the concept of unconscious motivation. He debated with himself for some time over whether or not he believed or did not believe in unconscious motivation. In recent years he has adopted eclecticism. He uses the concept of unconscious motivation in conjunction with conditioning principles when doing therapy, and no longer worries much about theoretical contradictions. He sees value in both psychoanalysis and behaviorism.

In fact, Walter's eclecticism spreads beyond psychoanalysis and behaviorism. He sees worth in humanistic psychology (see entry), and freely mixes its principles with the other two systems. He says, 'I practice a kind of therapy that I call multimodal – using as practical tools whatever I can find from any school of psychology to help my patients. I'm not much of a scientist, I suppose. But I try to be an effective healer.'

Connections
The word *eclecticism* is derived from two Greek roots: *ek*, meaning 'out,' and *legein*, meaning 'to select.' Thus eclecticism literally means selecting out. One who adopts eclecticism in psychology selects out the best ideas from several schools of psychology.

There are at least two important problems with eclecticism. One problem is that it is not intellectually satisfying. One feels that there is something wrong with a position in which one has to juggle ideas that contradict each other. It is a poorly advanced science that cannot resolve contradictions among competing principles.

A second problem with eclecticism is it can lead to a kind of apathy or lack of concern about the importance of theories. The eclectic may become apathetic about advancing our conceptual understanding of psychology. He or she may say in a superficial way, 'Oh, there's something of worth in every school of psychology.' However, this may lead to a kind of mental sloppiness and a lack of rigorous criteria for accepting or rejecting theoretical formulations.

EGO

Definition
The ego is the 'I' of the personality, the conscious self. It is oriented toward external reality.

Example
In psychoanalysis, a distinction is made between persons with a weak ego and a strong ego. Persons with a weak ego are impulsive, impatient, and tolerate frustration poorly. Persons with a strong ego exhibit opposite characteristics, and are generally what we call emotionally mature. Assume that two persons are waiting together in a fairly long cafeteria line. The first person, Richmond, is very irritated about the wait. He says to his companion, 'This is absurd! I have a good mind to just leave. Can't they do better than this?' He is actually beginning to turn slightly red with anger. The second person, his companion, Hugh, says, 'Well, what can we do? It will probably only take ten minutes to get to the head of the line at the most. I don't think there's any other place that we can go to at this time of day and get served

any faster. We might as well be patient.' Hugh appears to be calm and unruffled. Hugh is exhibiting, at the moment, a stronger ego function than is Richmond. He appears to be better oriented toward external reality in that he is making a logical evaluation of the facts.

Connections
The concept of the ego plays a significant role in psychoanalytic theory. However, ideas about the ego existed in philosophy before recent times. Scholastic philosophers of the medieval period thought of the ego as the whole person. The three sides of the ego were the soul, mind, and body. This early formulation has given way to the one identified in the definition in which the ego is reduced to a part of the personality, the conscious part.

The root word *ego* makes an appearance in other words. An *egotist* is a selfish and a conceited person. One of the characteristics of preoperational thought (see *cognitive development*) in children is *egocentrism*, meaning an inability to see any point of view other than their own.

ELECTRICAL STIMULATION OF THE BRAIN (ESB)

Definition
Electrical stimulation of the brain (ESB) is a process by which a weak electric current can be delivered to selected brain sites. This is accomplished by drilling tiny holes in the skull of the subject and implanting insulated microelectrodes with exposed tips into these sites.

Example
An experimenter implants a microelectrode into a rat's brain. It is placed in a region of the paleocortex, or 'old brain,' known as the septal area. The rat is put in an operant conditioning apparatus, or Skinner box, capable of delivering a bit of electric current to the septal area each time the rat presses a lever. The rat learns to self-stimulate the brain in order to receive the current. Apparently the reception of current in the septal area is a reinforcer for the rat because the rate of lever pressing increases as a function of the number of times current has been delivered.

ELECTROENCEPHALOGRAM (EEG)

Connections
The area being self-stimulated in the example has come to be informally referred to as 'the pleasure center.' We infer that rats feel pleasure, or something akin to it, when current is delivered to this area. Rats have been known to self-stimulate the pleasure center several thousand times in a single hour when given the opportunity. Also, they will cross painful shock grids in order to engage in self-stimulation. Much of the early work on electrical stimulation of the brain was pioneered by James Olds and Peter Milner at McGill University.

Electrodes have been implanted on an experimental basis in human beings, and the procedure has a number of potential clinical applications. A few possibilities include treatment of the following conditions: tumors, narcolepsy, psychomotor epilepsy, mental disorders, Parkinson's disease, and tremors associated with multiple sclerosis.

Critics of ESB in human beings point to its possible abuse as a form of unwanted behavior control.

ELECTROENCEPHALOGRAM (EEG)

Definition
An electroencephalogram (EEG) is a record over a given time period of fluctuating electrical potentials in the brain.

Example
One of the prominent EEG frequency bands is the *alpha rhythm*, appearing as a wave on the record with cycles per second ranging from eight to fourteen. When one is spontaneously producing the alpha rhythm he or she tends to be both relaxed and alert. It has been hypothesized that the voluntary production of more of the alpha frequency band will aid tense and anxious persons to find greater serenity. Early research in biofeedback training, pioneered by Joseph Kamiya, used increases in the alpha frequency as a reinforcer with positive results.

Connections
The informal term for the fluctuating electrical potentials of the brain is 'brain waves,' so named because the tracings on the EEG form a series of waves.

The EEG itself is a measure of gross electrical activity in the brain. Its source is the activity of millions of individual neurons (see entry) constantly fluctuating in electrical potential, or 'firing.'

There are three other prominent kinds of brain waves other than the alpha rhythm identified in the example. The *beta rhythm* has a frequency of about fourteen cycles per second. When persons are alert and highly aroused they will manifest increased amounts of the beta rhythm. The *theta rhythm* has a frequency of about six cycles per second. When persons are daydreaming they will manifest increased amounts of the theta rhythm. The *delta rhythm* has a frequency of about four cycles per second. When persons are in deep sleep they will manifest increased amounts of the delta rhythm.

An EEG is sometimes useful in the diagnosis of organic brain conditions such as epilepsy or minimal brain damage (MBD).

ELECTROSHOCK THERAPY

Definition
Electroshock therapy is a kind of therapy for mental disorders in which a low intensity electrical current is passed through the brain for between one and two seconds.

Example
Daniela is a thirty-eight-year-old married attorney with two children. For the past three weeks she has been hospitalized suffering from a major psychotic depression. It is Monday morning and her psychiatrist is about to administer Daniela's first electroshock treatment. The psychiatrist places a positive and a negative electrode on each of Daniela's temples. The electrodes lead out from a shock-generating apparatus attached to an ordinary wall plug. The throwing of a switch on the apparatus causes the brief flow of current through Daniela's brain. When the current flows she loses consciousness and has a seizure resembling the grand mal seizure associated with epilepsy. A muscle relaxant has been administered in advance to preclude any bone damage that might result from the contractions arising from the seizure. Twenty minutes later Daniela regains consciousness and has a very bad headache for several hours.

EMOTION

Connections
Two Italian psychiatrists, Ugo Cerletti and Lucio Bini, brought electroshock therapy into the mental health profession in 1937. There have been many hypotheses advanced to explain why electroshock therapy is effective in treating some mental disorders, particularly certain schizophrenic disorders and psychotic depression. A psychoanalytic hypothesis is that the patient perceives the shock treatment as punishment, and this can have the effect of alleviating guilt feelings causing depression.

A more contemporary hypothesis based on physiological psychology is that electroshock stimulates the brain to increase its production of certain neurotransmitters (see entry) such as norepinephrine. There is good reason to believe that some individuals suffering from a psychotic disorder have disturbed brain biochemistry. Shock therapy can help to restore a normal balance.

There has been much debate about the value of shock therapy. Critics argue that its long-run effectiveness for the treatment of mental disorders is questionable. They also assert that too many treatments may do some brain damage. Because of the criticisms, and also because of the development of antipsychotic drugs, electroshock therapy is not administered as often as it once was. However, it is not obsolete. And a majority of psychiatrists hold that it has a proper place in the treatment of mental disorders.

EMOTION

Definition
On a physiological level, an emotion is a bodily process involving sharp fluctuations in one's state of arousal. These changes are manifested by alterations in heart rate, breathing rate, production of moisture by the sweat glands, and so forth. On a psychological level, an emotion is experienced as either a highly pleasant or a highly unpleasant reaction to which we attach descriptive words such as *joy* or *anger*.

Example
Roger is attempting to return a defective electric toaster to a department store. The clerk in charge of adjustments is refusing a refund for reasons that seem adequate to the clerk but inadequ-

ate to Roger. Roger finds himself becoming increasingly angry as he attempts to make his point of view clear to the clerk. Prone to hypertension, Roger thinks, 'This is unfair! This clerk's a jerk! But I better watch it. My blood's beginning to boil and I can't afford to have a stroke over something as stupid as this.'

Connections
The word emotion is actually a contraction of two words, *exit* and *motion*. The ancient Greeks believed that the soul was, in a sense, coming temporarily out of the body when an emotion was displayed.

It is generally conceded that there are two primary dimensions to emotions. These are hedonic tone and arousal. *Hedonic tone* is the pleasant-unpleasant dimension of emotions. *Arousal* is the excitement-calm dimension. In anger there is excessive excitement. In depression there is excessive calm.

Wilhelm Wundt, the father of structuralism, argued that there are three dimensions to emotions. In addition to the two already noted, he proposed a strain-relaxation dimension. However, subsequent researchers have concluded that strain-relaxation is about the same thing as excitement-calm.

EMPIRICISM

Definition
Empiricism is the doctrine that all of our concepts and ideas are derived from experience. Experience, in turn, is based only on information coming in to us through the sense organs (i.e. the eyes, the ears, etc.).

Example
You are visiting a museum and pause to admire a particular statue. You think, 'This is a beautiful work of art.' An advocate of empiricism would argue that your judgment is based on a concept of beauty acquired by experience. As a child you were told what was and what was not beautiful. You were reinforced for certain judgments that were congruent with your culture. You had no inborn knowledge of how to rank objects in terms of beauty.

Connections
Contrary to empiricism is nativism (see entry). Nativism argues that some ideas, such as the idea of beauty, are inborn.

Two of the most famous empiricists in history were Aristotle and John Locke. Both philosophers taught that the mind at birth is devoid of ideas. (Locke wrote about the mind as a *tabula rasa* or blank slate.)

Empiricism has played an important role in the history of scientific research. The empirical attitude argues that it is essential to make observations, gather data, and do experiments to confirm principles. It is not enough to sit and ponder brilliantly.

Another doctrine contrary to empiricism is mysticism. Mysticism argues that higher knowledge about the universe or God is available through meditation. Meditation allows the intuitive power of the mind to make a transcendental contact. The tough-minded (see entry) followers of empiricism completely reject mysticism.

ENDOCRINE GLANDS

Definition
The endocrine glands are glands that secrete their products directly into the bloodstream.

Example
One of the endocrine glands is the *pituitary gland*, sometimes called the master gland because is partially controls the action of some of the other endocrine glands. The pituitary gland is comparable in size to a pea, and it is located at the base of the brain. One of its principal products is *growth hormone*, a hormone that regulates the rate of growth during one's developmental years. It also determines the limit of one's height.

Connections
Endocrine glands can be contrasted with *exocrine glands*, glands that secrete their substances into body cavities. Examples of exocrine glands are the *salivary glands* and the *digestive glands*.

The endocrine glands are important in psychology because their action can have a substantial impact on emotional states, and in turn both personality and overt behavior.

Other endocrine glands include the pineal gland, the thyroid glands, the parathyroid glands, the thymus gland, the adrenal glands, the pancreas gland, the ovaries in females, and the testes in males. Each of these glands plays its own unique role in regulating physiological processes.

An example of how an endocrine gland can play a role in behavior is provided by the *thyroid gland*. The thyroid gland secretes thyroxin. Thyroxin controls the metabolic rate, the rate at which one burns food. A person with an overactive thyroid gland will tend toward a high state of arousal. He or she will be likely to be quick to act, excitable, aggressive, and alert. A person with an underactive thyroid gland will tend toward a low state of arousal. He or she will be likely to be slow to act, apathetic, passive, and frequently drowsy.

ENDORPHINS

Definition
Endorphins are natural opiates produced in the brain and pituitary gland. They are classified as a kind of neurotransmitter (see entry).

Example
It has been found that a regular program of moderate exercise, such as taking a brisk daily walk of about twenty minutes, enhances one's sense of well-being. It has also been found that moderate exercise stimulates the production of endorphins. It is hypothesized that part of the sense of well-being that comes from moderate exercise may be due to opiate action of increased endorphin levels.

Connections
The word *endorphin* is a contraction of two words: *endogenous*, meaning 'produced within,' and *morphine*, an opiate. Thus an endorphin is, in a sense, a kind of morphine produced within the body.

Exercise is not the only procedure that may increase endorphin levels. There is evidence to suggest that the taking of a *placebo*, an inert pill with no actual pharmacological action, may stimulate the production of endorphins. This may account in some degree for the well-known ability of a placebo to provide some relief of pain.

EXISTENTIALISM

Definition
Existentialism is a philosophical point of view placing greater value on the inner world of experience than on the external world of objective criteria.

Example
The existential point of view can be made clear by means of a parable: Once there was a man named Glenn who went to a foolish physician. Glenn complained of depression and the physician tested Glenn's biochemistry. The biochemistry appeared to be normal. Then the physician obtained an electroenchephalogram (see entry). The electroencephalogram was normal. Then the physician tested Glenn's vitamin levels. The vitamin levels were normal. After all of the tests were concluded the physician announced to Glen, 'I have good news for you. You are not depressed!'

Glenn gave the physician a baleful stare and said, 'I say I *am* depressed. I believe my experience, not your tests.' Glenn's statement is consistent with existentialism.

Connections
The father of modern existentialism is usually said to be Sören Kierkegaard, often called 'the lonely Dane.' He placed a great value on the individual as an individual. Other leading figures in the founding of existential philosophy are Friedrich Nietzsche, Martin Heidegger, and Jean-Paul Sartre.

Existentialism can be used to 'solve' or throw a new light on many classical philosophical problems. For example, is the human will (see entry) free or determined? An objective train of logic may lead one to the conclusion that the will must obey the laws of cause and effect. The follower of existentialism can declare, 'I don't care what logic suggests. I *experience* my will as free. Therefore it is!'

In psychology, an existential frame of reference may contribute to mental health. There is a certain salutary effect that comes from trusting one's own experience and from believing in one's own free will.

EXPERIMENTAL METHOD

Definition
The experimental method is a method of gathering data in which measurements of the behavior of at least one control group are compared with measurements of the behavior of at least one experimental group.

Example
Dr Q. advances the hypothesis that students perform better on examinations in the morning than in the afternoon. He randomly assigns students from a large lecture class of sixty students to either a 9:00 a.m. or a 3:00 p.m. final examination over the course material, thus creating two groups of thirty students each. The 9:00 a.m. group is the experimental group because it is the group being subjected to the treatment of interest, taking an examination in the morning. The 3:00 p.m. group is the control group because its performance will provide a contrast to the performance of the experimental group. Because of the random assignment to conditions it is assumed that any differences in the performance of the groups can be assigned to the time of day the test is taken.

The average score of the experimental group turns out to be 84% correct. The average score of the control group turns out to be 76% correct. After subjecting the two averages to a statistical test designed to rule out chance variations between them, Dr Q. concludes that his experimental hypothesis is supported.

Connections
Of all of the methods available to psychology for the collection of data, the experimental method is considered the most powerful. Single sets of observations without control observations often lead an investigator astray. Many of the conclusions of contemporary psychology are squarely based on solid experimental findings.

The variable in an experiment assumed to affect behavior is called the *independent variable*, and it is under the direct control of the experimenter. In the above example *time of day* can be identified as the independent variable. The variable in an experiment associated with behavior is called the *dependent variable*. In the above example the *percent correct* on an examination was the dependent variable.

79

EXTINCTION

Experiments can become quite complex with sets of control groups and sets of experimental groups. It is also possible within a single experiment to study the effects of two or more independent variables. The joint effects of such variables, if they exist, are called *interactions*. Experimental methodology is a study in itself. However, at the core of every good experiment there remains the basic principle of comparing the measurements obtained from at least two groups.

EXTINCTION

Definition
Extinction is an active process in which the likelihood of occurrence of a conditioned response diminishes. It can also be thought of as the unlearning of a habit.

Example
Three-year-old Nancy has developed the habit of throwing a tantrum to get her way. Nancy's mother decides that she has been reinforcing the habit by paying too much attention to it. She decides to not allow Nancy to get her way by throwing tantrums, and she also decides that she will ignore Nancy's tantrums to whatever degree this is possible at a practical level. Much to Nancy's mother's gratification the tantrums eventually decrease in intensity and frequency.

Connections
The process of extinction has been studied extensively in the context of both classical and operant conditioning. Broadly speaking, it can be said that the most reliable way to bring about the extinction of a learned response is to withhold whatever reinforcer was involved in its original acquisition. If a rat has been trained to press a lever at a high rate to obtain food, the rat will decrease its rate of lever pressing markedly if its behavior is no longer effective in bringing forth food.

EXTRAVERT

Definition
According to Jungian theory, an extravert is a personality type characterized by behavioral traits designed to maximize contact

with the external world of physical objects and other persons in contrast to the internal world of thoughts and feelings.

Example
Dwight is a successful life insurance salesman. In his vocation he enjoys making calls, meeting people, and explaining insurance policies. In his private life he has many friends, enjoys the company of his wife and children, and enjoys traveling. People describe him with trait names such as *outgoing, cheerful, friendly*, and *self-confident*.

Connections
The *introvert* stands in contrast to the extravert. The introvert is described with trait names such as *inhibited, shy, reserved*, and *sober*.

It is important to realize that personality types can be spoken of only in extreme cases. In actuality Jung proposed a bipolar personality dimension called extraversion-introversion. Most people do not stand at one end or the other of the pole, but at various points in between. Thus it is, in most cases, probably better to speak of a personality profile in which extraversion is somewhat more dominant than introversion or vice versa.

Jung believed that one's characteristic personality profile on the extraversion-introversion dimension was determined primarily by inborn factors. This is, of course, a debatable point. It is possible to argue that learning during the developmental period is a more important factor than inborn ones.

F

FACTOR ANALYSIS

Definition
Factor analysis is a statistical tool designed to identify correlated clusters of items in standardized psychological tests. A given correlated cluster is called a *factor*.

Example
A psychological test that is both standardized and factor analyzed is the *Sixteen Personality Factor Inventory* constructed by psychometrician Raymond B. Cattell. Cattell was able to reduce a large array of seemingly unique questions into sixteen clusters, each of which measured approximately the same bipolar trait. For example, one factor on the test is: Reserved-Outgoing. Another factor is: Affected by feelings-Emotionally stable. Still another factor is: Humble-Assertive. A rating on each of the sixteen factors provides a rich personality profile when administered to a given person.

Connections
Factor analysis is considered a way of refining psychological tests, and has been used extensively to improve the quality of intelligence, personality, creativity, interest, and aptitude tests. Prior to the advent of factor analysis a test author drew up a test's personality dimensions, or areas of interest, based on a theory. Factor analysis, on the other hand, is empirical, being derived from actual data.

  L. L. Thurstone, associated with the University of Chicago, was a pioneer in factor analysis. His aim was to discover the structure of human intelligence (see entry). His factor analysis research suggested that intelligence consists of a general factor he referred to as *g* and seven additional specific abilities such as verbal comprehension, word fluency, reasoning, and others.

FANTASY

Definition

Fantasy is a mental process consisting of images produced by the imagination in contrast to images produced by the senses. The process can be said to apply to both daydreams and night dreams. Fantasy is also one of the classical defense mechanisms identified by psychoanalysis. The process of imagination can be used to distort reality and artificially enhance one's self-esteem.

Example

The Secret Life of Walter Mitty by humorist James Thurber tells the story of a meek man who is dominated by a bullying wife. He escapes into various absent-minded daydreams in which he sees himself as a sea captain rescuing a beautiful woman in distress, as a knight in shining armor fighting for the honor of his beloved, and so forth. All of the imaginary sequences star him as a heroic figure, the opposite of his real-world self. Thurber's tale illustrates both of the meanings of fantasy as given in the definition: first, the images produced by the imagination, and, second, the bolstering of a sagging ego.

Connections

The pathetic fantasizing of a Walter Mitty brings a smile to our lips. However, this is partly because we identify with Walter Mitty. Most of us use daydreams to give imaginary gratification to our secret desires. Fantasy is a defense mechanism. But it is more. It is normal to pursue in our minds the many options and possibilities that we automatically cut off by making choices in the real world.

The science-fiction writer Ray Bradbury has indicated in interviews and essays that he regards the ability to fantasize easily an important attribute of mental health. And the dreamer is, in turn, often eventually the doer. The poet and mystical philosopher Kahlil Gibran wrote, 'He who passes not his days in the realm of dreams is the slave of the days.'

FECHNER, GUSTAV THEODOR
(1801–1887)

Gustav Theodor Fechner was a professor of physics at the University of Leipzig in Germany. He was also a mystic, and he saw all objects in conscious terms. He asserted that the Earth, for example, was more than an object, but a conscious being like ourselves. He referred to it as Mother Earth.

Fechner's place in the history of psychology rests primarily on that fact that he is the father of *psychophysics*, an approach in experimental psychology allowing students of sensation and perception a means of relating these events to magnitudes of physical stimuli (see entry).

Fechner's real interest in psychophysics was in the hope that it could solve the classical mind-body problem (see *dualism*). Fechner believed that he had solved the problem, that he had demonstrated through psychophysics that mind and body are simply two different aspects of a single underlying reality. Unfortunately, although he convinced himself, he convinced very few others that he had proven anything of the sort.

Fechner's successful experimental work with psychophysics was an inspiration to Wilhelm Wundt (see entry), and Wundt founded the first psychological laboratory at Leipzig in 1879. Thus Fechner is an important forerunner of contemporary experimental psychology. Psychophysics remains a useful scientific tool to this day.

FIELD DEPENDENCE

Definition
Field dependence is an attribute of cognitive style characterized by a tendency to rely heavily upon external cues in the making of perceptual judgments.

Example
Assume that Natalie is a subject in an experiment. She is brought into a dark room and seated in a chair. All she can see is a glowing frame and a rod seemingly suspended within the frame. She is given a remote control apparatus capable of rotating the rod within the stationary frame. She is instructed to align the rod so that it is at right angles to the Earth's horizon *independent* of the orientation of the frame. Natalie is not told that the frame is deliberately set at a somewhat odd angle to the actual horizon in order to provide a misleading cue. Given several different opportunities to align the rod, Natalie scores rather poorly in contrast to other subjects. She tends to depend on the frame too much as opposed, for example, to correct cues arising from her own

vestibular sense. Natalie has exhibited, on this test, a high degree of field dependence.

Connections

The opposite of field dependence is field independence. It has been hypothesized that persons with a high level of field dependence tend to be less autonomous, more passive, more socially adapted, and more suggestible than people in general. Conversely, it has been hypothesized that persons with a high level of field independence tend to be somewhat more autonomous, assertive, less conforming, and less suggestible than people in general.

There are times when field dependence can be an undesirable perceptual trait. Studies conducted by Stanley Schachter on overeating behavior suggest that one characteristic of some obese persons is a tendency to rely heavily on external cues as a trigger for eating. The sight of food, the smell of food, the presence of others eating, and the time of day when food is usually eaten are all powerful cues that induce eating behavior. Normal weight persons are more field independent, relying on internal cues such as amount of food in the stomach and blood sugar levels.

FIGHT-OR-FLIGHT REACTION

Definition

The fight-or-flight reaction is an inborn behavioral sequence triggered by a real or perceived threat to the safety of the organism. Blood flows to the striated muscles (i.e. the muscles that move the skeleton), the heart rate increases, the pupils constrict, and the overall level of arousal increases. Whether the situation demands combat or provides the opportunity to run away, the physiological preparations of the body will serve the organism well.

Example

Grant, age ten, is cornered on the way home from school by a boy in his class who has the reputation of being a bully. He is prevented from running away by two of the bully's friends. The bully challenges Grant to a fight and Grant refuses. The bully punches Grant in the nose, and says, 'Fight back, sissy!' Grant's body has been reacting to the rising threat with the fight-or-flight reaction. At a subjective level, he feels a rage welling up in him

85

against the injustice of the bully's behavior. At a physiological level, there are the changes in arousal described in the definition. Grant stops trying to avoid the fight after the bully's direct aggression, and begins to fight back.

Connections
The fight-or-flight reaction is obviously a survival mechanism, and often serves us well. Grant, in the example, needed it. In primitive settings, members of hunting and gathering tribes need it when confronted with the hazards arising from confrontations with various dangerous animals.

One of the problems with the fight-or-flight reaction is that it can be triggered in 'civilized' settings in which no physical combat is allowed. A sarcastic remark made by one's employer, a criticism by one's spouse, can often trigger the fight-or-flight reaction. When one is unable to fight back adequately or to run away, the fight-or-flight reaction can take a toll on the body. Stress-complicated disorders such as ulcers and high blood pressure can be aggravated by the frequent provocation of a fight-or-flight reaction without adequate outlet.

FIGURE-GROUND RELATIONSHIP

Definition
There is a tendency in perception to segregate one or more objects (i.e. figures) out of a perceptual field (i.e. ground). The perception of a figure with a well-defined shape or pattern standing out from the ill-defined and rather formless ground is the figure-ground relationship.

Example
You look up into the night sky and seek out a familiar constellation, the Big Dipper. As you attend to its form it becomes figure. The rest of the stars spread out in the sky become ground.

Connections
That which constitutes figure in perception can change. In the example given of the Big Dipper as figure, one could shift one's attention to a different nearby constellation. And the stars in the Big Dipper would become ground.

Gestalt psychology (see entry) asserted that the figure-ground relationship is an inborn organizing tendency in perception.

86

There is good evidence that this is so. As soon as infants are testable in any meaningful sense, they display behavior suggesting the presence of figure-ground perception. And research reported on newly sighted adults, persons blind from birth with congenital cataracts, indicates that their first perception is figure-ground, even before they can perceive shapes and forms.

The figure-ground relationship applies to all of the senses, not just vision. One hears a melody played on a piano in a noisy room; the melody is figure and the noise in the room is ground. One eats a hamburger with a very sour pickle; the sour taste of the pickle becomes figure and the other taste sensations from the hamburger become ground.

FREE ASSOCIATION

Definition
Free association is a technique used in psychoanalysis to explore a patient's unconscious mental life. The basic instructions given to the patient require that he or she report anything and everything that comes to mind during an analytic session without regard to its logical, moral, sexual, or aggressive content.

Example
Jason is a thirty-seven-year-old professor of English literature undergoing a classical psychoanalysis. He suffers from an obsessive-compulsive disorder (see entry) and chronic neurotic anxiety. This is his seventeenth session, and he is reclining on a couch staring at a blank wall. The psychoanalyst is seated behind his head, out of view. As Jason free associates he talks at random about his unsatisfactory sexual relationship with a female colleague who also teaches English literature, his resentments toward his parents, an emotionally disturbing event that occurred when he was seven years old, and his hostility toward the all-knowing stance of the analyst.

Connections
A key assumption of free association is that much of the material brought forth during an analytic session was formerly repressed at an unconscious level. Free association unlocks the repressed content and makes it available to consciousness where it can be dealt with more realistically and effectively.

It was Freud who introduced free association into the therapy process. Prior to free association he had used hypnosis (see entry) to uncover the contents of the unconscious, but gave it up. He found that quick cures achieved through hypnosis were usually temporary. Also, he found that many of his patients resisted hypnosis.

FREUD, SIGMUND
(1856–1939)

Sigmund Freud was an Austrian physician who in the early stages of his career specialized in neurology. This led him to work with patients suffering from *hysteria*, a neurotic reaction in which emotional conflicts are converted into physical symptoms such as paralysis or deafness. (The preferred contemporary term for 'hysteria' is *conversion disorder*.) Freud first attempted to relieve the symptoms of hysteria with hypnosis and electromagnets, but soon discovered that the 'cures' effected were temporary. Seeking a permanent cure, he invented a psychological tool for exploring the personality called *free association* (see entry), and this tool revealed to him the unconscious realm of mental life.

The exploration of the unconscious mental life of his patients was the primary inspiration for *psychoanalysis* (see entry), and Freud's primary claim to fame rests on the fact that he is its father. Psychoanalysis is at once both a method of therapy and a personality theory.

Freud is by far the most famous psychologist who ever lived. If lay persons have heard of no other psychologist, they have usually heard of Freud. Freud's contributions to the psychology of the unconscious side of mental life are many and include the study of *abnormal behavior, amnesia, anxiety, dreams, personality, psychosexual development,* and *unconscious motives* (see entries).

Freud's most important single hypothesis was that unconscious ideas, motives, and memories play an important part in daily life. From an unseen realm they exert a kind of remote control over much of our behavior. Their existence is revealed by slips of the tongue, dreams, neurotic symptoms, and so forth. If correct, the doctrine of unconscious elements is of tremendous importance. Freud has had many critics, of course, and the hypothesis of an unconscious mental life has not won universal acceptance in psychology.

The two great themes in Freud's work are sex and aggression.

He believed that sex was the great upward theme in life. It is the force that accounts not only for the individual's life but also the life of future generations. The set of instincts, essentially biological drives as Freud conceived them, associated with survival Freud called *Eros* after the Greek god of love (see *id*). Aggression, including self-aggression, Freud believed arose from the *death instinct* (see entry) which he called *Thanatos* after the Greek god of death. These two forces struggle against each other throughout the organism's lifetime. In the beginning *Eros* is stronger, but in the end *Thanatos* wins.

Even if the concepts of *Eros* and *Thanatos* are somewhat romantic, it is true that therapists find that much maladaptive behavior is expressed in terms of sexual difficulties and aggressive impulses. Thus Freud was pointing mental health workers in generally the right direction.

Freud was a prolific author. One edition of his works contains over twenty volumes. Among his more well-known books are *The Interpretation of Dreams* (1900), *The Psychopathology of Everyday Life* (1901), *Introductory Lectures on Psychoanalysis* (1917), and *The Ego and the Id* (1923).

FRUSTRATION

Definition
The primary meaning of frustration is the blockage of a motivated organism from either attaining a positive goal or avoiding a negative one. A secondary meaning of frustration is the feeling experienced by the organism when such blockage takes place.

Example
Madeline, a homemaker and part-time nurse, is in a hurry to go to the grocery store and buy some ingredients for cookies she wants to bake for a get-together that evening at her home. As she slips rapidly into the driver's seat of her automobile, she inserts a key into the ignition switch. She turns the key only to find that the battery is dead. In vain, she turns the key several more times. She is frustrated because she has been thwarted in attaining her goal (i.e. a quick trip to the grocery store).

Connections
The definition notes that some goals can be negative. An example of a negative goal is a person one dislikes. If one has been

cornered by this person at a social gathering one will be frustrated.

An important hypothesis in psychology is the *frustration-aggression* hypothesis (see the entry on aggressive behavior) which asserts that aggressive behavior is a common reaction to frustration. Madeline might get out of the automobile and give one of its tires an angry kick. The individual cornered at a social gathering might make hostile remarks veiled by a double meaning designed to discount the disliked person.

FUNCTIONAL AUTONOMY

Definition
Functional autonomy is a quality associated with certain motives. The functional autonomy of motives takes place when (1) a motive no longer serves its original purpose, and (2) it still continues to motivate the organism.

Example
Edward escaped in his youth from the slums of a big city by becoming a successful clothing salesman. Eventually he became a highly prosperous manufacturer of women's apparel. The money-making motive in his youth was energized primarily by memories of an impoverished childhood. Edward is now sixty-eight years old and he still works ten hours a day, six days a week, and seldom takes a vacation. He is a wealthy man, but the money-making motive still dominates his behavior. It provides its own current satisfactions, such as the feeling of pride he gets from running a large business. But it is independent of its origins. It has become functionally autonomous.

Connections
The concept of functional autonomy was introduced into psychology in the 1930s by the personality theorist Gordon Allport. Allport was to some extent inspired by the earlier writings of the psychologist Robert S. Woodworth who stated that mechanisms of behavior may be transformed into drives. An example of this principle at a very fundamental level is provided by a rat experiment published by W. C. Olson in 1919. An irritating chemical was placed on the ears of a group of rats. The rats began to scratch their ears on a regular basis. Long after the irritating effects of the chemical had worn off the rats continued

to scratch their ears with a high level of frequency. It is reasonable to hypothesize that ear-scratching had become an end in itself, or was functionally autonomous.

FUNCTIONALISM

Definition
Functionalism is a school of psychology based on the assumption that the primary aim of psychology should be to study the uses, or functions, of mental faculties associated with consciousness such as attention, perception, intelligence, will, and memory.

Example
Julia A., an experimental psychologist, specializes in research on ways of improving memory. She has presented a number of weekend seminars for grade-school teachers demonstrating to them the practical applications of her findings. Although Julia does not think of herself as belonging to a particular school of psychology, her work is clearly in the spirit of functionalism.

Connections
The father of functionalism was William James (see entry). Functionalism was to a large extent a protest against *structuralism*, which argued that the primary aim of psychology was to study the structures of consciousness (see entry). James was unhappy with structuralism, declaring it to be too static and useless to be of much interest to practical persons. James, instead, was interested in the question: what is consciousness for? Functionalism was well-suited to the spirit of Yankee ingenuity abounding in the New England area of the United States during the early part of this century. James' approach met with enthusiasm, and has had much to do with the growth of applied psychology.

G

GALTON, FRANCIS
(1822–1911)

Francis Galton was an English explorer and scientist with a wide range of interests. He did not occupy a formal university position, but conducted most of his research under his own auspices. His many contributions received formal recognition when he was knighted at the age of eighty-seven.

Galton emphasized the importance of one's *nature*, or set of inborn endowments, as a determinant of success in life. In order to demonstrate the importance of nature, Galton studied eminent men. He found that eminent fathers tend to have eminent sons, and believed that this could be explained primarily in terms of nature, not *nurture* (see entry). In order to make an analysis of the data he collected Galton hired the mathematician Karl Pearson, and Pearson devised a tool known as the *correlation coefficient* (see entry). This is one of the principal descriptive statistics, and is widely employed in a variety of research settings.

Galton was also interested in measuring intelligence, and favored an approach to its measurement known as the *biometric method* in which intelligence is assessed by the evaluation of physical characteristics such as strength of grip, circumference of the head, and reflex reaction time. Although the biometric method of assessing intelligence is out of favor today, the biometric method itself has a place in biology, research on exercise, and physiological psychology.

If Galton's work has any focus at all, it is the general assertion that heredity is more important than environment. Although this general point of view has been relatively unpopular among behavioral scientists throughout most of the twentieth century, it is beginning to regain some strength (see *nativism* and *sociobiology*).

GAME

Definition
The definition of a game given here is not the general one used in everyday language, but a specialized one based on transactional analysis, a school of psychotherapy. According to transactional analysis, a game is a contest, or a power struggle, between at least two persons involving hidden messages and manipulative ploys. At the end of the game one person will be emotionally defeated; a second person will be emotionally triumphant at the expense of the first person.

Example
Transactional analysis identifies a number of games and gives them labels. One game frequently played by married couples is called *If It Weren't for You*. A husband tells his wife that if it wasn't for her they would be wealthy today. He had great ideas for trading in the stock market, but she stopped him. If he can make her feel guilty and/or depressed about her lack of confidence in him, then he has 'won' a round of the game. In this case, the protagonist of the game is the one who is doing the blaming, the husband.

Connections
The idea that people play destructive life games comes from Eric Berne, a psychiatrist. Berne wrote a book called *Games People Play* that became a bestseller in the 1960s. Berne is also considered to be the father of transactional analysis.

An important part of any game is a hidden agenda, particularly on the part of the protagonist. The protagonist instigates the game because he or she has a secret psychological aim. In the example given it is quite likely that the husband lacks the self-confidence to trade in stocks, and avoids admitting this to himself. Therefore he projects the blame onto his wife. Every game has an *antithesis*, a move that will put a stop to the game. In this case the wife need only give her husband her 'permission' to buy and sell stocks, and the game would be over.

GENERAL ADAPTATION SYNDROME

Definition
The general adaptation syndrome is a physiological reaction

pattern induced by chronic stress. Its aim is to fight off the effects of stress and conserve the resources of the body. The three stages of the pattern are: (1) the alarm reaction, (2) the stage of resistance, and (3) the stage of exhaustion.

Example
A chronic irritant such as a high-pitched whistle is introduced into the environment of a rat. At first its arousal increases markedly: the heart rate increases, the rat is more alert, and blood vessels in the striated muscles constrict. This is the alarm reaction. Then the organism settles down. Its adrenal glands pump out extra adrenal hormones on a regular basis, and the behavior of the animal seems to be almost normal. This is the stage of resistance. In time the animal dies prematurely of heart disease. This is the stage of exhaustion. A post-mortem examination reveals swollen adrenal glands. The rat was fighting off the effects of stress and using up its coping reserve. Although superficially the cause of death was heart disease, on a deeper level the cause of death was chronic stress.

Connections
The physiologist Hans Selye originated the concept of the general adaptation syndrome, and conducted quite a large number of experiments with lower organisms to demonstrate its effects.

The implications of the general adaptation syndrome have not been lost on psychologists and physicians. Psychosomatic illness (see entry) is in part explained by referring it to chronic stress. We have all heard the advice that it is not a good idea to burn the candle of life at both ends. Folk wisdom says that those who live at too rapid a pace often die young. Briefly, people should avoid introducing excessive stress into their lives. The general adaptation syndrome gives a scientific basis to informal observations.

GENERAL DRIVES

Definition
General drives are hypothesized to be inborn drives aiming to provide the organism with certain kinds of stimulation or the opportunity to express certain kinds of behavior. Important differences between general drives and biological drives are that general drives do not serve known tissue needs or follow the principle of homeostasis.

Example
One of the general drives is the *activity drive*, a drive to be doing something, to be moving, even if the activity serves no instrumental purpose. People appear to want to walk, talk, and play games even when such activities do not bring immediate gratifications in the form of food or water. Sitting through a boring meeting one may doodle on a piece of paper just to be doing something.

Connections
Other examples of general drives are the affectional drive and curiosity behavior (see entries).

It has been suggested that the maternal drive is one of the general drives. Experiments with rats indicate that a mother rat will endure quite a bit of pain in order to engage in the opportunity to feed her pups.

GESTALT PSYCHOLOGY

Definition
Gestalt psychology is a school of psychology that asserts organized wholes are prior in both perception and behavior to the parts that make up the wholes. The German word *Gestalt* is translated into English as 'organized whole,' 'pattern,' or 'configuration.'

Example
You hear a song being played on the piano. The perception of the melody is dominant over the sensations associated with individual notes. In fact you have to work at hearing the notes; they have to be abstracted from the flow of the melody. A further indication of the dominance of the melody over individual notes is given by the fact of transposition. The entire melody can be transposed to a different key. Now every note is *different*, but one hears the *same* melody. The perception of the melody is a Gestalt, or organized whole.

Connections
The father of Gestalt psychology was Max Wertheimer (see entry). Gestalt psychology arose as a protest against structuralism (see entry), a school of psychology that assumed simple sensations were the building blocks of complex perceptions, and

thus prior to them in experience. Wertheimer argued that the simple sensations of structuralism were found only by an effort of will on the part of a subject. Thus they were, in a sense, created entities, not the building blocks of perception.

The general line of reasoning of Gestalt psychology is that wholes in perception and behavior must be studied in and of themselves without an analysis downward into parts. This approach was used by Wolfgang Köhler (see entry) with some success to attack behaviorism. Köhler argued that the behaviorist breaks down the organized wholes of behavior, such as insight learning, into parts such as conditioned reflexes. This analysis destroys the whole, and the parts that are studied cannot be put together again to make the whole. Gestalt psychology argues that behavioral scientists must not put themselves in the position of the king's horses and men by breaking Humpty Dumpty (i.e. an organized whole) into parts and then trying to put him together again.

GOAL

Definition
A goal is an end or objective of motivated behavior. A goal can be positive, in which case the organism seeks to move toward the goal. Or a goal can be negative, in which case the organism seeks to move away from the goal.

Example
Bradford is a student in a medical school. A dominant goal in his life is the M.D. degree. He has organized his life around this goal. It determines when he will study, when he will sleep, and when he will socialize.

Connections
Goals can be short-term or long-term. In the example, Bradford's goal is a long-term one. If on a particular day he is trying to get to a class on time, that is a short-term goal.

Psychologists have made use of the concept of a goal on many levels. In maze-learning experiments with animals it is common to speak of the *goal box*, a region at the end of the maze often baited with food. Frustration is seen in terms of a goal being blocked (see entry). It is possible to speak of a *conflict* between goals when one is forced to make a choice among two or more goals.

H

HABIT

Definition
A habit is a learned behavior pattern characterized by being both well-established and capable of automatic performance.

Example
James has the habit of shaving every morning with a safety razor. The smaller units of behavior associated with shaving such as opening the medicine cabinet, lathering his face, changing blades, rinsing the razor, and so forth can be performed with little conscious attention. In fact he often thinks about what clothing he wants to wear for the day while he is shaving.

Connections
In view of the fact that much human behavior is acquired through learning psychologists have been very interested in studying habits. The work of Ivan Pavlov on classical conditioning and B.F. Skinner on operant conditioning are essentially studies of habit formation (see entries).

Because habits are capable of automatic performance they are often referred to as 'second nature,' meaning that once they are entrenched they seem to have almost inborn status. The author Raymond Radiguet wrote, 'It is not in novelty but in habit that we find the greatest pleasure.'

HALO EFFECT

Definition
The halo effect is a tendency on the part of an observer to make a biased rating, either positive or negative, of another person based on outstanding, but irrelevant, traits or characteristics displayed by that person.

Example
Mr C. is a fourth-grade teacher who admires neatness and cleanliness in his students. One of his students, Faith, is a particularly clean and well-dressed little girl. He thinks of her as very intelligent, and, when a subjective evaluation is required, tends to give her work higher marks than it merits.

Connections
A halo is a circle of light surrounding the head of a saint or holy person. So it is easy to understand the derivation of the term *halo effect* in social psychology. As the word *halo* would suggest, the halo effect is usually thought of as a biased positive perception. However, it is possible to speak of a negative halo effect, as the definition indicates. Thus one of Mr C.s students, Leon, is thought of as unintelligent because he wears ill-fitting wrinkled clothes, has poorly combed hair, and washes carelessly.

HEDONISM

Definition
Hedonism is the point of view that the prime motivating factor in human behavior is a bipolar pain-pleasure dimension.

Example
Porter is a well-meaning father who believes he can be an effective disciplinarian by the use of appropriate rewards and punishments. When he approves of the behavior of one of his children, he gives the child a reward in the form of candy, money, or some other small treat. When he disapproves of behavior, he withholds a privilege or spanks the child. The giving of rewards and punishments as a means of training children is based on hedonism.

Connections
The principal early advocate of hedonism as an explanatory frame of reference for human behavior was Aristotle (see entry). Hedonism appeals to common sense, but in some ways it breaks down as an explanation. Hedonism is hard put to handle *masochism*, a tendency of some persons to seek pain. It can be said, as it often is, that such people enjoy suffering. In other words, they derive pleasure from pain. This is an appealing application of hedonism, but it weakens the general principle because it makes

hedonism circular. Hedonism is simply assumed to be true and all behavior is made to fit the hedonistic model. For this reason psychologists interested in studying human motivation have looked to other factors in behavior such as biological drives, general drives, curiosity behavior, functional autonomy, observational learning, and operant conditioning (see entries).

A *hedonist* is a person who lives mainly for pleasure. In *Don Juan* the poet Lord Byron had his protagonist express the hedonistic philosophy in this manner:

Let us have wine and women, mirth and laughter.
Sermons and soda-water the day after.

HOMEOSTASIS

Definition
Homeostasis is a tendency for the organism to maintain a stable and optimal internal environment either through automatic physiological processes or through overt behavior.

Example
An internal body temperature of 98.6° Fahrenheit is normal for human beings. If the temperature falls below the normal level, the metabolic rate may increase, the person may shiver, extra clothing may be put on, and so forth. If the temperature rises above the normal level, the matabolic rate may decrease, the person may sweat, clothing may be discarded, and so forth. All of the physiological processes as well as any overt behavior exhibited have one aim: to return the body temperature to 98.6° Fahrenheit.

Connections
Homeostasis is an important principle in both physiology and psychology. It is important in psychology because the biological drives (see entry) tend to follow the homeostatic principle, and these drives are considered to be foundation stones for human behavior. Eating behavior is affected by blood sugar levels. Sexual behavior is affected by hormone levels. Thus an understanding of homeostasis provides a certain amount of insight into some aspects of human behavior.

HOMOSEXUAL BEHAVIOR

Definition
Homosexual behavior is erotic activity or sexual relations between persons of the same sex.

Example
Two men are lovers. At times that they consider to be opportune they hold hands, kiss, embrace, and bring each other to orgasm.

Connections
Homosexual behavior may be between two men or between two females. Homosexual behavior in females is referred to as lesbianism because of the ancient legend that the females on the Greek island of Lesbos, followers of Sappho, practiced homosexual behavior.

In classical psychoanalytic theory homosexual behavior was looked upon as a form of pathology. It was seen as caused by infantile fixations associated with pregenital psychosexual development.

More recently psychiatry has tended to take the view that homosexual behavior is not a form of pathology in and of itself. However, it *is* a problem if the person attracted by or engaging in such behavior is distressed by it. Psychiatry identifies a form of homosexuality called *ego-dystonic homosexuality* in which the troubled person states that the homosexual arousal is unwanted and a source of emotional upset.

HORNEY, KAREN
(1885–1952)

Karen Horney was one of the pioneers of early psychoanalysis. She received a medical degree in Germany, was a member of the Berlin Institute of Psychoanalysis, and eventually moved to New York City in the United States. A pioneer feminist, she added to our understanding of the psychology of women.

Although Horney remained faithful to the spirit of Freud's ideas, she was a rebel in terms of the letter of his ideas. She made a lifetime commitment to the idea of unconscious motivation (see entry), but disagreed with Freud on a number of specific points. For example, she felt that Freud made too much out of the sex drive as such. In the case of the Oedipus complex (see entry) Horney felt that the emotional difficulties associated with it were due primarily to a power struggle between parent and child, not to an incest wish on the child's part.

Horney is perhaps best known for moving psychoanalysis away from a limited emphasis on biology and the maturational processes. She directed psychoanalysis instead toward an emphasis on the impact of society and culture and their joint role in personality development.

Two of Horney's books are *The Neurotic Personality of our Time* (1937) and *Our Inner Conflicts* (1945).

HUMANISTIC PSYCHOLOGY

Definition
Humanistic psychology represents a point of view asserting that we ourselves shape the quality of our existence. We do this by making conscious choices, by exercising the will, and by looking toward the future. Thus each individual is responsible for the course his or her life may take.

Example
Richard is thirty-three years old, married, has two children, and works in a grocery store as a clerk. He also battles with frequent feelings of depression. It turns out that Richard's depression is neither biochemical nor traceable to early childhood experiences. In counseling with a humanistic psychologist, he realizes that his life has taken a wrong turn. He has always wanted a musical career. He wants to both perform and teach young people. But he gave up his high aspirations when he married and had children, thinking his musical ambitions were impractical. With the support of his wife he decides to pursue a musical education on a part-time basis while he continues to support his family. Even though he is working somewhat harder, and the pathway is somewhat rougher, his depression lifts. He feels that his life now leads in the correct direction.

Connections
Humanistic psychology has acquired the label, the *third force* in psychology. This contrasts it with the other two principal forces in contemporary psychology, psychoanalysis and behaviorism (see entries). Humanistic psychology rejects the emphasis that psychoanalysis places upon the unconscious aspects of mental life. It also rejects the emphasis that behaviorism places upon

learned aspects of behavior. Although a humanistic psychologist might agree that we have both unconscious motives and habits, they don't have us! We can break free from psychological chains by asserting ourselves as conscious beings.

Humanistic psychology is thought of as a fairly recent trend in psychology, rising to prominence in the 1960s. Nonetheless, it is apparent that it has historical roots going back at least to the Middle Ages and St Thomas Aquinas' teaching that human beings have free will with responsibility for their actions.

Two of the principal founders of humanistic psychology are Abraham Maslow and Carl Rogers (see entries).

HYPERKINETIC BEHAVIOR

Definition
Hyperkinetic behavior is behavior characterized by restlessness, inattention, and excessive muscular motion.

Example
Randolph is an eight-year-old boy who suffers from a behavioral disorder known as the *hyperactive child syndrome*. At school he has difficulty paying attention for any sustained length of time when a teacher is offering an explanation of a subject. At home he flits from one activity to another in a restless unsettled manner. He is often aggressive and rude, having little frustration tolerance. He is receiving poor marks in school. Although his intelligence is basically normal, he has a difficult time displaying that it is.

Connections
Various explanations have been offered for hyperkinetic behavior in children. It has been suggested that they suffer from minimal brain damage acquired during the birth process, a vitamin deficiency, low blood sugar, emotional conflicts, and excessive intake of artificial food additives. Kinds of therapy include the prescription of drugs, the administering of vitamins, removal of refined sugar from the diet, child psychotherapy, and an eating regimen of unprocessed foods.

Although hyperkinetic behavior is more common in children than adults, it is nonetheless possible to speak of this kind of behavior in adults. The explanations of the behavior and the kinds of therapy for it are essentially the same as those described in connection with children.

HYPNOSIS

Definition
Hypnosis is an altered state of consciousness characterized by narrowly focused attention and heightened suggestibility.

Example
Elena is a subject presently in a deep trance. She has been hypnotized a number of times, learning with each experience to become a more facile subject. The hypnotist suggests that her hand is numb and incapable of feeling pain. He punctures it deeply with a thick needle and Elena gives no evidence of feeling injured. He then suggests that an amusing motion picture is being projected on the wall, and Elena appears to hallucinate the sights and sounds of the film. She laughs and reacts as if the film is present. Although extremely attentive to the voice and instructions of the hypnotist, Elena is unaware of other potential objects of perception in her environment.

Connections
Hypnosis derives its name from Hypnos, an ancient Greek god of sleep. Thus the term *hypnosis* is something of a misnomer because during hypnosis the subject is *not* sleeping, but is in fact more attentive to certain specific stimuli. The state has a superficial resemblance to sleep because of the subject's lack of attention to many general stimuli.

During the eighteenth century Franz Anton Mesmer was one of the first practitioners of hypnosis. The word *mesmerized* is still sometimes used as a synonym for hypnosis. Mesmer thought that a trance in a subject was due to an animal magnetism flowing from Mesmer's body. The subject was 'caught' in Mesmer's spell the way an iron filing is caught in the field of a magnet.

Freud used hypnosis in his early work in psychoanalysis, but gave it up in favor of free association (see entry). In recent times there has been a rebirth of interest in the uses of hypnosis in psychotherapy.

Not all researchers are convinced that hypnosis is an altered state of consciousness. A relatively small number of skeptics argue that hypnosis is possibly a kind of role playing in which the subject acts as he or she imagines a hypnotized person should act.

HYPOGLYCEMIA

Definition
The basic meaning of hypoglycemia is simply low blood sugar. Persons who suffer from a clinical case of hypoglycemia have a tendency toward chronic low blood sugar, a debilitating condition.

Example
Selby, a thirty-seven-year-old accountant, suffers from an undiagnosed case of hypoglycemic disorder. Between meals he often feels listless, fatigued, apathetic, and slightly confused. He has learned that he can obtain quick relief from a candy bar, a soft drink, a cookie, or ice cream – any high-sugar food. As a consequence, he has become dependent upon such foods. They provide quick relief from his distress, and his quick relief reinforces his undesirable eating habits. Selby's hypoglycemic disorder is as a consequence complicated by obesity.

Connections
A person with a hypoglycemic disorder may exhibit what is mistakenly thought to be neurotic behavior (see entry). Before psychotherapy is begun it is prudent to have a physical check-up. If hypoglycemia is suspected, a physician can order *a glucose tolerance test*, a test capable of detecting a clinical case.

HYPOTHETICAL CONSTRUCT

Definition
A hypothetical construct is an explanatory concept authored by a theoretician in order to explain observed phenomena. It is hypothetical because it is not itself directly observed, and therefore not known for certain. And it is a construct because it is 'constructed' by the mind of the theoretician.

Example
Freud's formulation of the id (see entry) is a hypothetical construct. Freud never saw an id, nor did anyone else. What he did observe were a group of behavioral tendencies, including sexual and aggressive ones, that were not easily explained in terms of learning. It thus seemed reasonable to him to postulate the

existence of an agent in the personality of inborn origin account-
ing for the observed behavior.

Connections
Psychology makes use of many hypothetical constructs. Many of
the words defined in this book represent hypothetical constructs.
A few examples are: achievement motive, cell assembly, complex motives, innate ideas, learning set, personality, and trait.
Upon hearing that psychology is heavily dependent upon
hypothetical constructs, some people become hostile and negative toward the field. They think that hypothetical constructs are
somehow not respectable because they are not 'real' and never
can be completely proven to exist. However, the philosophy of
science identifies hypothetical constructs in all fields of science.
The concept of a field of energy in physics is a hypothetical
construct. The atom is also a hypothetical construct. And so are
subatomic particles such as proton, neutron, and electron.

Science represents not only facts, but *ideas*. Many of these
ideas may be fictions of a sort, useful for tying together sets of
observations. It is really impossible for a science to advance
without the ideas of its theoreticians. And these ideas are often
expressed in the form of hypothetical constructs.

I

ID

Definition
In Freudian theory, the id is the primitive and basic part of the personality. It is roughly equivalent to the biological drives taken as a group.

Example
John is a prisoner in a concentration camp. He and his fellow prisoners are slowly starving to death. One day, after he has eaten his own bread ration, he steals bread right out of the hands of a weaker fellow prisoner. This is unusual behavior for John. But the behavior can be explained in part by referring it to the id. Under stress, John has regressed to a primitive level of his personality – the id. The id presents to the conscious mind an image of and a desire for food without regard for reality or the rights of others.

Connections
Freud was inspired to develop his concept of the id by the writings of a physician named Georg Groddeck, author of *The Book of It*. Groddeck's theme was that instead of consciously living our lives (as we prefer to think), we are *lived by* an impersonal force that controls us. He called this impersonal force the *it* of the personality. Neither Freud nor Grodeck spoke of the *id*, simply of the *it*. The word *id* is Latin for *it*, and first appeared when Freud's works were translated to English.

IDENTICAL TWINS

Definition
Identical twins are siblings originating from the same zygote. In consequence, they share identical genetic structures.

Example
Paula and Pearl are identical twins seventeen years old. They both have light brown hair, fair skin, blue eyes, and a mole on the right cheek. There are slight physical discrepancies. Paula is five-feet three-inches tall and weighs one-hundred twenty pounds. Pearl is five-feet two-inches tall and weighs one-hundred fifteen pounds. They have similar personalities. Both are cheerful, optimistic, and extraverted persons with career aspirations in a scientific field. Only people who know them well can tell them apart readily.

Connections
Because identical twins share identical genetic structures they provide helpful subjects when an investigator wants to explore the interaction of heredity and environment. A number of studies have involved a research plan in which identical twins who were separated in infancy are located as adults. Raised in different homes, they have identical hereditary input, but varying environmental input. If such twins are significantly different in intelligence or in personal adjustment, then one can conclude that environment is the source of this difference. If such twins are significantly similar in intelligence or in personal adjustment, then one can conclude that heredity is the source of this similarity.

Studies utilizing the described research plan have shown very convincingly that environment is not the only factor that plays an important role in development. Heredity is an important factor, and has a great effect on intelligence and personal adjustment. However, one does not want to end up with the simplistic statement that one factor or the other is the primary cause of human development. Sophisticated investigators point to the interaction, the joint effects of heredity and environment, as the meaningful source of variation.

ILLUSION

Definition
An illusion is a perception that does not correspond to objective facts.

Example
When the moon is near the horizon it appears to be much larger

than when it is high in the sky. The moon does not change its size as it moves. It is the perception that changes. This is a striking and well-known illusion. It is known, obviously, as the *moon illusion*.

Connections
Many illusions have been identified, and attempts to explain them revolve around either inborn factors or learned factors in perception. Gestalt psychology (see entry) has traditionally been very interested in studying the illusions as a way of gaining a greater understanding of perception in general. Gestalt psychology tends to give greater importance to inborn factors than to learned factors. In the case of the moon illusion the misinterpretation seems to arise from the way in which the nervous system uses cues arising from linear perspective. When the moon is near the horizon it is also near the vanishing point for parallel lines moving toward the horizon. The moon appears large in contrast to other perceived or remembered objects. The assumption that learning plays a small role in the illusion is supported by the informal observation that pre-schoolers see the illusion as readily as do adults, and are quite impressed by it. If learning were the key factor in the moon illusion, one would expect that the illusion might become greater with development and more experience, but it does not.

On the other hand, learned factors can and do play a role in explaining some illusions. One of the most well-known demonstrations of the importance of learning in perception is the distorted room designed by Adelbert Ames. Seen from the front, the vantage point of most observers, the room appears to be normal in design. Seen from above, the left back wall is much farther from the front wall than is the right back wall. When two people of approximately the same objective size stand against the two back corners, the one on the left seems tiny and the one on the right seems gigantic to an observer viewing from the front. The angled back wall sets up a misleading cue suggesting to the observer that both of the persons in the room are the same distance from him or her. It is argued by Ames that our perceptual habit, acquired by experience, is to judge object A as smaller than object B if (1) the two objects seem to be the same distance away from us, and (2) object A presents a smaller image on the retina.

IMPOTENCE

Definition
First, impotence at the most general level is any state of helplessness or powerlessness in a given situation. Second, applied to sexual relations, impotence is an inability on the part of the male to either achieve or maintain an erection adequate for an act of sexual intercourse.

Example
Madison is forty-seven years old and has been married for twenty-two years to the same partner. About seven years ago he was in the midst of sexual intercourse with his wife, was sexually excited, and had achieved penetration. Rather abruptly he felt his penis becoming flaccid. He was surprised because this had never happened to him. He tried to continue, but felt anxious, and his penis became more flaccid. He was unable to reach an orgasm and discontinued in disappointment. Both Madison and his wife were puzzled. He felt embarrassed, and she felt rejected.

At present he loses his erection more than half of the time when he attempts sexual intercourse. He has developed a considerable amount of *performance anxiety*, perceiving every sexual union as a test of his manhood. And this anxiety is compounding his sexual dysfunction.

Connections
The noted sexual research team of William H. Masters and Virginia E. Johnson distinguish two kinds of impotence: primary and secondary. *Primary impotence* is a kind of impotence in which the male has never had an erection adequate for sexual intercourse. *Secondary impotence* is a kind of impotence in which the male has had prior successful sexual relations, but now has frequent erectile difficulties. Of the two kinds of impotence, the second is much more common.

Early attempts on the part of psychotherapists to treat impotence usually depended on a psychoanalytic approach in which it was believed necessary to uncover unconscious guilt or anger as the source of the problem. Contemporary sex therapy does not necessarily reject the importance of emotional factors such as guilt and anger, but it tends to focus more on maladaptive learned responses, in consequence seeking a reconditioning of the male with sexual complaints.

In view of the fact that the word *impotence* has the literal

109

meaning 'lack of power,' the term is somewhat pejorative. It is for this reason that some clinicians favor terms such as *inhibited sexual excitement* or *erectile insufficiency* over impotence.

IMPRINTING

Definition
Imprinting is a form of both rapid and irreversible learning associated with critical periods of development in the early life of some organisms.

Example
Ducklings tend to follow their mother about. This tendency does not appear when a duckling is first hatched, but will appear within a few hours. If deprived of the opportunity to follow for more than thirty hours, the following behavior will not be acquired. The fixed tendency of the duckling to follow the mother duck is imprinted behavior.

Connections
Imprinting is a form of learning, and not a tendency to follow only a mother duck, because it has been possible to show that ducklings can imprint on various moving objects presented during the critical period such as decoys, blocks of wood, and toy trucks.

Imprinting has been studied primarily by *ethologists*, students of *instinctive behavior* (see entry). The subjects of their research have been animals. The question has naturally arisen: Do human beings imprint? Human beings do not imprint in the rigid and fixed way that animals imprint. Strictly speaking, the term *imprinting* should be reserved for animal behavior. However, human infants do display behavior that is somewhat similar to imprinting. They form an emotional attachment to a primary caretaker when they are about six months old. Some researchers assert that this attachment is an essential feature of normal infant development.

INCIDENTAL LEARNING

Definition
Incidental learning is learning that occurs without particular intention, effort, or purpose.

Example
One day you find yourself humming a melody. You are not sure at first where it comes from. Then you recognize it as the theme song of a certain television series. You have learned the melody in an incidental way as you watched the program.

Connections
Several variations exist on a game called Trivia. The participants are required to recall the names of popular film stars, historical events, book titles, advertising slogans, and so forth. Even those of us who do not excel at playing Trivia acquire thousands of items of more or less irrelevant information. Incidental learning is the explanation of this phenomenon.

Incidental learning is of considerable theoretical importance in learning theory because it demonstrates that the two essential processes in learning are (1) attention and (2) contiguity (see entry). It does not seem that reinforcement in the form of some distinct pay-off or value is required in all cases of learning. This last statement is open to debate, but a minority of psychologists would disagree with it.

INFANTILE AUTISM

Definition
Infantile autism is a behavioral disorder associated with infancy and early childhood characterized by lack of interest in other people, disturbed language development, hyperactivity, aggressiveness, self-destructiveness, and excessive attention for prolonged periods to irrelevant stimuli in the environment.

Example
Six-year-old Lyle is an autistic child. His parents assert that even when he was a few weeks old he seemed odd to them. He hated to be touched and would arch his back away from his mother even when she was nursing him. If given the opportunity, he will spend hours in a corner of a room in a pointless repetitive activity such as spinning a favorite red ball. He bites his fingers and several are mutilated. He almost never gives anyone, including his parents, a social smile. Most of the time he is mute, but he sometimes displays *echolalia*, the immediate repetition of a word or phrase said to him.

111

INNATE IDEAS

Connections
The psychiatrist Leo Kanner first described infantile autism in 1943, distinguishing it from childhood schizophrenia. The onset of infantile autism is earlier than childhood schizophrenia. And the autistic child does not have the bizarre thinking, delusions, and hallucinations associated with a schizophrenic disorder.

At first researchers thought that infantile autism was caused by an authoritarian and rejecting parental style. The present thinking is that the cause of the disorder is primarily *biogenetic*, a disorder arising from constitutional factors inherent in the child.

There have been many attempts to devise a successful therapy for infantile autism including prescriptions of megavitamins, psychoanalysis, and behavior therapy. Behavior therapy (see entry) seems to be the most effective approach, but it is not a cure for the condition. Most autistic children will spend a large part of their lives in institutions. Those who do respond well to behavior therapy may live relatively adequate lives at home.

Approximately four or five children out of every 10,000 suffer from infantile autism, a relatively low incidence of occurrence.

INNATE IDEAS

Definition
Innate ideas are ideas that are hypothesized to be present in the organism at birth. They do not necessarily exist in their mature and full-blown final form, but at least in seminal form.

Example
The philosopher Plato (427–347 BC) asserted that many important ideas are inborn. An example is the idea of beauty. Plato said we perceive some objects and persons as having exceptional beauty because we have an inborn idea of perfect beauty. We compare every person and object with this inborn standard and rank each accordingly. Perhaps culture and personal experience have an effect on the way in which the inborn idea of beauty takes mature form. But the core image is in its essence fixed.

Connections
The philosopher Immanuel Kant (see entry) agreed with Plato that some ideas are innate. He called such ideas *a priori* ones, meaning they exist in the mind prior to experience. Kant asserted that our basic ideas about space and time are inborn.

Other thinkers have disagreed. John Locke (see entry) argued that all ideas are acquired by experience. Advocates of behaviorism (see entry) reject the doctrine of innate ideas.

INSIGHT

Definition
First, in Gestalt psychology, insight is the sudden perception of how parts relate to an organized whole. Second, in psychoanalysis, insight is a patient's accurate grasp of the meaning of ideas, motives, and memories recovered from the unconscious level of the personality.

Example
This example is associated with Gestalt psychology. Add the following numbers as rapidly as possible and state their sum: $2 + 8 + 1 + 9 + 4 + 6 + 3 + 7 + 7 + 3$. Most of us on seeing this problem add the numbers to each other one-by-one and arrive rather slowly at the correct sum, fifty. A few people exclaim abruptly, 'Fifty!' The people in this second group are demonstrating insight. They perceive that each pair of two numbers starting from the beginning of the series is equal to ten. There are five such pairs of ten. So the sum is obviously fifty, and rote addition is not necessary.

Connections
The two definitions of insight from Gestalt psychology and psychoanalysis differ only in emphasis, not in any essential feature. They are in fact quite congruent. Both assume the capacity at a conscious level to *understand*.

Gestalt psychology stressed the value of insight in learning. Max Wertheimer (see entry) felt that too much teaching encouraged memorization and rote learning without creativity or imagination.

INSTINCTIVE BEHAVIOR

Definition
Instinctive behavior is behavior that meets these criteria: (1) It has an inborn basis, (2) it is more than a reflex; it involves a complex repertoire, (3) it is more dependent on maturation than

on learning, and (4) it appears full-blown at the first appropriate opportunity.

Example
The nesting behavior of most birds fits the definition of instinctive behavior. The mother bird must find a suitable place for the nest, collect appropriate materials for its construction, actually put the materials together in an adequate way, sit on the eggs, and so forth. The entire behavior pattern appears to be much more dependent on some kind of innate programming than on learning.

Connections
It was popular in psychology for about three decades starting in the 1920s to deny the existence of instincts in both animals and human beings. This was due primarily to the influence of behaviorism which attempted to explain virtually all behavior in terms of conditioning.

Today a more moderate view prevails, a view that allows for the concept of instinctive behavior, at least in animals. This view has arisen in part because of the highly respected investigations of *ethologists*, a group of researchers who have studied the behavior of many animals in their natural habitats. The work of these scientists clearly indicates that there are *species-specific behaviors*, behaviors that are exhibited on a universal basis by the members of a given species. Although the term *instinctive behavior* is an older usage, species-specific behaviors and instinctive behaviors have about the same meaning.

More recently the concept of instinctive behavior has been given renewed vigor by *sociobiology*, a research orientation stressing the importance of genetic factors in behavior (see entry).

INTELLIGENCE

Definition
The literature of psychology contains numerous definitions of intelligence because intelligence is an abstraction conceptualized differently by different psychologists. However, it seems fairly safe to say that intelligence is usually associated with these traits: the ability to (1) learn quickly, (2) adapt to new situations, (3) use abstract reasoning, (4) understand both verbal and mathe-

matical concepts, and (5) perform tasks in which a relationship must be grasped. David Wechsler, author of the *Wechsler Adult Intelligence Scale* and the *Wechsler Intelligence Scale for Children*, defines intelligence as follows: 'The global capacity of the individual to act purposefully, to think rationally, and to deal effectively with the environment.'

Example
Mallory is stranded in a remote area when one of the water hoses in the engine of his automobile bursts. At first it appears that he will be forced to wait a long time for assistance. Then he recalls that in the trunk of his car there is an old garden hose and some friction tape. On his person he has a pocket knife. He is able to make a rough repair of the broken water hose with the materials at hand, and he is on his way again. It is certainly appropriate to say that Mallory's behavior was intelligent.

Connections
Psychologists hotly debated for many years this question: is intelligence mainly inborn or acquired? Today most of the dust of battle has settled and a consensus seems to have arisen. It is now conventional to say that intelligence is the result of an *interaction*, the complex joint effects, of heredity and environment working together.

Another question that was discussed for many years is this one: is intelligence a global capacity or does it consist of a set of specific abilities? Research using factor analysis (see entry) suggests that there is a general capacity underlying intelligence, and, in addition, there are several specific abilities augmenting it.

INTELLIGENCE QUOTIENT

Definition
The intelligence quotient (IQ) is a single index number indicating an individual's intelligence level relative to other individuals in a standardized sample. The IQ tends to be relatively stable over time.

Example
The Wechsler Adult Intelligence Scale (WAIS) is administered by a clinical psychologist to Madge, and she obtains an IQ score

of 122. This places her in the classification *Superior*. Only 8.9 per cent of individuals in a standardized sample associated with the WAIS scored as high or higher than Madge.

Connections
The measure known as the IQ was first proposed by William Stern, a psychologist working in Germany during the early part of this century. Original measures of intelligence reported the subject's mental age. But because mental age increases over time a subject's score constantly changes, and the stability of intelligence cannot be discerned. Stern noted that if mental age is compared with chronological age a stable measure emerges. Thus Stern proposed that the following formula be used:

$$\frac{\text{Mental age}}{\text{Chronological age}} \times 100 = \text{IQ}$$

This formula will automatically give anyone with an identical mental and chronological age an IQ of 100. Thus by definition 100 is a normal IQ. IQs higher than 100 fall into three ascending classifications: Bright normal, Superior, and Very Superior. IQs below 100 fall into three descending classifications: Dull Normal, Borderline, and Mental Defective. Approximately 50 percent of the population is within the normal range. Only 2.2 per cent are in the Very Superior classification. And only 2.2 percent are in the Mental Defective classification.

In recent years Stern's formula has been replaced by a different method of computing the IQ based on the *standard deviation*, a measure of the dispersion of a set of scores (see entry).

INTIMACY

Definition
According to transactional analysis, intimacy is a state of emotional closeness with another person characterized by an absence of manipulation and the presence of authentic communication.

Example
Andrew and Jeannine are a married couple with a number of interests and values in common. They are both authentic persons (see entry). Both detest falsehoods and deception of any kind. When they talk to each other they are prone to be quite self-disclosing about both ideas and feelings. The personality traits

being described have brought their relationship to a high state of intimacy, a state that is a joy to both of them.

Connections

Transactional analysis identifies intimacy as one of the most important goals of human relationships. It is the opposite of a relationship characterized by games (see entry). The psychiatrist Eric Berne was the father of transactional analysis, and he confessed that he had had great difficulty in finding intimacy in his own life.

J

JAMES, WILLIAM
(1842–1910)

William James was a professor at Harvard University in the United States, and is known as both a philosopher and a psychologist. In the area of philosophy he is known as a leading figure in *pragmatism*, the point of view that the truth of an idea or a concept can be tested in terms of whether or not it has any practical value.

In the area of psychology, James is recognized as the father of *functionalism*, a school of psychology emphasizing the importance of studying the purposes of consciousness (see entry). Functionalism inspired some psychologists to move in an applied direction toward industrial psychology, intelligence testing, educational psychology, and so forth.

James opened up many avenues of exploration for psychology when he published his classic two-volume work *Principles of Psychology* in 1890. Topics in the work included sensation, perception, the functions of the brain, habit, the stream of consciousness, the self, attention, memory, thinking, emotion, and will. James broke much ground in all of these areas, and foreshadowed much of the psychological landscape for the coming twentieth century.

JUNG, CARL GUSTAV
(1875–1961)

Carl Gustav Jung was a Swiss psychiatrist. In his early days of practice he was impressed by Freud's theories, and made it a point to visit Freud in Austria. They became quite friendly, and Freud began to look upon Jung as an intellectual heir-apparent to the leadership of the psychoanalytic movement. There was

118

almost a twenty-year gap in their ages, and the older Freud began treating Jung something like a surrogate son. With Freud's help, Jung became in 1910 the first president of the International Psychoanalytic Association.

Jung began to disagree with Freud on a number of theoretical points, resented to some extent Freud's patronizing attitude toward him, and eventually the two men became alienated. Jung went on to do much original work in personality theory and psychotherapy. He founded his own school of psychology called *Individual psychology.*

Like Freud, Jung accepted the hypothesis of an unconscious mental life. However, Jung went farther than Freud. Jung said that the unconscious level of the personality contains much more than personal repressions. There is also a *collective unconscious,* an unconscious level common to all human beings. And the contents of the collective unconscious are *archetypes,* inborn patterns and images (see entry). The related concepts of the collective unconscious and the archetypes are probably the most striking single set of concepts in Jung's theory. They have been widely rejected by many psychologists as being too mystical and not fitting the facts of evolutionary theory. However, the relatively recent findings and interpretations of sociobiology (see entry) have given a kind of general support to Jung's way of looking at behavior.

Jung is also famous for his theory of personality types, a primary distinction being the one between the extravert and the introvert (see *extravert*).

Seen in a large frame of reference, Jung's work can be thought of as a reappearance of the platonic doctrine of innate ideas (see entry). Also, his approach rests on the doctrine of nativism (see entry).

Jung was a prolific writer. One edition of his collected works consists of fourteen volumes. Among his books are *The Theory of Psychoanalysis* (1913), *The Structure of the Unconscious* (1916), *Psychological Types* (1921), and *The Archetypes and the Collective Unconscious* (1936).

K

KANT, IMMANUEL
(1724–1804)

Immanuel Kant was a professor of philosophy at the University of Königsberg in Germany. His most famous work is *The Critique of Pure Reason* published in 1781. A lifelong bachelor, Kant led a regular and unexciting life. He took a daily walk, and it is said that the people of Königsberg could set their clocks by his comings and goings.

Kant said that some of the ideas in the human mind are *a priori*, meaning they are present at birth. This is essentially the same as Plato's doctrine of *innate ideas* (see entry). Kant's prestige lent additional credibility to the doctrine, and was intended as a rejection of John Locke's teaching that the mind at birth is a blank slate (see *empiricism* and *John Locke*).

Kant also argued that there is a distinction that must be made between a *phenomenon* and a *noumenon*. A *phenomenon* refers to an idea or a perception. It is the way things appear in the mind. A *noumenon*, on the other hand, refers to the thing-in-itself, the actual existence of an object. This distinction suggests that we can never know reality directly, that we are prisoners of our sense organs and the perceptions of our minds. The modern study of *perception* and *psychophysics* (see entries) to some extent preserves Kant's distinction.

Kant's general approach to the study of the mind can be seen as a variety of *nativism* (see entry), and has much in common with the earlier teachings of Plato (see entry).

KÖHLER, WOLFGANG
(1887–1957)

Wolfgang Köhler was a German psychologist, and one of the

principal personalities giving birth to Gestalt psychology (see entry). The father of Gestalt psychology is identified as Max Wertheimer (see entry). And the two leading founders are Wolfgang Köhler and Kurt Koffka. Of these two men, Köhler is generally considered to have made the more significant contributions to Gestalt theory. Köhler emigrated to the United States prior to the outbreak of World War II, and completed his academic career at Swarthmore College.

Köhler did much to advance the concept of *insight learning* (see entry). Experiments conducted with apes on the island of Tenerife during World War I are described in Köhler's book *The Mentality of Apes* published in 1925. He demonstrated that apes learn from wholes to parts, that they show abrupt jumps in performance, and that they exhibit, on the whole, what most of us would be willing to call reasoning ability. Köhler argued that what is true of apes is certainly even more true of human beings, and he took behaviorists to task for their overly mechanical way of looking at human learning.

L

LATENT CONTENT

Definition
According to psychoanalysis, the latent content of a dream is the true meaning of a dream, a meaning hidden by the *manifest*, or surface, content.

Example
A man dreams that he is locked in a deserted department store at night. The female mannequins take on life and start converging on him. It appears that they want to strangle him. He realizes that there is a gun in his hand, and he begins to shoot it at the stomachs of the mannequins. One-by-one they are stopped in their tracks, returned to their inanimate states, but they have large swollen stomachs where the bullets entered.

The manifest content of the dream refers to the actual story told by the dream containing the events having to do with the deserted department store, the female mannequins, and so forth. The latent content of the dream, applying a psychoanalytic approach, suggests feelings of hostility toward women. Here is a possible interpretation of the dream: The man is afraid of women, feels that they are controlling his life. He unconsciously believes that if he can use his penis (i.e. the gun) in an aggressive way (i.e. shooting women in the stomach) he can impregnate women and take away their power. It is possible to hypothesize that the dream is the expression of a rape fantasy. One dream is not enough to make these kinds of interpretations with reliability. One needs a series of dreams and knowledge about the patient's behavior in actual life.

Connections
Freud was convinced that every dream had a latent content associated with unconscious concerns. The aim of the manifest

content is to protect the ego against self-knowledge. It disguises the dream so that the emotional release can take place without damaging one's self-esteem.

Jung took issue with Freud's point of view. Jung asserted that the images of a dream are meant to *express* meaning, not to hide it. The dream follows the principle that a picture is worth a thousand words. Far from hiding the meaning of the dream, the dream symbols bring the meaning forth. For example, the fact that the dreamer in the example uses a gun in an aggressive way suggests the way in which he looks upon his penis: it is a weapon against women. Note that both Freud and Jung might be willing to interpret the gun in the dream as a penis. The difference is that Freud says the gun is chosen to *hide* the fact that the man is dreaming about his penis. Jung says the gun is chosen to *express* the way in which the man is thinking about his penis.

LATENT LEARNING

Definition
Latent learning is learning that is dormant and unexpressed in performance at the time it is acquired.

Example
A first rat is allowed to explore a maze a number of times without the reinforcement of food in the goal box. Subsequently the goal box is baited with food. The first rat displays a much more rapid rate of learning than a second rat that has never explored the maze. It can be inferred that the first rat must have been learning the maze while it was exploring it, but this learning was not displayed in performance until an appropriate incentive was introduced.

Connections
The example is adapted from a classic experiment using three groups of rats conducted by H. C. Blodgett in 1929 at the University of California. The experiment was of substantial theoretical importance because it demonstrated that learning without reinforcement is possible. The attention that a rat pays to relevant cues as it explores a maze seems to be a sufficient condition for learning it.

Latent learning is of practical importance because parents, teachers, and others offering instruction often are discouraged by the performance of children and students, sometimes believing that little or no learning is taking place. It is possible that the subject has little or no motivation to learn, but that the learning acquired will nonetheless surface in an encouraging manner at some future time.

Latent learning should not be confused with incidental learning (see entry). Although both appear to take place without reinforcement, incidental learning is not necessarily dormant, and may be displayed at any time in performance.

LAW OF EFFECT

Definition
The law of effect states that if a response to a stimulus is satisfying to an organism, the response will be learned and 'stamped into' the nervous system.

Example
A cat is confined in a puzzle box. In order to escape the cat must learn to claw an overhead string. Clawing the string will release a latch making an exit possible. When the cat is free from confinement it finds a bowl of food outside of the box. The first time the cat is placed in the box it makes many random and fruitless efforts to escape. Stated differently, it makes many responses to the stimulus situation. One of these responses (i.e. clawing the string) is successful. After the cat has been placed in the puzzle box about twenty times, it escapes in a few minutes and we can say that learning has taken place. The process of learning was gradual, and the cat displayed no sudden burst of insight. The law of effect says that the kind of trial-and-error learning described proceeds in a mechanical way, that each time the successful response is displayed it is 'stamped into' the nervous system by the satisfaction it provides for the organism in the form of escape and the opportunity to eat.

Connections
The law of effect was formulated by the learning theorist Edward L. Thorndike (see entry). Thorndike's view of learning was mechanical. He saw it as a set of connections between stimuli and responses, and conducted many experiments suggesting that both animals and human beings learn by a trial-and-error process. We, like animals, retain responses that bring us satisfac-

tion. So the law of effect can be used to explain much of our acquired behavior.

The law of effect is the forerunner of the concept of a *reinforcer* in *operant conditioning* (see entries). Thorndike's work was an inspiration to B. F. Skinner (see entry).

LEARNING

Definition
Learning is a more or less permanent change in a behavioral tendency as a result of experience.

Example
A human infant is not born able to walk. Although maturation plays a significant role in the ability to walk, so does learning. A toddler must take a number of tumbles before walking becomes a well-defined capacity. Repeated efforts to walk are a form of practice, and the aim of practice is to increase the toddler's range of experience. With enough experience walking becomes second nature, meaning a well-established learned behavior.

Connections
Numerous examples of learning can be given. We learn to talk, write, ride a bicycle, swim, play cards, make computations, and so forth. In fact the *acquired* aspect of any behavior is its learned aspect. So pervasive is learning that some psychologists have made it their primary concern in the study of behavior. Ivan Pavlov, B. F. Skinner, Edward L. Thorndike, and John Watson (see entries) all identified learning as the most important single process in the explanation of human behavior.

LEARNING SET

Definition
A learning set is the ability to effectively transfer learned behavior acquired in association with an original set of tasks to a novel task.

Example
One of Donald's avocations is solving crossword puzzles. He has solved so many crossword puzzles that he can usually complete a

new puzzle in half of the time taken by the average person. He is well-prepared, or *set*, to solve crossword puzzles.

Connections
A principal investigator into the phenomenon of learning sets was Harry Harlow, well-known for his research on the affectional drive. Harlow found with rhesus monkeys that they become progressively better at solving problems of a given class such as discriminating between two containers with different shapes. (The choice of the 'correct' container was reinforced with a grape.) They seemed to develop what might be called 'insight.' (See entry on insight.) However, Harlow reasoned that insight was descriptive of the behavior, but not explanatory. The insight itself had to be explained, and it was explained by pointing to the learning history of the organism. Experience with groups of similar problems results in the gradual formation of a learning set. And this learning set is the foundation beneath the phenomenon of insight.

Gestalt psychology (see entry) disagrees with Harlow's formulation. It looks upon insight as an innate ability.

LEVEL OF ASPIRATION

Definition
One's level of aspiration is a subjective standard by which one sets goals and evaluates one's own accomplishments.

Example
Karen and Eva are friends, and they are taking together a college course in geography. Karen is working to earn an A in the course and Eva is working for a C. Karen has a high level of aspiration in regard to the course, and Eva's level of aspiration is moderate.

Connections
Level of aspiration is related to self-esteem. William James (see entry) offered this formula for self-esteem:

$$\frac{\text{Success}}{\text{Pretensions}} = \text{Self-esteem}$$

In this formula the word *pretensions* is equivalent to the concept of level of aspiration. Let's apply the formula to the example of Karen and Eva. Convert letter grades to numerical equivalents: An A = 4, a B = 3, a C = 2, a D = 1, and a F = 0. If success and pretensions are a perfect match, then the self-esteem score will be unity or one. Say that Karen is awarded the A she wanted. Dividing a 4 for pretensions into a 4 for success equals 1. The same is true for Eva. Say she is awarded the C she worked for. Dividing a 2 for pretensions into a 2 for success equals 1. The self-esteem of both students has not been greatly affected by the outcome of the course.

However, assume that both students are awarded B grades at the end of the semester. For Karen we divide a 4 for pretensions into a 3 for success and obtain a self-esteem score of .75. For Eva we divide a 2 for pretensions into a 3 for success and obtain a self-esteem score of 1.5. Although both students received the same objective grade, Karen's self-esteem comes down a notch and Eva's moves up a notch. Karen may think, 'I'm not as smart as I thought I was.' And Eva may think, 'Maybe I'm smarter than I thought I was.'

The limited example of Karen and Eva's grades can be applied to life in general. Although we tend to admire persons who have high ambitions and great expectations, such persons are subject to equivalent disappointments if their objective achievements fall short of their dreams.

LIBIDO

Definition
According to Freud, libido is psychosexual energy. Its source is *Eros*, the group of life instincts. And this group includes hunger, thirst, and sex – with an emphasis in early psychoanalytic theory on sex. Libido is the energy that makes possible the activity of the mind.

Example
Donna is a young woman with a very strong interest in the opposite sex. She has fantasies about men she has not yet met, is preoccupied with male-female relations, and is sexually active. The source of her thoughts, mental images, and overt behavior is, according to Freudian theory, libido. When she becomes a very old woman it is likely that her sexual interest will diminish because Eros will also diminish, and there will be in consequence a reduction of libido.

LIFE CHANGE UNITS

Connections
Reduction in, or loss of, libido can result from organic factors such as old age or chronic illness. Or libido can diminish as a result of emotional conflict. It is this second kind of reduction in libido that is the primary concern of psychoanalysis. Persons who become disinterested in life and experience an apathy about sexual activity are manifesting diminished libido.

The concept of libido is in fact vague. Its definition is too general to assert that libido has any sound scientific status. Thus the nature of libido has been much debated. Jung (see entry) argued that libido was simply psychological energy with no particular emphasis on its sexual aspect. Freud insisted that the sexual character of libido was its dominant feature.

LIFE CHANGE UNITS

Definition
Life change units (LCUs) are numerical values assigned in rank order to stressful events associated with human existence. The assignment of values generates a measuring instrument called the Social Readjustment Rating Scale.

Example
During a one-year period the following changes occurred in Lionel's life: his wife died, he was fired from his job, and his mother developed a serious chronic illness. The death of a spouse on the Social Readjustment Rating Scale receives a value of 100, the maximum value on the scale. Being fired is given a value of 47. Change in the health of a family member is given a value of 44. Thus within a single year Lionel has piled up 191 LCUs.

Connections
LCUs and the Social Readjustment Rating Scale are the work of two researchers, R. H. Rahe and T. H. Holmes. Their work indicates that LCUs have something to do with illness. If more than 300 LCUs are acquired in a single year, this may be a substantial contributing factor to a health problem.

It is interesting to note that the Social Readjustment Rating Scale assigns LCUs even to positive life changes. For example, getting married receives a value of 50 LCUs. And a vacation receives 13 LCUs.

128

LOCKE, JOHN
(1632–1704)

John Locke had several careers. He was the personal physician to the Earl of Shaftesbury. He was a political activist, and this led to his temporary exile in Holland in 1683. And he was a philosopher, author of *An Essay Concerning Human Understanding*, published in 1690. The ideas advanced in the *Essay* were fundamental ones in establishing the school of philosophy known as *British empiricism*, a school that emphasized that all knowledge comes from the sense organs (see *empiricism*).

Locke said that the mind at birth is a *tabula rasa*, a blank slate. Nothing that is in the mind is there at birth. All ideas are formed from the sensory processes of vision, hearing, taste, touch, and smell. In brief, ideas come from experience. The doctrine of the blank slate directly contradicts the teachings of Plato, and the doctrine of *innate ideas* (see entry). Empiricism is also a foe of *nativism* (see entry).

Locke has been a great inspiration to those psychologists who stress the importance of the acquired aspects of behavior. His focus is primarily on *learning* (see entry). Thus *behaviorism* as a school of psychology (see entry) rests squarely on the Lockean tradition.

LOGOTHERAPY

Definition
Logotherapy is a kind of psychotherapy designed to help a troubled person rediscover lost meaning in life.

Example
Kendall is a married man with three children. His wife and one of his children are killed in an automobile accident. Three months after his wife's death he has reached a low point in his existence. He feels that life makes no sense at all, that nothing is worth doing, and that he can't go on. He seeks psychotherapy for his chronic depression and his therapist sees that Kendall's problem originates neither in a biochemical disorder nor a neurotic conflict. He correctly perceives that Kendall is suffering from an *existential vacuum*, a loss of meaning in life. Therapy consists of a set of discussions aimed at helping Kendall reaffirm values that he has lost sight of – for example, the importance of being a good

father to his two remaining daughters. The therapist helps point the way toward values that Kendall has forsaken, and in time he finds it possible to rebuild his shattered life.

Connections
The father of logotherapy is the European psychiatrist Viktor Frankl. Frankl himself was imprisoned in Nazi concentration camps during World War II, and noted that those most likely to survive the camps were individuals who felt that life remained meaningful in the face of even the worst adversity.

In subsequent work with troubled persons, Frankl noted that the existential vacuum was a common phenomenon and could be experienced by persons who had not had a great objective loss such as the death of a loved one or bad news about their health. Frankl asserts that *nihilism*, the point of view that nothing is of any real value, is pervasive in our age. So even people with health, good vocations, and property may feel that their lives have no meaning.

Frankl takes the position that values are real, that they actually exist. We fall into the existential vacuum not because values go out of objective existence, but because we lose sight of their enduring presence. Logotherapy does not create imaginary values. It is incapable of doing that. However, as already noted, it does help a troubled person rediscover lost values.

M

MASLOW, ABRAHAM
(1908–1970)

Abraham Maslow was a professor of psychology at New York University (formerly Brooklyn College) and Brandeis University. He was a principal founder of *humanistic psychology* (see entry). Maslow and Carl Rogers (see entry) were leading figures in establishing humanistic psychology as a third force among psychologists in the United States, the other two principal forces being *psychoanalysis* and *behaviorism* (see entries).

One of Maslow's principal contentions was that there resides in human beings an inborn tendency to make the most out of their talents and potentialities. He called this tendency *self-actualization* (see entry).

Maslow's approach to both psychology and life has an inspirational quality. He did not see human beings as pawns of fate, as victims of life. True, people do fall into various psychological traps leading to despair and demoralization. But they can through the use of will and intelligence climb out of these traps and find life worth living again. In fact, Maslow felt that people could do more than just find life worth living. They could from time-to-time have moments of joy or ecstasy that he called *peak experiences* (see entry).

Maslow's most influential book is *Toward a Psychology of Being* (1962).

MASOCHISM

Definition
Masochism is a tendency to extract pleasure from pain. The two basic kinds of masochism are *sexual masochism* and *masochistic personality traits*. Sexual masochism is a tendency to experience

131

sexual excitement from one's own suffering. Masochistic personality traits are tendencies such as a desire to fail at a task or a
need to be embarrassed.

Example
Irma is unable to become sexually aroused unless her lover
insults her, binds her, or beats her. She cooperates in this
behavior. Indeed she provokes it. This is a chronic pattern with
Irma, and it has been going on for a number of years. Sometimes
when she is alone she masturbates with fantasies of being raped,
kicked, and called foul names by a violent and aggressive male.

Connections
The most interesting feature of masochism is its paradoxical
nature. How is it possible to extract pleasure from pain? The
classical psychoanalytic explanation sees the masochistic person
as having an overly strict and punitive superego (see entry). If,
for example, one's sexual behavior is perceived as 'bad' or 'dirty'
or 'wrong,' then arousal is inhibited unless some sort of price is
paid for the arousal. The suffering experienced by the individual
with masochistic tendencies is the psychological pound of flesh
given in tribute for the permission to have an erotic experience.

MEGAVITAMIN THERAPY

Definition
Megavitamin therapy is a kind of therapy for mental or physical
disorders characterized by the prescription of very large quanti-
ties of selected vitamins.

Example
Isabella is hospitalized for a schizophrenic disorder (see psychotic disorder). Her psychiatrist has reason to suspect that some of
Isabella's symptoms can be explained in terms of a deficiency of
the B-complex vitamins. He prescribes daily doses ten times
larger of these vitamins than usually recommended levels. After
one month of this regimen Isabella seems to be noticeably
improved, and the psychiatrist believes that a large part of the
improvement is due to the megavitamin therapy.

Connections
When megavitamin therapy is used as a treatment for a mental

disorder it is also called *orthomolecular psychiatry*. The biochemist and Nobel laureate Linus Pauling was a poineer in this kind of psychiatric practice.

The effectiveness of megavitamin therapy is an open question. Some studies suggest that it is remarkably effective. Critics of these studies suggest their methodology is faulty, and therefore their conclusions are unreliable. Megavitamin therapy provides a promising avenue for further research.

MEMORY

Definition
Memory is a mental process involving the encoding, storage, and retrieval of information.

Example
You are introduced to a person and are informed that his name is Jim. Two weeks later you meet the person and say pleasantly, 'Hello, Jim. Nice to see you again.' The name was encoded in the form of the symbols J, I, and M. It was stored in your memory bank, also sometimes referred to as the *apperceptive mass* or the *subconscious mind*. When you recalled the name *Jim* you retrieved the information.

Connections
In classical philosophical terms memory is one of the faculties, or powers, of the mind. Consequently it was believed for centuries that some people had 'bad' memories and that others had 'good' memories. Today's approach focuses less on memory as a mental faculty and more on the conditions that facilitate encoding, storage, and retrieval. Mnemonic devices (see entry) and effective teaching methods are both aimed at helping the learner be competent as opposed to judging the innate quality of his or her memory.

Memory is such a common human experience that we tend to take it for granted. Seldom do we ask, 'How is it done?' Psychologists have been curious about this question and have tried to answer it with experiments and theories of memory. One major theory is that the biological basis for memory is groups of neurons that are mutually facilitating called cell assemblies (see entry). Another major theory is that information is retained in the brain and nervous system by changes taking place in the structure of *ribonucleic acid* (RNA) molecules in the nuclei of neurons. (See entry on deoxyribonucleic acid, DNA.) The two theories are not mutually exclusive.

MENTAL DISORDER

Definition
A mental disorder is a pathological state characterized by confused thinking, emotional turmoil, and maladaptive behavior. The origins of the pathology may be either organic or functional in nature.

Example
Hilton is a patient in a mental hospital, and he has been diagnosed as suffering from a *schizophrenic disorder, paranoid type*. His thinking is bizarre, bearing little relation to reality as most of us know it. For example, he believes that beings situated on the fourth planet circling the sun Anatres are poisoning his food by remote control. He also sometimes sees devils and dragons that tell him he is destined to be the ruler of the planet Earth in the year 2003.

Connections
Modern psychiatry recognizes several kinds of mental disorders including mental retardation, personality disorders, and psychotic disorders (see entries). As noted in the definition, mental disorders may be either organic or functional in nature. *Organic* mental disorders have a biological basis. For example, there may be a disturbance in the brain's biochemistry. Or there may be damage to the central nervous system. *Functional* mental disorders have a psychological basis. For example, emotional conflict may be present. Or 'bad' habits may have been formed.

Some clinical psychologists and psychiatrists do not have much of a liking for the word *mental* in mental disorders. They feel too much emphasis is being put on the thinking of the troubled person, a process that is not directly observable. They suggest that the term *behavioral disorders* is preferable because behavior *is* directly observable, and is the actual basis for deciding that a pathological state exists.

MENTAL RETARDATION

Definition
The basic meaning of mental retardation is severely impaired general intelligence. A formal definition for clinical purposes is an IQ score of 70 or below.

Example
Laurette suffers from Down's syndrome, a pattern of development caused by a chromosome defect. (A prior name for Down's syndrome was *mongolism*.) Laurette's intelligence is tested at the age of eight, and her IQ score is 68. This is interpreted to mean that she suffers from mild mental retardation.

Connections
The four subtypes of mental retardation are: (1) mild (IQ = 50–70), (2) Moderate (IQ = 35–49), (3) Severe (IQ = 20–34), and (4) Profound (IQ = Below 20).

The cause of mental retardation is usually biological in nature. Down's syndrome cited above falls in the biological category. Brain damage during childbirth is another cause, also biological. However, mental retardation can be due to psychosocial factors. Some biologically normal children are raised by mentally retarded adults, and these children may become mentally retarded themselves. Such retardation is called *familial retardation*.

The incidence of mental retardation is a little over two percent of the general population. This incidence is subject to reduction by the application of methods such as genetic counseling and improved birthing techniques.

MENTAL SET

Definition
A mental set is a disposition or state of preparation to think or perceive in a given way. It is a determining tendency in cognition.

Example
You need to add ten columns of numbers and produce a sum for each column. When you begin to work on the first column you give yourself a mental set to add. When you begin to work on the second column you do not have to give yourself the mental set again; it simply exists at a subconscious level, but nonetheless

enters into the way you think about and perceive the numbers. You do not suddenly switch to subtraction. The mental set determines that you will produce ten sums, but is not a part of the content of your consciousness as you work.

Connections
The concept of mental set developed out of the work of the German psychologist N. Ach in the early part of this century. Ach was associated with a school of psychology known as the Würzburg school. A principal feature of the Würzburg school was the assertion that thought without an image was possible. This was in direct opposition to the more established teachings of Wilhelm Wundt and structuralism (see entries) that thought always had a conscious content that could be discovered by introspection. Ach and the Wurzburg school argued that a mental set, for example, determined cognition but resided below it and was not itself a part of consciousness. The eventual acceptance into psychology of the concept of a mental set was something of an embarrassment to Wundt.

A mental set can help one solve a problem. But it can also interfere with a problem's solution. Let's say that in a certain situation it would be useful to perceive a pair of pliers as a hammer in order to pound a nail. If one persists in the mental set that a pair of pliers is used to enhance grip, then no tool exists for pounding the nail. A certain degree of flexibility and ability to break mental sets is an attribute of creative thinking (see entry).

METHODS OF PSYCHOLOGY

Definition
Methods of psychology are a set of traditional ways by which behavioral data are gathered and evaluated.

Example
The *clinical method* is one of the time-honored methods of psychology. It was the method used by such famous psychologists as Freud, Jung, Adler and Horney (see entries). The method consists of the formulation of hypotheses about personality and human nature from numerous observations made during psychotherapeutic sessions. Two criticisms of the method are that it is unsystematic and that there are no control observations. Defenders of the method say that the many cross-

comparisons made between patients provide a natural set of control observations for the experienced researcher. Also, no other method provides the wealth of information about the deepest concerns of human beings.

Connections
The most systematic of the methods is the experimental method (see entry).

Naturalistic observation is a method characterized by the observation of organisms in their usual habitats. Go to a department store and take notes about how people behave, and you are using naturalistic observation.

The *survey method* involves collecting data by having people respond to an interview or a questionnaire. The famous Kinsey surveys of sexual behavior used this method.

The *one-subject case study* probes deeply into the behavior of one person. Often it overlaps with the clinical method. The case of Anna O. was the first psychoanalytic study reported, and it employed both methods.

The *phenomenological method* asks a subject to report his or her thoughts and perceptions. It was the primary method used by Gestalt psychology (see entry). Say that a subject describes his or her perception of an optical illusion to a psychologist. The method is called *phenomenological* because the subject is describing *phenomena* (i.e. conscious ideas) in the mind.

The *correlational method* is a statistical method in which the magnitude of a relationship between at least two variables is assessed (see entry).

Although some sort of criticism can be leveled against any one method of psychology, together they form a formidable battery allowing psychologists to approach behavior from more than one avenue.

MIND

Definition
The word *mind* has several meanings, all of them quite general and somewhat imprecise. First, in the philosophical position called *dualism* (see entry), the mind is one of two basic aspects of existence, the second one being matter. Thus it is possible to say that the mind of each individual represents a primary and irreducible principle of innate consciousness. Second, the mind

is a group of conscious mental processes such as thinking, perceiving, remembering, imagining, and willing. Third, the mind is the activity of the brain and nervous system, subjectively experienced as consciousness.

Example
Elaine is reading a novel. As she does so, she must use all of the processes we associate with mind. She thinks about what she is reading, perceives the words and sentences, remembers much of what she has read, imagines the characters in various settings, and decides to continue reading the book. (Deciding is one aspect of willing.)

Connections
To most of us it is so obvious that we each have a mind that to doubt the existence of minds in people seems absurd. And yet, John Watson, the father of behaviorism, did just that (see entries for *Watson* and *behaviorism*). Watson said that the concept of the mind is unnecessary for psychology, that it neither explains nor predicts behavior. He argued that psychology without the idea of mind is more scientific, the mind being a mushy philosophical concept. It is sometimes jokingly said that Watson is the psychologist who made up his mouth that he didn't have a mind.

Watson's position is too radical for most people, including most behavioral scientists. However, research on behavior can be done in many cases without employing the concept of mind. There is, of course, a difference between saying that the concept of mind is not necessary for a scientific analysis of behavior and saying that the mind does not exist. It seems that much of the confusion arises from alternate frames of reference. If one is an external observer of a second person's behavior, then one does not experience the other person's mind. The mind is inferred from observations of behavior. Thus one observer may find the concept of mind·useful to explain behavior (e.g. Freud). And a second observer may find the concept of mind useless to explain behavior (e.g. Watson). However, if one is an internal observer of one's own behavior, the frame of reference is entirely different. We actually experience ourselves thinking, perceiving, and so forth. So we have first-hand knowledge that such mental processes have reality, and each of us knows that at least one mind exists, our own.

MINNESOTA MULTIPHASIC PERSONALITY INVENTORY (MMPI)

Definition
The Minnesota Multiphasic Personality Inventory (MMPI) is a paper-and-pencil personality test consisting of 550 items. Subjects respond to the items by indicating *true, false*, or *cannot say*. When the test is scored it yields a profile of the personality based on ten clinical scales, each measuring an aspect of mental health.

Example
One of the clinical scales of the MMPI is the *schizophrenia scale*. (Subjects who receive a standard score between 30 and 70 on any clinical scale are considered to be in the normal range.) If Mara were to receive a score of 60 on this scale she would almost certainly be free of a schizophrenic disorder. If Lawton were to receive a score of 90, twenty standard units above the normal range, it would indicate that there is a high likelihood that he is suffering from a schizophrenic disorder. Of course, this elevated scale would have to be evaluated in terms of other tests, interviews, and his general behavior.

Connections
The MMPI is an important test in the history of psychological testing. It was one of the first tests to be validated by comparing scores on clinical scales with the diagnoses made by psychiatrists. Thus the test was built on a firm empirical basis, not the theories of the test authors.

The long cumbersome name *Minnesota Multiphasic Personality Inventory* often unsettles people. The word 'Minnesota' appears in the name because the test was devised by a group of psychologists at the University of Minnesota. The word 'Multiphasic' appears because the test measures several phases, or aspects, of the personality.

The MMPI has been a controversial test. Critics have poked fun at many of the questions. The test may ask a question such as, 'Do you talk to the angels?' Or, 'Do you use telepathy often?' Although the questions may on their surface seem absurd or silly, a person with a schizophrenic disorder might very well answer both questions *true*.

The MMPI has proven to be quite popular with clinicians, and has been used extensively since the 1950s.

MNEMONIC DEVICE

Definition
A mnemonic device is a cognitive strategy used to assist the functioning of memory.

Example
Lindsey has difficulty remembering how to spell the word *recommend*. Sometimes he spells it r-e-c-c-o-m-e-n-d and sometimes he spells it correctly. He is tired of looking it up every time he wants to write it. (It also happens that Lindsey is fond of a candy known as M & M's.) He makes up the following mnemonic device, 'One can see that recommend is sweet like candy because it has an M & M.' The first three words of the device tell him that recommend has *one c* (i.e., one can see = 1C). The last letters tell him it has *two ms*. Lindsey never mispells recommend again.

Connections
Through the adroit use of mnemonic devices it is possible to remember long lists of arbitrary items and all sorts of random information. However, this approach to the art of mnemonics is nothing more than a series of stunts. The application of mnemonic devices is a serious and practical business when it is used to remember names of people, the spelling of some words, and the content of courses of instruction.

A basic principle that resides behind mnemonic devices is *association with something familiar*. By doing this the subject obtains a free ride on prior learning. For example, Lindsey already knew that a kind of candy existed with the brand name M & M. By using this prior learning and 'plugging it into' the word *recommend*, he had less to recall when writing the problem word.

MOTIVE

Definition
Objectively defined, a motive is a hypothetical state in an organism used to explain its choices and goal-oriented behavior. Subjectively defined, a motive is experienced as a desire or wish.

Example
The status-seeking motive is a common one in human beings. Howard makes a real effort to be elected president of a club,

drive an expensive car, win honors, and so forth. His friends see him as a person who is always trying to attain greater social rank. From the point of view of Howard's friends, external observers of his behavior, the status-seeking motive in Howard is hypothetical. It is a convenient explanation of Howard's behavior. However, it may or may not exist in him. If Howard himself is conscious of an inordinate need for status, then the motive exists as a desire in Howard. And it is certainly not hypothetical from his point of view.

Connections
The word *motive* is associated with other words such as *motion* and *movement*. In a fundamental sense, a motive is anything that sets an organism in motion, that makes it move.

The concept of motive is very similar to the concept of biological drives (see entry). However, a motive is more general than a drive, and may include both learned and unlearned components (see *complex motives*).

The subject of motivation is a basic one in psychology, playing a part in more than one important theory. For example, psychoanalysis (see entry) makes extensive use of the concept of motivation.

MULTIPLE PERSONALITY

Definition
Multiple personality is a kind of mental disorder characterized by the alternating appearance of two or more contradictory personalities.

Example
One of the most famous cases of a personality disorder was presented in the book *The Three Faces of Eve* by C. H. Thigpen and H. M. Cleckley. Eve White was a twenty-five-year-old homemaker, and this was her first dominant and 'good' personality. As Eve White, the homemaker was stable and responsible. A second personality, Eve Black, was coconscious with Eve White. That is to say that Eve Black knew about Eve White, but Eve White did not know about Eve Black. When Eve Black manifested herself from time to time the homemaker would become reckless and irresponsible. Eve White had a blackout for these episodes. Therapy produced a third personality, Jane, who was

coconscious with both Eve White and Eve Black, and appeared at first to be more stable than the two prior ones.

Eventually there was a fourth face to Eve, Evelyn Lancaster. It is assumed that she was able to integrate in a meaningful way the characteristics of the other three.

Connections

Although multiple personality has received a great deal of publicity because it is such a colorful disorder, it is in fact a rare one. It could be argued that many of us act like Dr Jekyll and Mr Hyde, sometimes manifesting a 'good' personality and sometimes manifesting a 'bad' one. But this is hardly multiple personality in the clinical sense. Most of us have no dissociation of one personality from the other. When multiple personality exists as a mental disorder the minor and aberrant personalities know about the main one (i.e. are coconscious with it), but the main personality is unaware of the existence of the aberrant ones. Thus an aberrant personality can take over behavior for a time, and the 'good' or socialized personality may have a blackout, a complete loss of memory, for what behaviors took place during a given time frame.

N

NARCISSISM

Definition
Narcissism is an ego defense mechanism characterized by excessive preoccupation with oneself. *Self-love, self-admiration, self-absorption,* and *egotism* are all words we can associate with narcissism.

Example
Elwin is a twenty-year-old college student of mediocre academic ability. His parents are very disappointed in his lack of scholastic accomplishment, and his self-esteem is suffering as a consequence. Elwin has decided that he is very good-looking and that he has unusual attraction to the opposite sex. He spends a great deal of time on his grooming and his clothing. His favorite pastime on weekends is shopping for clothes. When he combs his hair he will sometimes recomb it six or seven times until it is exactly to his liking. When he is alone he will on occasion simply admire himself in a mirror for five or ten minutes. It is possible to hypothesize that Elwin's narcissistic behavior is one way that he copes with low self-esteem concerning his academic performance.

Connections
The word *narcissism* is derived from the myth of the Greek youth Narcissus who fell in love with his own reflection in a pool of water. He could not, of course, take possession of the reflection. However, he continued to pine over the reflection, and he eventually starved to death. There is a message in this: excessive self-absorption can be destructive to the person. *The Picture of Dorian Grey* by Oscar Wilde tells a similar story. A handsome youth wishes that a painting of himself will age and that he will remain young indefinitely. His wish is granted. The painting ages

and also shows his sins. He eventually stabs the painting in a fit of rage, seeking to destroy it. Instead, the act of stabbing the painting causes his own death. When he is found subsequently the painting has been restored to its original beauty, and an old man is a corpse. Both the myth of Narcissus and the *Picture of Dorian Grey* are warnings against the dangers of narcissism.

NATIVISM

Definition
Nativism is the doctrine that many, perhaps most, important behavior patterns are determined by innate (i.e. inborn) factors.

Example
It is a common behavior for people to protect their real property. They lock doors, secure windows, build fences, and put up no trespassing signs. It can be argued that these actions are an expression of an inborn urging called *territoriality*.

Connections
Sociobiology (see entry) argues that both animals and human beings protect territories, and that this protective behavior has its roots in genetic predispositions. This way of explaining behavior is essentially nativistic.

Nativism finds many expressions in philosophy and psychology. Plato believed that many ideas are inborn. Immanuel Kant spoke of *a priori* concepts, meaning concepts in the mind before birth. Carl Jung asserted that the collective unconscious has archetypes (see entry), and that these are inborn. More than one researcher has said that both human beings and animals display instinctive behavior.

An interesting and fruitful contemporary application of nativism is found in the ideas and research of the noted and highly influential linguist Noam A. Chomsky (1928–). Chomsky contends that language development in human beings cannot be explained in terms of the learning process only. His research suggests that children take to words in somewhat the way in which ducklings take to water – it is natural for them. This tendency is explained in terms of a *biological predisposition*, an inborn tendency to use words and sentences in a direct and immediate way with a minimum of experience and reinforcement. Chomsky's approach does not say that experience and reinforcement play no role in verbal ability, but they are not all-important. The inborn tendency of human beings to speak, to use grammatical constructions, and to express themselves symbolically is the foundation of language development.

NEGATIVE PRACTICE

Definition
Negative practice is a method of habit-breaking in which one consciously and voluntarily repeats the error tendencies associated with a maladaptive habit.

Example
Lyris has the habit of spelling *exercise* with a *z* instead of an *s*. Using negative practice, she writes incorrectly the misspelled word *exercize* twenty times, saying to herself all the while, 'This is *not* the right way to spell it. This is the error I want to avoid.' The conscious repetition of the error helps her avoid making it involuntarily in the future.

Connections
Negative practice was introduced by the psychologist Knight Dunlap in the 1930s. It is also called the *beta method of extinction*, and has been applied with some success by practitioners of behavior therapy (see entry) to a range of maladaptive behaviors including stuttering, smoking, and overeating.

NERVE

Definition
A nerve is a bundle of axons arising from neurons within the peripheral nervous system. Sensory nerves transmit information toward the central nervous system, and motor nerves transmit information away from the central nervous system.

Example
The optic nerve is one of the body's nerves. Arising from neurons located within the retina, the optic nerve transmits visual information toward the brain.

Connections
A nerve should not be confused with a neuron. A neuron is a

145

single living cell, and a nerve is made up of the axons from many such cells. (See the entry for *neuron* to find a definition of the word *axon*.)

The words *nerve* and *tract* are similar, but not identical. Both are bundles of axons. However, as already indicated, nerves are found in the peripheral nervous system. Found within either the brain or the spinal cord, tracts transmit information within the central nervous system.

NERVOUS SYSTEM

Definition
The nervous system is the body's communication network. It is made up of millions of neurons working in harmony to make possible all of the coordinated functions of behavior.

Example
One of the two principal divisions of the nervous system is the *central nervous system*, consisting of two substructures, the *spinal cord* and the *brain*. The spinal cord has several functions: (1) it transmits information from sensory neurons to the brain, (2) it transmits information from motor neurons to the muscles, (3) it mediates reflex arcs, and (4) it regulates autonomic functions of the body. Broadly speaking, the brain is a central control system, and it makes consciousness possible (see *brain*).

Connections
The other principal division of the nervous system is the *peripheral nervous system*, consisting of two subsystems, the *autonomic nervous system* and the *somatic nervous system*. The autonomic nervous system controls all of the involuntary functions of the body such as heart rate and disgestion. The somatic nervous system contains the sense organs, making awareness of the external world possible. It also contains the motor nerves, making voluntary movement of the body possible.

NEURON

Definition
A neuron is a cell specializing in the communication of information. It is the basic functional unit of the brain and nervous system.

Example
Sensory neurons constitute one kind of neuron. They are found in the receptor organs of the body (e.g. the eyes, the ears, the skin, the tongue, and the nose), and they transmit information toward the brain. Other kinds of neurons include *association neurons* and *motor neurons*. Association neurons link sensory neurons to motor neurons. And motor neurons transmit information to glands and muscles.

Connections
Although a neuron is a single living cell, it is articulated into distinct structures. The *dendrite* transmits information toward the cell body. The *cell body* itself contains the nucleus of the cell. Leading off of the cell body is the *axon*, a threadlike filament transmitting information toward another neuron, a gland, or a muscle. Neurons are connected to each other through junction points called *synapses* (see entry).

The word *neurotic* is derived from neuron, and originally indicated some kind of organic problem in the nervous system. The popular term *nervous breakdown* is also obviously inspired by the concept of the neuron. It has no formal clinical meaning, and is a wastebasket term meaning in ordinary language anything from an anxiety disorder to a psychotic disorder.

NEUROTIC BEHAVIOR

Definition
Neurotic behavior is inflexible maladaptive behavior associated with one or more of the following attributes: (1) excessive anxiety, (2) emotional conflicts, (3) irrational fears, (4) somatic complaints lacking an organic basis, and (5) a tendency to avoid certain kinds of stress-arousing situations instead of effectively coping with them.

Example
Quentin, age twenty-four, is plagued by chronic anxiety. If he hears the slightest unexpected squeak when he is driving, he begins to worry about getting stranded on the road. He wants to become a novelist, and has written a book. But he can't bring himself to submit it to a publisher because he fears that its minor flaws will lead to its rejection. Consequently he has compulsively revised the manuscript seventeen times. He believes himself to

147

be in love with Jane, but tortures himself about whether or not he should marry her. He suffers from what he describes as 'a weakness in my muscles,' but physicians have been unable to find any organic basis for the complaint. In spite of much self-defeating behavior, Quentin is employed, has basically good reality contact, and is far from needing hospitalization as a mental patient.

Connections
The original meaning of the term *neurosis* was a weakness or disability of the nervous system. This was assumed to produce all sorts of tensions, weaknesses, anxiety states, and complaints. Gradually it became apparent to physicians that in many, perhaps most, such cases there was no organic problem with the nervous system. Thus the concept of *psychoneurosis* came into being. Freud was one of the early pioneers who recognized that a psychoneurosis could be rooted in emotional conflicts. So common are psychoneurotic conditions that today when we speak of neurotic behavior, it is the psychoneurotic variety that is being thought of.

The concept of neurotic behavior played an important part in the development of both psychoanalysis in particular and psychotherapy in general. Almost any condition in which the patient complained of subjective distress and displayed even moderate maladaptive behavior came to be labeled *neurotic*. Thus we obtain cliché remarks such as, 'Everybody's neurotic.'

So general is the term *neurosis* that some systems of psychiatric nomenclature reject it. In the United States, the American Psychiatric Association no longer recognizes a single mental disorder called *neurotic disorder*. There are disorders such as phobic disorder and obsessive-compulsive disorder (see entry) that are, broadly speaking, 'neurotic.' But many psychiatrists prefer to limit themselves to the specific limited disorder than to speaking in vague general terms of a neurotic disorder.

In spite of its problems such as vagueness and overgeneralization, the concept of neurotic behavior has a place in psychology. First, it has historical meaning, and the developments of psychotherapy must be understood in light of that meaning. Second, it points toward a broadly conceived class of behaviors suggesting a troubled person who is to at least some degree sustaining himself or herself in the struggle of life. The important thing to realize is that when one speaks of neurotic behavior one is not speaking of a precise clinical disorder, but a very general set of behavioral characteristics.

NEUROTRANSMITTER

Definition
A neurotransmitter is a chemical messenger allowing one neuron to either excite or inhibit the depolarization (i.e. 'firing') of an adjacent neuron.

Example
One of the important neurotransmitters is *norepinephrine*. Neuron 1 may excite neuron 2 to depolarize in the following manner. Molecules of norepinephrine are released from the end foot of the *axon* of neuron 1. These move across the *synapse*, or gap, between the two neurons. When the molecules of norepinephrine reach either the *dendrites* or *cell body* of neuron 2 they upset the resting state of neuron 2 and it depolarizes or ·'fires.' (See the entry for *neuron* to find definitions of the words *axon, synapse, dendrite*, and *cell body*.)

Connections
Note from the definition that a neurotransmitter does not always function to excite the depolarization of an adjacent neuron. Sometimes a neurotransmitter is released in order to inhibit or 'turn off' another neuron's activity.

Contemporary research on neurotransmitters and their functions is an important aspect of psychobiological research, and has led to some important practical findings. For example, there is a substantial body of research indicating that persons suffering from severe and chronic depression often have low levels of norepinephrine in their nervous systems. Electroshock therapy (see entry) temporarily stimulates the production of norepinephrine, and this may be one reason why electroshock therapy has beneficial results in some cases.

A drug frequently prescribed for *bipolar disorder* in which the mood of the patient swings between extremes of mania and depression is *lithium carbonate*. There is evidence suggesting that lithium carbonate functions by a regulatory action upon norepinephrine.

Norepinephrine is but one among a number of neurotransmitters.

NONSENSE SYLLABLE

Definition
A nonsense syllable consists of a consonant, a vowel, and another consonant producing an unfamiliar and meaningless 'word.'

Example
The letters Y, I, and T may be combined to form the nonsense syllable YIT.

Connections
The nonsense syllable was invented about one hundred years ago by Hermann Ebbinghaus. He used it to study verbal learning and memory, using himself as his own experimental subject. The virtue of nonsense syllables is that they have fewer memory associations than do actual words, and therefore provide advantages when used as stimuli in verbal learning experiments.

There are about 2,300 usable nonsense syllables. A contemporary name for them is the *CVC trigram*, meaning three letters made up of a consonant, a vowel, and a consonant. The older and more colorful term *nonsense syllable* is the one that experimental psychologists tend to use in informal discourse.

NORMAL CURVE

Definition
The normal curve is a theoretical probability distribution in which the relationship between a random variable and its frequency traces a function approximating the shape of a bell. The normal curve is also known as the *bell-shaped curve* and the *Gaussian curve*.

Example
Although the normal curve is itself a mathematical model, not a curve of actual data, it is useful because some sets of data tend to approximate its shape. Intelligence quotients (see entry) tend to distribute themselves in a bell-shaped fashion, particularly when a large set of scores are gathered. Because of certain properties of the normal curve it can be applied in a practical way to intelligence quotients to define formal categories of intelligence.

150

This application also defines the percentages of subjects likely to be found in the given categories.

Connections
The mathematician primarily responsible for studying and articulating the properties of the normal curve was Karl Friedrich Gauss, working in the middle of the nineteenth century.

One of the important attributes of the normal curve is that approximately 68 percent of scores reside within one standard deviation (see entry) above or below the mean. This makes it possible to define the concept of 'normal' in reliable statistical terms. If a behavior lends itself to any kind of scoring or quantification, that behavior can be thought of as 'normal' if it is found in the band between the first standard deviation above or below the mean (i.e. the arithmetical average).

(The term *random variable* was used in the definition. A random variable is a variable distributed according to the laws of chance.)

NURTURE

Definition
Nurture is the nourishment required by an organism to grow and thrive.

Example
In order for the human infant to grow and thrive he or she must be nurtured in a number of ways. There must be adequate food, water, affection, and so forth.

Connections
Note in the example that *affection* is included in the concept of nurture. Broadly conceived in psychology, nurture refers to virtually anything in the environment that fosters the development of the person. Thus it is possible to speak of training and education within the context of nurture.

One of the ongoing issues in psychology for many years was the *nature-nurture controversy*. Assume that Jessica is a particularly intelligent eight-year-old child. Was she 'born smart?' (Is this her basic *nature*?) Or did she receive excellent training and enriching experiences in early childhood? (Is her high intelligence due to *nurture*?)

NURTURE

The debate can be resolved to some extent by pointing out that nature and nurture are *both* important and that they work together. A certain genetic potential (i.e nature) must exist in the organism for a given trait such as high intelligence. This is the 'seed.' But optimal experiences (i.e. nurture) will draw out the best from the genetic potential and allow it to reach its highest level. (In the same sense, adverse conditions may provide a poor quality nurture and inhibit growth.)

OBJECT CONSTANCY

Definition
Object constancy is the tendency of an object to retain its perceived size, shape, color, brightness, or other attributes relatively independent of variations in the retinal image.

Example
Assume that you are looking at two people standing a moderate distance away from you. The first person is about four feet away and the second person is about twenty feet away. The size of the two images cast on your retina by each person differ substantially. The first person casts a large image and the second person casts a small one. Nonetheless, allowing for individual differences, both persons appear to be approximately of the same size.

Connections
Object constancy is an important feature of perception. If the tendency did not exist, we would see a bizarre world in which objects appeared to expand and shrink as they either approached or receded from our view. Coins would seem to become elliptical instead of circular if seen at an angle.

How do we maintain object constancy across a broad band of stimulus variations? Broadly speaking, two general classes of explanations exist. First, theorists who emphasize learning hypothesize that we adapt to variations in stimuli, compensating in such a way that we perceive the 'true' nature of the stimulus. Hermann Ludwig Ferdinand von Helmholtz (1821–1894), the great German physicist and physiologist, said that we make an *unconscious inference* about the nature of the stimulus. This unconscious inference, an educated guess made without conscious deliberation, is based on our experiences with the real world.

Second, theorists who emphasize inborn abilities hypothesize that the built-in data-processing abilities of the sense organs, brain, and nervous system allow these structures to abstract invariant features of a stimulus from a flow of information. We 'pick out' that which is *actually constant* in a stimulus. This general line of reasoning was advanced by the Gestalt psychologists, particularly Wolfgang Köhler (see entry).

Both classes of explanation have their advocates, and both appear to have some utility.

OBSERVATIONAL LEARNING

Definition
Observational learning is learning in which one organism copies, mimics, or imitates the behavior of another organism. This kind of learning is also called *modeling* and *social learning*.

Example
Eight-year-old Darlene has watched her mother peel an orange a number of times, but has never peeled one herself. One day when her mother is out of the kitchen, Darlene picks up a paring knife and peels an orange for the first time. She works slowly, and achieves a fair degree of success. Some learning must have taken place without overt practice or obvious reinforcement during the observation sessions.

Connections
The concept of observational learning has come back into vogue in psychology only relatively recently. (The idea that organisms imitate, particularly human organisms, was more or less taken for granted by psychologists such as William James during the early part of this century.) For a substantial period of time classical and operant conditioning (see entries) were thought to be the dominant learning processes. However, contemporary psychologists recognize that cognition (see entry) plays a role in learning. In the example, Darlene *knows* what her mother is doing and takes advantage of what she knows.

The experimental psychologist Albert Bandura and his co-workers have had a lot to do with establishing the credibility of the concept of observational learning. One series of experiments by them demonstrated convincingly that children will sometimes copy the aggressive behavior of an adult model. This line of research has led to a substantial amount of concern about the effects on the actions of a child from watching adults model aggressive behavior on television.

OBSESSIVE-COMPULSIVE DISORDER

Definition
An obsessive-compulsive disorder is a mental disorder characterized by (1) involuntary irrational thoughts and (2) repetitive behaviors aimed at the reduction of anxiety associated with the irrational thoughts.

Example
Clifford is obsessed with the idea that other people's hands and the utensils in restaurants are contaminated with particularly deadly viruses. After he shakes hands with someone he must wash his own hands as quickly as possible. When he eats in a restaurant he wipes all the utensils with the napkin on the table and then refuses to use that napkin on his mouth. He regards his contamination idea as silly and groundless, and looks upon his compulsive behavior as foolish. Nonetheless, he cannot use will power to control either the idea or the compulsion.

Connections
In traditional terms, an obsessive-compulsive disorder can be looked upon as a kind of neurotic behavior (see entry). The classical explanation of an obsessive-compulsive disorder is in terms of unconscious wishes of either a sexual or aggressive nature. For example, Clifford may have a great deal of repressed hostility toward other people. Unconsciously, he wishes to 'do them dirt.' Consciously, this wish is unacceptable in terms of his superego (see entry). So the unconscious wish is converted into a projection. Other people and things are perceived as the agents carrying dirt (i.e. harm or injury) to Clifford. These underlying psychodynamics produce the obsession and the compulsion.

An alternate explanation can be found in the domain of learning theory. Perhaps Clifford suffered from a life-threatening viral infection as a child. During his early developmental years he became hypersensitized to the idea that viruses can be very dangerous. As an adult he overreacts to the fact that viruses can be found in plentiful supply almost everywhere.

Psychodynamic explanations of the obsessive-compulsive disorder are more colorful and have more literary appeal than those arising from learning theory, but this is no basis for selection. A reasonable approach is to evaluate the troubled person's life history. Either a psychoanalytic or a learning theory explanation may be useful depending upon the features of an individual case.

OEDIPUS COMPLEX

Definition
An Oedipus complex is, in psychoanalytic theory, a repressed wish for sexual intercourse with the parent of the opposite sex. (The term *Electra complex* is sometimes used when speaking of a female's wish. However, the term *Oedipus complex* is often used in a generic sense, and can refer to either males or females.)

Example
Freud believed that the following scenario was typical of most conventional households. Lloyd, a boy five years of age, is developing an incest wish toward his mother. As the wish gathers strength, it also creates guilt. The superego (see entry) says the wish is wrong. Also, Lloyd fears possible retribution from his father, possibly in the form of castration. The combination of fear and guilt energizes the ego (see entry) to take action, and the wish itself is repressed to an unconscious level of the personality. Aiding the repression is a reaction formation (see entry) in which the unconscious incest wish appears at a conscious level as disgust at the idea of sexual relations with one's own mother. Assuming the repression is maintained, as it is in most cases, a boy such as Lloyd will be sexually interested in females other than his mother when he reaches puberty.

Connections
Freud derived the term *Oedipus complex* from the ancient Greek tragedy *Oedipus Rex* (i.e. Oedipus, the King) in which a man inadvertently marries his own mother.

The existence of the Oedipus complex has been one of the most controversial hypotheses advanced in psychoanalytic theory. The principal problem seems to be that Freud claimed the Oedipus complex was a universal phenomenon in Western culture. This is a highly debatable contention. If, on the other hand, one were to say that *some* people do give evidence of an Oedipus complex, then much of the theoretical conflict abates. In actual work with certain patients in psychoanalysis, particular-

156

ly those with highly ambivalent feelings toward a parent of the opposite sex, the hypothesis of an Oedipus complex complicating the relationship may be of some use.

Karen Horney (see entry) felt that Freud's emphasis on an actual sexual wish in a child of five years of age was exaggerated. She suggested that a child might wish to usurp the power and status of the parent of the same sex, thus gaining the limelight and more love from the parent of the opposite sex. To Horney, the Oedipus complex was psychosocial in nature, not psychosexual.

OPERANT CONDITIONING

Definition
Operant conditioning is a kind of learning in which an organism's behavior has an effect upon its immediate environment. The organism, so to speak, 'operates' upon its local world.

Example
A rat is placed in an *operant conditioning apparatus*, informally known as a 'Skinner box.' The operant conditioning apparatus contains a lever. If the rat will press this lever, it will obtain a small food pellet. At first the rat explores the box, sniffs around, places its paws on the walls, etc. These various individual behaviors fall into a general class of behavior known as *emitted behavior*, behavior 'sent out' by the organism without regard to any particular stimulus. One of the emitted behaviors is an inadvertent lever press. Informally, we would say that the rat in its exploration of the apparatus accidently presses the bar. The lever press quickly brings about the appearance of the food pellet in a tray. The food pellet acts as a reinforcer (see entry) for lever pressing, and the probability of lever pressing increases with every reinforcement of the behavior. In time the rat's rate of lever pressing is quite high.

The operant behavior in this example is pressing the lever. The immediate environment is transformed from one in which there is a scarcity of food into one in which there is plenty of food.

Connections
B. F. Skinner (see entry) was the psychologist who coined the term *operant conditioning*. And he invented the operant conditioning apparatus or Skinner box. Skinner's work was a natural

outgrowth of the earlier work on trial-and-error learning conducted by E. L. Thorndike (see entry). Both men studied a kind of learning in which an organism's behavior brings it 'satisfaction' (Thorndike) or reinforcement (Skinner).

Skinner's work is of broad general interest because it establishes very clearly an important principle: *behavior is shaped by its own consequences.* The principle applies across a broad spectrum of organisms including rats, pigeons, monkeys, and human beings. If an action 'pays off,' if it has a positive consequence, it tends to appear with increasing frequency. If an action does not 'pay off,' if it brings no consequence of positive value to the organism, it tends to drop out of the organism's behavioral repertoire.

ORGANIC MENTAL DISORDER

Definition
An organic mental disorder is one in which a pathological condition of the body, particularly of the brain and nervous system, produces maladaptive behavior.

Example
Amnestic syndrome is one of the organic mental disorders. Victims of amnestic syndrome often display an impairment of both short-term and long-term memory. Short-term memory loss is displayed by an inability to learn anything new. Long-term memory loss is displayed by an inability to recall formerly familiar facts about one's life history or information relating to one's vocation.

Connections
Various pathological conditions can cause an organic mental disorder. Some of these are: a brain tumor, a biochemical imbalance, a deficiency of certain hormones, a cerebrovascular accident (i.e. a 'stroke'), chronic alcoholism, and degenerative disorders of the brain and nervous system (e.g. Alzheimer's disease).

It is important in clinical work to distinguish an organic mental disorder from a functional one. A *functional mental disorder* is one in which there is no obvious pathology at a biological level. Under such conditions it can be hypothesized that the maladaptive behavior is the result of emotional conflicts or learned behavior. A problem arises, however, when one considers that some bodily pathology may be subtle and difficult to detect. For example, a shortage of the neurotransmitter norepinephrine (see *neurotransmitter*) may be involved in certain cases of depression. This condition may easily be missed, and an organic mental disorder may appear incorrectly to be a functional one.

ORGANISM

Definition
An organism is any living entity.

Example
A human being is an organism.

Connections
The spectrum of the concept of an organism is very wide, encompassing one-celled creatures, plants of all kinds, worms, fish, birds, rats, monkeys, and human beings.

The behavior of organisms is the subject matter of psychology (see entry), and therefore one could argue that the behavior of *any* organism can be included in psychology. In practice, the focus of interest in psychology has been on the behavior of organisms with a highly organized brain and nervous system.

ORGASM

Definition
In males, an orgasm is a reflex action in response to sexual stimulation producing rhythmic contractions of the penis and the ejaculation of semen. In females, an orgasm is a reflex action in response to sexual stimulation producing rhythmic contractions of the *pubococcygeus muscle*, a muscle surrounding the vagina. Subjectively, in both sexes, an orgasm is experienced as the peak of pleasure in sexual arousal.

Example
A male and female are engaging in an act of sexual intercourse. He provides adequate erotic stimulation to her clitoris and vagina, and she reaches an orgasm before him. He then main-

tains steady penile stroking and within a few minutes reaches his own orgasm.

Connections
The *clitoris*, mentioned in the example, is an erectile structure analogous to the penis, and is located above the vaginal opening. The studies of sex researchers William H. Masters and Virginia E. Johnson indicate that stimulation of the clitoris, often indirect, is the most common pathway for the induction of an orgasm in a female. The stimulation can be autoerotic, as it is in masturbation, or it can be supplied by a partner.

Physiological investigations conducted by Masters and Johnson indicate that the sexual response cycle in both males and females consists of four stages: (1) excitement, (2) plateau, (3) orgasm, and (4) resolution. Although there are many individual differences, they found that females tend to move through the cycle at a somewhat slower pace than males. Many females move through the cycle in ten to twenty minutes. Many males move through the cycle in two to four minutes.

OUT-OF-BODY EXPERIENCE

Definition
An out-of-body experience is one in which the individual experiences the self as dissociated from the physical body.

Example
Winifred, age thirty-three, suffers a brief clinical death during surgery. (A clinical death takes place when the heart stops and respirations cease.) She is resuscitated by the physician using standard techniques. Note that it is debatable whether or not she was 'actually' dead. For example, she did not suffer a brain death, the neurons in her brain remaining alive during the clinical interlude. After she regains consciousness, she reports that she had an out-of-body experience during the surgery. And it is quite likely that this event is associated with the clinical death. Winifred says that she was floating and looking down at her body on the table. Then she passed through the walls of the hospital and met a beautiful guide bathed in light. The guide led her towards a group of deceased family and friends in the distance. They were smiling and welcoming her. But something called her back. She told the guide that her work on Earth was not yet done.

He smiled and understood, and she returned once again through the walls of the hospital to the surgical room. Without pain she reentered her body. The experience has left her convinced that there is spiritual life after biological death.

Connections
Reports of out-of-body experiences in association with clinical deaths, near-death encounters, and great pain are relatively common. Two interpretations of such experiences are available. One interpretation suggests that the experiences reflect objective reality, and that they prove the existence of an immortal soul. A second interpretation suggests that the experiences are produced by an inborn program that is triggered by certain biological events, but that this program is subjective in nature. Thus the experiences prove nothing definite about immortality.

P

PARENTAL STYLE

Definition
Parental style is the characteristic pattern of behavior exhibited by a given parent toward a particular child.

Example
Ralph, age forty-two, tends to be stern, controlling, and demanding toward his twelve-year-old son. With his seven-year-old daughter, Ralph tends to be relaxed, agreeable, and undemanding. Ralph's parental style toward his son may be described as *authoritarian*, and toward his daughter it may be described as *permissive*.

Connections
Parental style tends to vary along two independent dimensions. The first dimension may be described as authoritarian-permissive. The two ends of the dimension are made clear by the adjectives used in the example. In the middle of the dimension there is a style called *democratic*, suggesting a reasonable style between the two extremes.

The second dimension may be described as accepting-rejecting. The accepting style is characterized by a substantial amount of unconditional love and spontaneous expressions of affection. The rejecting style is characterized by emotional distance and 'coldness.'

A substantial amount of research over the years on developmental psychology converges to suggest that an optimal combination of parental styles, one that fosters high self-esteem in children, is the combination of the democratic style with the accepting style.

PARTIAL REINFORCEMENT EFFECT

Definition
The partial reinforcement effect is the tendency of an operant response to display greater resistance to extinction when it has been acquired under conditions of intermittent reinforcement than when it has been acquired under conditions of one-to-one reinforcement.

Example
Rat 1 is placed in an operant conditioning apparatus (see *operant conditioning*). It learns to press a lever in order to obtain reinforcers in the form of food pellets. Each lever-press brings a pellet. So the reinforcement schedule is one-to-one.

Rat 2 is also placed in an operant conditioning apparatus. And, again, it learns to press a lever in order to obtain reinforcers in the form of food pellets. However, in the case of Rat 2, food pellets are obtained on the basis of every other lever-press. So the reinforcement schedule is two-to-one (i.e. two lever-presses = one pellet).

Although Rat 2 takes a longer time, both rats eventually learn the response and reach a high rate of response. Now both rats are placed on an extinction schedule (see *extinction*). No food is obtained for lever pressing, and the rate of response declines for both rats. However, Rat 2 shows more *resistance to extinction*. It unlearns the habit more slowly than Rat 1.

Connections
More than one kind of partial reinforcement schedule is possible. Rat 2 was receiving what is called a *fixed-ratio schedule* in which a fixed number of lever presses produces a reinforcer. A *fixed-interval schedule* is one in which a reinforcer is given after a fixed time interval passes. A *variable-ratio schedule* is one in which a reinforcer is given after a variable, or random, number of operant responses are given by the organism. A *variable-interval schedule* is one in which a reinforcer is given after a variable, or random, time interval passes. All of these schedules of partial reinforcement produce greater resistance to extinction than does a schedule of continuous reinforcement.

Why does the partial reinforcement effect take place? A number of explanations have been advanced. One explanation is the *expectancy hypothesis*. Referring to the example, the expectancy hypothesis states that Rat 1 expects to be reinforced with

163

every lever-press, and Rat 2 does not. Thus when reinforcement is stopped, Rat 1 quickly ceases to expect reinforcers. However, Rat 2 continues to expect them. A second explanation is the *frustration hypothesis*. Rat 1 is frustrated very little during the training phase. Rat 2 must endure more frustration during training. Thus when reinforcement stops, Rat 2 has more tolerance for frustration and persists longer in the unreinforced behavior. Other explanations have been advanced, and quite a bit of experimental work has gone into comparing them with each other.

The partial reinforcement effect has important practical applications. Let's say that a parent is trying to teach a child a good habit. If the child is reinforced with a little money, a bit of candy, or even praise every single time the habit is performed, the child will become dependent upon these reinforcers. The habit will not be self-sustaining, and when reinforcement is withdrawn, as it must be someday, the habit will tend to extinguish quickly. In order to get the habit *started* it may be advantageous to give a reinforcer every time the child demonstrates the habit. However, after some regularity is established, it is best to switch to a schedule of partial reinforcement.

PAVLOV, IVAN PETROVICH
(1849–1936)

Ivan Petrovich Pavlov was a Russian physiologist and a winner of a Nobel Prize in 1904 for his research on the functioning of the digestive glands. This research led him to an interest in what he termed *psychic secretions*, secretions produced by the salivary glands without direct stimulation by food in the mouth. He noted that when experimental dogs heard the sound of the footsteps of caretakers who usually fed them they salivated before actually being presented with food. If they heard unfamiliar footsteps, they did not salivate. These observations inspired Pavlov's many investigations into *classical conditioning* (see entry).

Pavlov refused to explain classical conditioning in terms of the commonsense viewpoint that dogs salivate to a cue because it leads them to expect food. He rejected explanations in terms of dog consciousness, and instead insisted on strictly physiological ones. He never saw himself as a psychologist, and remained in his own eyes a physiologist to the last day of his life.

Pavlov's work is considered to be seminal. He was the first person to conduct systematic investigations of many of the important phenomena of learning such as conditioning itself, *extinction*, and *stimulus generalization* (see entries).

Although Pavlov was not the father of behaviorism, he is its most important single forerunner. John Watson (see entry) was impressed by Pavlov's research, and made the conditioned reflex a cornerstone of his system.

PEAK EXPERIENCE

Definition
A peak experience is a high point in one's life during which one experiences a great rush of joy, ecstasy, or similar positive emotion.

Example
A parent is watching a pre-schooler take his or her first steps. Suddenly the parent is hit in an overwhelming way by the idea that the generations of human life form a long unbroken chain. A powerful sense of identification with *this* child, with potential grandchildren, and future generations is felt. A sense of great rapture fills the parent's whole being. The experience is brief, but it retains its meaning and is remembered for the parent's lifetime.

Connections
The concept of a peak experience was suggested by Abraham Maslow (see entry) in association with his more general concept of self-actualization (see entry). Maslow's hypothesis was that self-actualizing persons are somewhat more likely to spontaneously have peak experiences than persons who are less self-actualizing.

A peak experience is just that, a *peak*. Like climbing to the mountaintop, one does not stay there long. Similarly, a peak experience is by its very nature short in duration. Maslow was not suggesting that we can exist in a steady state of bliss or rapture.

PERCEPTION

Definition
Perception is a process by which sensations, bits of information arising from the sense organs, are converted into organized and meaningful wholes (i.e. perceptual objects).

Example
You are looking at four dots on a piece of paper. The dots are arranged in the form of a square, and you say that you can 'see' the square. The 'seeing' of the square based on sensory information arising from four disconnected dots is an act of perception.

Connections
Perception is a process that goes on continuously as we see, hear, taste, touch, and smell the world around us. Perception is necessary in order for us to experience order instead of chaos. William James (see entry) asserted that we are not born perceiving the world. He said that the world of the infant is a 'buzzing, blooming confusion.' Thus James took the position that learning is required for perceptions to form, a position that has been taken by many theoreticians.

The Gestalt psychologists (see entry), on the other hand, argued that there are a number of inborn organizing tendencies that make perception possible. Therefore, not even the infant's world is chaos. The Gestalt psychologists did not deny that learning is important, but argued that its role is to improve perception, not create it.

PERSONALITY

Definition
Personality is a global concept with several meanings. First it is one's character, the set of behavioral traits usually associated with a given individual. Second, it may be construed as the conscious self, or ego. Third, it is one's social mask. Fourth, it is the total impact that one has on other people.

Example
Most of Ellen's friends would agree that she is creative and ambitious. *Creative* and *ambitious* are examples of traits (see

entry). And, in this case, they describe two aspects of Ellen's personality as others see her. If we were to obtain more of Ellen's traits, we would have a more or less complete picture of her personality in terms of the first definition given in the example. We would, of course, have to assure ourselves that the traits assigned to Ellen were basically correct, often a difficult task to do on a reliable basis.

Connections
The study of personality is a very large subject, and many psychologists have given it much of their attention. Much of Freud's work was an effort to describe the structure of the human personality. His concepts of the id, ego, and superego (see entries) were an attempt to grasp key processes of the personality. Examples of other personality theorists of prominence are Alfred Adler, Karen Horney, Carl Jung, Abraham Maslow, and Carl Rogers (see entries).

An early attempt to describe and explain personality was made by Hippocrates (c. 460–377 BC), often identified as the father of medicine. Hippocrates said that high levels of blood make people cheerful or *sanguine*. High levels of conventional bile make them tend to be angry or *choleric*. High levels of black bile make them depressed or *melancholic*. High levels of phlegm make them apathetic or *phlegmatic*. This is known as the theory of the four humors, or body fluids. And our word *humor* in reference to temperament is derived from Hippocrates' theory.

PERSONALITY DISORDER

Definition
A personality disorder is a kind of behavioral disorder characterized by substantial problems in the making of social adaptations. The person suffering from a personality disorder does not necessarily experience himself or herself as troubled, but is often seen as troublesome or irksome by other people.

Example
Redmond suffers from an *antisocial personality disorder*. He may be said to be *undersocialized* and unwilling to abide by the conventions of society. He hops from job to job, seldom lasting more than a few months with a single employer. He steals, lies,

and cheats when he thinks he can get away with it. He has lived with several women out of wedlock and has also been married twice, but no relationship seems to endure. He is cross and aggressive, often getting into fights. Now divorced from his second wife, he refuses to contribute to the support of the child he had with her. In general he leads a reckless and wayward life, but does not define himself as troubled. He thinks other people are the problem, and blames them for the difficulties he encounters in life.

Connections
Terms such as *psychopath* and *sociopath* have also been used as labels in association with personality disorders. There is no quick and easy explanation of why some people develop personality disorders. There is, of course, the folklore that some children come from a 'bad seed.' Although temperament may to some degree be associated with inborn factors, it is doubtful that a personality disorder is caused primarily by such factors.

The consensus view in psychology seems to be that a personality disorder is caused primarily by experiences during childhood and early adolescence. For example, if parents combine rejecting and authoritarian styles (see *parental style*), there is some evidence that such a combination may foster an antisocial personality disorder.

PHOBIC DISORDER

Definition
A phobic disorder is a kind of mental disorder characterized by irrational fear, fear that the subject himself or herself easily recognizes as exaggerated and groundless.

Example
Nicole, a thirty-three-year-old homemaker, has made herself into a house prisoner. She has not left the yard of her home for two years, and is most comfortable when she stays inside of her house's walls. She suffers from a phobic disorder known as *agoraphobia*, a fear of public places or large open areas. Her house and yard have become security blankets 'protecting' her from the outside world. She is unhappy with her own behavior and is self-critical about it. Her husband is frustrated by their

inability to have a normal social life including going out to dinner and visiting friends.

Connections
Many phobias have been identified. Some common ones are: *acrophobia* (a fear of high places), *ailurophobia* (a fear of cats), *androphobia* (a fear of men), *cynophobia* (a fear of dogs), *gynophobia* (a fear of women), *haptephobia* (a fear of being touched), *nyctophobia* (a fear of darkness), and *zoophobia* (a fear of animals).

Explanations of the phobic disorders tend to fall into two broad categories. The explanation associated with psychoanalysis is that the object of a phobia is a *symbol*. It stands for an unconscious mental conflict. Thus, in the example, it is possible that Nicole has an unconscious wish to have sexual relations with males outside of her marriage. Her moral code, however, does not permit her to act on this wish. At a conscious level, she wishes to be a 'good' wife. The solution is to stay home where it is safe and not go outside to 'play.'

The second broad category used to explain phobias is learning theory. Perhaps Nicole had a very bad experience when she was away from home that made her hypersensitive to unfamiliar places. Her problem is an adverse conditioned response.

Psychoanalysis and behavior therapy (see entries) have both been used to treat phobias. A solid body of objective research supports the hypothesis that behavior therapy offers effective strategies for the extinction of phobic behavior. The effectiveness of psychoanalysis is much more debatable.

PIAGET, JEAN
(1896–1980)

When Jean Piaget died in 1980 he was the most famous and highly regarded child psychologist in the world. Appointed in 1929, he was for many years the director of the Institute Jean-Jacques Rousseau of Geneva. Although he was very influential on the European continent, his impact on the English-speaking psychological world was delayed until the late 1950s. This was in part due to his emphasis on exploring the inner world of childhood, an approach that was at odds with behaviorism (see entry).

Piaget asserted that the thinking of children is of a very

different quality from the thinking of adults (see *cognitive development*). For example, why does a stone released from one's hand fall to the ground? An adult might explain this familiar phenomenon in terms of *gravity*, a principle derived from physics. A child of four or five years of age might explain the event in terms of loneliness. The stone released from the hand is lonely and homesick for other stones, and therefore rushes to join them when given the opportunity.

A substantial set of changes in modes of thought take place with maturation. This set of changes Piaget spoke of as a *metamorphosis*, a term used in biology to describe a substantial change of form in development such as the transformation of a caterpillar into a butterfly. Piaget argued that the transformation in the modes of thought used by children to the modes of thought used by adults is quite as profound in its way as the transformation of the caterpillar into a butterfly.

The method used by Piaget to explore the thought processes of children was the *phenomenological method* (see *Methods of Psychology*). The phenomenological method is by its very nature subjective, requiring interpretation on the part of the researcher. It is also low in reliability. This provides additional explanation of why Piaget's research was resisted for a long time by psychologists disposed in favor of behaviorism. Nonetheless, the phenomenological method has its favorable points. In particular, it is the only method that provides a deep look at the inner world of the child. And this is something Piaget wanted to do.

It should be understood that it is today conventional to identify Piaget as a child psychologist. However, his claim to fame rests on a broader base. He studied children primarily because of his interest in *epistemology*, the study of how human beings acquire knowledge. The exploration of cognitive development in children seemed to Piaget the most fruitful way to make a contribution to epistemology.

There is a 'cognitive revolution' in modern psychology. In recent times there has been a great rebirth of interest in cognition, concept formation, and thinking (see entries). Much of the current enthusiasm can be traced to the influence of Piaget.

A prolific author, Piaget wrote a number of books describing children's mental development. Among his works are *The Language and Thought of the Child* (1926), *The Construction of Reality in the Child* (1954), and *The Child's Conception of Time* (1969).

PLACEBO

Definition
A placebo is a substance or a treatment with no actual medicinal or therapeutic value. Sometimes a positive response is obtained to such a substance or treatment, and this positive response is called the *placebo effect.*

Example
Otto has a headache in the middle of the night, arises from bed, fumbles about in the kitchen, and takes two aspirin tablets. After a short time back in bed, he begins to feel better, relaxes, and goes to sleep. The next morning, refreshed, he congratulates himself on taking the aspirin. Then he sees the 'aspirin' bottle on the kitchen counter where he left it during the night. Except it isn't a bottle of aspirin at all. It is a bottle of vitamins that resembles the aspirin bottle. Much to his chagrin he realizes that any relief he experienced was entirely due to the placebo effect.

Connections
Placebo in Latin means, 'I shall please.' Thus a placebo has the effect of 'pleasing' or sometimes pacifying a patient.

The early history of medicine is to a large extent the history of the placebo effect. Countless worthless remedies have gained great popularity because of the beneficial psychological response to a treatment of almost any kind. The administration of placebos has been a fertile ground for quacks and charlatans.

A rather interesting recent development in the history of the placebo effect is the finding that a placebo may stimulate the production of endorphins (see entry). And thus in some cases a placebo may have an actual pain-relieving ability.

PLATO
(427–347 BC)

Plato was a principal founding father of Western philosophy, and is among the greatest of the ancient Greek philosophers. He established the Academy of Philosophy near Athens, influenced many young men of his time, and left a substantial set of writings including *The Republic, The Symposium*, and *Phaedo.*

Plato believed in the immortality of the soul. In *Phaedo* he writes, 'I have good hope that there is something after death.' If the soul is immortal, it is not part of the material world. If it is not part of the material world, then it need not obey the natural principles of cause and effect. This leads directly to the idea of the freedom of the will, a concept articulated in clear form by St Thomas Aquinas (see entry). Both Plato and Aristotle were influences on Aquinas. Although Aquinas was impressed by the natural science of Aristotle, he considered Plato to be more of an authority on the nature of the soul. Thus it is clear that Plato played a large part in the formation of one of the most important and debatable concepts in the history of philosophy and psychology, free will.

Plato taught that there are ideas in the mind at birth, or at least their seeds. This is the controversial doctrine of *innate ideas* (see entry).

Plato also taught that there is a distinct separation of appearance from reality. He gave the example of a prisoner in a cave. The prisoner sees shadows on the wall projected from outside of the cave, and takes these shadows to be the real thing. In a similar way, the soul is temporarily trapped within the body (i.e. the cave), and incorrectly takes what it sees and hears in daily life as reality itself. But reality will not be revealed to the soul until it is free of the body after death. This distinction between appearance and reality was preserved by Kant (see entry) in his distinction between a *phenomenon* and a *noumenon*. The distinction is also preserved in the experimental study of perception. It is assumed that we do not experience the external world directly, but construct a psychological world out of sensory data, expectations, and motives (see *sensation, perception*, and *cognition*).

PREJUDICE

Definition
A prejudice is a judgment, attitude, belief, or opinion made before sufficient experience or information exists to reach a firm conclusion. A prejudice is, literally, a prejudgment.

Example
Jacob is convinced that most of the members of ethnic minority X are lazy, dirty, and irresponsible. This prejudice is based not on first-hand experience with members of ethnic minority X, but on opinions expressed by his family and friends.

Connections
A prejudice may be either positive or negative. Thus it is possible to be convinced on the basis of little or no evidence that members of Group Y are bright, talented, and creative.

The acquisition and retention of prejudices is an important research area for social psychology. Prejudices, once well-formed, are tenacious. They often resist change even in the face of quite a bit of contrary evidence. A stereotype (see entry) is often a component of a prejudice.

A prejudice is not limited to attitudes about other people or groups. One can have a prejudice toward almost anything. Many people have a negative prejudice concerning the eating of snails. The prejudice is so strong that they will never test it and try to eat a snail.

Obviously the concepts of attitude (see entry) and prejudice overlap to a large extent. In fact the word *attitude* was included in the definition of prejudice. The difference is that an attitude as such is not necessarily formed beforehand. It *may* be based on experience, fact, or first-hand knowledge. If, on the other hand, it *is* formed beforehand, then we are speaking of a prejudice.

PREMACK PRINCIPLE

Definition
Assume that two actions in an organism's behavioral repertoire are exhibited with varying degrees of probability, one action having a low probability of occurrence and a second action having a high probability of occurrence. The Premack principle states that an action with a high probability of occurrence can be used to reinforce an action with a low probability of occurrence.

Example
Rhoda is eight years old, and she often neglects her chores. Doing her chores may be identified as an action with a low probability of occurrence. Rhoda spends quite a bit of time relaxing in front of the television set. This may be defined as an action with a high probability of occurrence. If the opportunity to watch television is made conditional by Rhoda's parents on doing her chores, the probability of doing chores will go up. Thus watching television becomes a reinforcer for doing chores.

PROJECTION

Connections
The Premack principle was stated by learning theorist David Premack, and he has conducted a number of experiments establishing its effectiveness. Premack points out that an informal name for the Premack principle is 'Grandma's law.' Grandma's law simply states that one must do one's work *before* one has fun.

Premack's principle is of substantial help to exasperated parents who declare that they are unable to find any effective ways to reinforce or reward the behavior of their children. By arranging the *order* in which actions take place a high-probability action can *become* a very effective reinforcer.

The Premack principle can also be very helpful in the self-management of behavior. A tendency to procrastinate and avoid responsible tasks can be combated by promising oneself a pleasurable activity *after* the task is done. If the pleasurable activity precedes the responsible task, the Premack principle is defeated.

PROJECTION

Definition
Projection is an ego defense mechanism characterized by assigning to other persons and things attributes arising from one's own unconscious mental life. Broadly speaking, it is the perception of the world in terms of one's own personality.

Example
Louise is a person with a great deal of repressed hostility, hostility that she does not recognize in herself at a conscious level. She tends not to trust other people, is suspicious of their intentions, and imagines that they are planning to take advantage of her. Her mistrust is a projection arising from her own hostility. The hostility within herself she sees in others.

Connections
The concept of projection is an important one in psychoanalytic theory. It is used to explain a great deal of maladaptive behavior in which one assigns blame for one's own failings and transgressions to external sources.

Two personality tests based on projection are the Rorschach inkblot test and the Thematic Apperception Test (see entries).

PSI ABILITIES

Definition
Psi abilities are hypothesized abilities of the mind allowing it to act and perceive in such a manner that it transcends natural laws.

Example
One of the psi abilities is *telepathy*, the power of one mind to communicate with another mind directly without the use of a physical medium. Telepathy has been called 'mental radio.'

Connections
The word *psi* is derived from the twenty-third letter of the Greek alphabet, and is the symbol for *psyche*, or soul. Thus *psi* is a very apt word for mental powers that presumably go beyond the earthly body's capacities. Psi abilities are sometimes called 'wild talents.'

Telepathy is a part of a group of three psi abilities known as *extrasensory perception* (ESP). Extrasensory perception is the hypothesized power of the mind to perceive or be aware of events in the present or future without the use of the sense organs. Telepathy has already been identified. The other two types of extrasensory perception are *clairvoyance* and *precognition*. Clairvoyance is 'clear seeing,' and the power allows one to know the details of what is happening in a place sometimes far removed from one's own location. For example, a man in New York City on a business trip might 'see' that his wife in Kansas is dating his best friend. *Precognition* is to 'know ahead,' or the ability to read the future. This is an ability presumed to be possessed by fortune tellers and famous prophets such as Nostradamus.

The other principal psi ability is *psychokinesis* (PK), and it is not a form of extrasensory perception. It stands on its own as a talent. Psychokinesis is the ability of the mind to directly affect or move matter. With psychokinesis one can bend a spoon or lift an object off of a table by mental power alone.

We have a rich history of legends, anecdotal reports, and folklore supporting the existence of psi abilities. As a consequence, experimental psychologists have attempted to study psi abilities in laboratory settings. One of the most famous researchers to explore psi abilities was J. B. Rhine, long associated with Duke University. Rhine was convinced that his many studies proved the existence of psi abilities beyond a reasonable doubt.

Other psychologists have not been so convinced. And some have criticized both Rhine's methodology and interpretations of his data. There is no consensus in psychology as a field of study concerning the very existence of psi abilities. The issue continues to be debated.

PSYCHOANALYSIS

Definition
Psychoanalysis has two principal meanings. First, psychoanalysis is a method of treating mental disorders utilizing such techniques as free association and dream interpretation. Second, psychoanalysis is a personality theory built upon such concepts as unconscious motivation, the id, the ego, and the superego.

Example
Stephanie is a self-referred psychoanalytic patient. She has a number of vague emotional complaints including mild depression and several phobias. She is intelligent, talkative, has a profession, and is interested in psychoanalysis from an intellectual point of view. Loosely speaking, she is in colloquial terms somewhat 'neurotic.' Psychoanalytic treatment for Stephanie consists largely of reclining on a couch and engaging in free association (see entry). Her psychoanalyst from time-to-time offers an interpretation of the material Stephanie produces. In brief, the *meaning* of Stephanie's ideas, emotions, and behavior is sought. Usually, in psychoanalysis meaning will be discovered in terms of early childhood experiences and unconscious motives. The whole process for Stephanie is one of gradual growth in which she finds a certain freedom from her emotional conflicts and a greater sense of well-being.

Connections
The undisputed father of psychoanalysis was Sigmund Freud (see entry). It is considered the first of the modern verbal psychotherapies. However, the terms psychoanalysis and

psychotherapy (see entry) should *not* be equated. Psychoanalysis is but one kind of psychotherapy.

Although psychoanalysis has been highly influential, its effectiveness has been hotly debated. It is not possible to give a simple *yes* or *no* answer to the question, 'Is psychoanalysis effective?' Much depends upon the art of the psychoanalyst, the motivation of the patient, and the kind of disorder being treated. In general terms it can be said that psychoanalysis is not particularly useful in treating psychotic disorders (see entry), and Freud never intended it for that purpose. Freud's principal aim with psychoanalysis was to treat disorders in which the repression of ideas and motives produced maladaptive symptoms generally called 'neurotic.'

PSYCHOBIOLOGY

Definition
Psychobiology is the study of behavior in terms of its biological foundations.

Example
One of the principal areas of investigation in psychobiology is *physiological psychology*, the study of the relationship of behavior to the sense organs, brain, nervous system, and endocrine glands. Let us say that a particular researcher discovers that variations in a certain neurotransmitter (see entry) in the brain are related to depression. This researcher's work is in the psychobiological domain.

Connections
The other principal area of investigation in psychobiology is comparative psychology (see entry).

Psychobiology assumes a certain kind of link between what we call 'mind' and 'body.' The nature of that link is such that 'mind' is the name we give to certain activities of the body, particularly the 'firings' of neurons (see entry). Unlike dualism (see entry), which assumes that mind and body have an equal status, psychobiology assigns a sort of supremacy to the biological level of discourse. Biological events are used to explain psychological ones. Implicit in psychobiology is a philosophy known as *materialistic monism*, meaning that some sort of material 'stuff' (e.g.

177

the atom) is the basis of everything, including neurons, thought, and behavior.

Psychobiology does not have to proceed on the conviction that materialistic monism is an actual truth. It can operate with the assumption that materialistic monism is only a working hypothesis. Using this hypothesis, a great deal of important research is being conducted on the biological sources of behavior, or, simply, psychobiology.

PSYCHOLOGICAL TEST

Definition
A psychological test is an objective, standardized measuring instrument used to evaluate an attribute or set of attributes such as intelligence, personality, creativity, aptitudes, or interests.

Example
A set of related tests called the *Differential Aptitude Tests* provides an example of a measuring instrument designed to evaluate aptitudes (see entry). The tests are scored in categories such as Verbal Reasoning, Numerical Ability, Abstract Reasoning, and others. The results of the test are useful when vocational guidance is required. Schools, large corporations, and the armed forces often find aptitude tests useful.

Connections
Other examples of psychological tests are the Minnesota Multiphasic Personality Inventory (MMPI), the Rorschach inkblot test, the Rotter Internal-External Scale, the Stanford-Binet Intelligence Scale, the Thematic Apperception Test (TAT), and the Wechsler Adult Intelligence Scale (WAIS) (see entries).

There has been much discussion concerning the ethical use of psychological tests. For example, the MMPI (see entry) has been sometimes used by corporations in making personnel decisions. In view of the fact that the MMPI was designed for psychiatric use and tends to flush out mental disorders, it may be inappropriate to use it in nonclinical settings. A person who on a behavioral level has never exhibited a mental disorder may be thought of as 'paranoid' or 'schizophrenic' by his or her superiors on the basis of a test result alone. On the other hand, if psychological tests are used by qualified persons, the results of such tests can be applied in many helpful ways.

Two of the problems with psychological tests are their *validity* and their *reliability* (see entries). Some tests are low on one or both of these important attributes, and such tests are next to useless.

PSYCHOLOGIST

Definition
A psychologist is a person who makes a vocation of studying the behavior of organisms.

Example
Pia C. has earned a doctor of philosophy (Ph.D.) degree in psychology, and teaches courses in the subject at a university. She also does research in learning theory. It is appropriate to call her a psychologist.

Connections
There are various kinds of psychologists because there are various fields of psychology. Pia in the example would probably be classified as a *teaching psychologist* or an *experimental psychologist*. On the other hand, another field of psychology is *clinical psychology* in which the psychologist's principal work activities consist of giving psychological tests and doing psychotherapy (see entry). Additional fields of psychology are *industrial psychology, school psychology*, and *counseling psychology*.

It is important to distinguish a psychologist from a psychiatrist. A psychologist is *not* a medical doctor, and holds at the minimum a master's degree (MA or MS) in psychology. Clinical psychologists, for example, cannot prescribe drugs. A *psychiatrist*, on the other hand, holds a doctor of medicine (MD) degree. A psychiatrist is, essentially, a medical doctor who specializes in the treatment of mental disorders. As a physician, he or she can prescribe drugs.

It is also important to distinguish a psychoanalyst from either a psychologist or a psychiatrist. The confusion arises from the similarity of the terms involved, and the fact that psychoanalysts usually come from the ranks of psychiatrists. A *psychoanalyst* is one who helps troubled persons by employing as a principal

179

assumption the existence of an unconscious mental life (see *psychoanalysis*). Most psychoanalysts are first psychiatrists. However, some training institutes accept psychologists. In a few instances the prior academic background of a psychoanalyst is neither medicine nor psychology.

PSYCHOLOGY

Definition
Three definitions of psychology, all related to each other, will be offered. First, the oldest definition of psychology is that it is the study of the soul. Second, a bridging definition between the first and the third is that psychology is the science of mental life. Third, the most widely accepted contemporary definition is that psychology is the science of the behavior of organisms.

Example
It is not uncommon for a beginning student in a psychology course to protest that a lecture on rats learning to press bars in order to obtain food pellets is not 'really' psychology. Nothing at all is being said about what the rats think or feel, and, worst of all, they are not even human beings! The instructor will usually make an effort to explain that what he or she is discussing most definitely *is* psychology because a rat is an organism and it is most certainly behaving. The instructor is, of course, basing his or her usage of the word *psychology* on the third definition given above.

Connections
Defining psychology in terms of the soul is associated with the ancient Greeks. Plato (427–347 BC) and Aristotle (384–322 BC) thought of psychology as the study of the soul. It was assumed that consciousness was associated with the soul. Thus the study of consciousness and its associated mental processes was a part of the study of the soul.

Remaining in the domain of philosophy for many centuries, psychology was thought of as the study of the soul and its conscious aspects. Psychology split off from philosophy and attained independent status in 1879 when Wilhelm Wundt (see entry) founded the first psychological laboratory. As a consequence, William James (see entry) recognized that psychologists no longer needed to keep referring to the soul, and so he proposed around 1890 that psychology be defined as the science of mental life. His approach to psychology (see *functionalism*) opened up the study of thinking, attention, perception, intelligence, will, and memory.

John Watson (see entry) was dissatisfied with James's definition. He felt that James had taken only a half-step in dissociating psychology from philosophy. And so Watson proposed the no-nonsense definition that psychology is the science of the behavior of organisms. In this definition he quite deliberately excluded the assumption that the organism is conscious (see *behaviorism*). He also wanted to broaden the scope of psychology beyond human behavior. Thus the behavior of worms, fish, monkeys, pigeons, rats, and so forth is included in the subject matter of psychology.

PSYCHOPHYSICS

Definition
Psychophysics is the study of the functional relationship between magnitudes of physical stimuli and the sensory response to those stimuli.

Example
Research has shown that the relationship between the intensity of a sound, a *physical* quality, and the loudness of a sound, a *psychological* quality, is not a straight line as common sense would have it. When *j.n.d.*'s or *just noticeable differences* in loudness are plotted against increases in sound pressure level, it turns out that geometric increases in sound pressure level must be produced in order to obtain arithmetical increases in j.n.d.'s. Thus the *decibel scale*, the scale used to measure sound pressure level, is a logarithmic scale. To illustrate, ten decibels = 10 units of physical intensity, 20 decibels = 100 units of physical intensity, 30 decibels = 1,000 units of physical intensity, and 40 decibels = 10,000 units of physical intensity. A decibel level of 120 is 1,000,000 times more intense than a decibel level of 10!

Connections
The father of psychophysics was Gustav Theodor Fechner (1801–1887), a professor of physics at the University of Leipzig in Germany. Although Fechner worked out several classical

methods for gathering psychophysical data, his primary interest in psychophysics was philosophical. He believed that psychophysics 'solved' the mind-body problem (see *dualism*), and that he had demonstrated, because of their lawful functional relationships, that mind and body are aspects of a single reality. No consensus exists in psychology or philosophy concerning the adequacy of Fechner's solution of the mind-body problem, but his practical work in psychophysics is highly regarded, and has formed the basis of much modern research on sensory processes and perception.

PSYCHOSEXUAL DEVELOPMENT

Definition
Psychosexual development is the combination of maturation and learning that produces changes in both sexual behavior and personality from infancy to and through adulthood.

Example
Prior to puberty one has little overt sexual interest in the opposite sex. After puberty, and during adolescence, partly as a result of certain hormones released by the endocrine glands (see entry), erotic attraction toward the opposite sex undergoes a marked increase.

Connections
The most influential single theory of psychosexual development has been Freud's. Freud hypothesized that a person goes through five distinct stages of psychosexual development. The five stages are: (1) *oral* (birth to 18 months), (2) *anal* (18 months to 3 years), (3) *phallic* (3 to 6 years), (4) *latency* (6 to 12 years), and (5) *genital* (puberty to and through adulthood). During the oral period the *libido* (see entry) is focused on the oral zone of the body. The infant obtains erotic satisfaction from oral activities such as sucking, biting, chewing, spitting, and so forth. During the anal period the libido changes its focus to the anal zone of the body. The toddler obtains erotic satisfaction from anal activities such as holding and expelling fecal bulk. During the phallic period libido changes its focus again and the pre-school child obtains satisfaction from autoerotic manipulation of either the penis or the clitoris. During the latency period the libido is repressed and the

school-age child experiences little conscious erotic satisfaction at all. This is the period during which the Oedipus complex forms (see entry). During the genital period the libido becomes strongly manifest once again, and interest in the opposite sex on a more or less mature genital basis buds and blooms.

Although Freud's psychosexual theory has been very influential, it must not be accepted as a completely accurate description of psychosexual development in all cases. The theory has been much criticized. For example, contemporary research indicates that only some, not all, children display autoerotic activity during the phallic period. And the great importance that Freud attached to the Oedipus complex is widely questioned. Nonetheless, the theory is useful up to a point, and it has inspired a great deal of research on psychosexual development.

PSYCHOSOCIAL DEVELOPMENT

Definition
Psychosocial development is the growth of the personality in relation to other persons and as a member of a society from infancy throughout life. It is the formation, over time, of a *social self*, a self that identifies with the family, the culture, the nation, and so forth.

Example
At age sixteen Harlan was confused about what vocation he would follow. He also wondered whether or not he would really want to marry and become a father when he was an adult. He was confused about future roles, and questioned many values held by his parents and grandparents. The behavior described is suggestive of an *identity crisis* (see below). By the time Harlan was twenty years old he had made a vocational choice and had met a young woman he wanted to marry eventually. Future goals had become clear, and much of his identity was now defined. However, he still faced other developmental tasks of a psychosocial nature (see below).

Connections
The single most influential theory of psychosocial development is the one proposed by the psychoanalyst Erik H. Erikson. Erikson said that there are eight distinct stages of psychosocial

development: (1) *basic trust versus basic mistrust* (birth to two years), (2) *autonomy versus shame and doubt* (2 to 3 years), (3) *initiative versus guilt* (3 to 5 years), (4) *industry versus inferiority* (5 to 11 years), (5) *identity versus role confusion* (11 to 18 years), (6) *intimacy versus isolation* (18 to adulthood), (7) *generativity versus stagnation* (middle age), and (8) *integrity versus despair* (old age).

It is that task of the individual at each developmental stage to bring forth primarily the positive quality (i.e. trust, autonomy, initiative, etc.). If this can be done, a basically healthy social self will emerge. If this cannot be done, the person will develop inadequately and maladaptive behavior patterns may emerge.

PSYCHOSOMATIC ILLNESS

Definition
Psychosomatic illness is illness either induced or aggravated by psychological factors such as stress, life changes, personality variables, and emotional conflicts.

Example
Alexander is a hard-driving professional man who takes on many responsibilities and insists on completing work to a high standard of excellence. He and his wife have a stormy relationship, often spending hours bickering over trifles. Although relatively successful, he is not happy with his level of income and dreams of earning more money. Recently he developed a *peptic ulcer*, an open sore in the intestinal tract. His physician has explained to Alexander that the peptic ulcer is probably caused by superfluous gastric acid associated with chronic anxiety. The acid is actually eating a small hole in Alexander's intestines. Treatment for such a condition may include tranquilizing medication, psychotherapy, and self-management of stress-inducing behavior patterns.

Connections
The word *psychosomatic* is derived from the Greek words *psyche* (i.e. soul or mind) and *soma* (i.e. body). Thus a psychosomatic illness is a 'mind-body' illness.

Research on the general adaptation syndrome, life change units, and type A behavior (see entries) supports the generalization that psychological factors play an important role in many illnesses. There is nothing wildly speculative or far-fetched about the concept of psychosomatic illness.

Examples of common illnesses in which psychological factors play either a dominant or particularly important role are various kinds of colitis, gastritis, certain respiratory disorders (e.g. bronchial asthma), irregular heart rhythm, hypertension (i.e. high blood pressure), both tension and migraine headaches, premenstrual syndrome, some skin rashes, and backaches.

PSYCHOSURGERY

Definition
Psychosurgery is surgery performed on the brain for the purpose of treating a mental disorder.

Example
The *prefrontal lobotomy* is a surgical procedure in which the frontal lobes of the brain's cortex are severed from subcortical structures. The surgery has been most often performed to alleviate the symptoms associated with either chronic schizophrenia or intractable aggressive behavior. A popular form of psychosurgery during the 1940s, the present use of prefrontal lobotomy is infrequent because of both ethical considerations and unreliable results.

Connections
In addition to the prefrontal lobotomy, two principal kinds of psychosurgery are readily identified: (1) cutting the corpus callosum, and (2) electrical stimulation of the brain. The *corpus callosum* is the structure connecting the two cerebral hemispheres (see entry), and it is sometimes cut to control severe epilepsy. *Electrical stimulation of the brain* (see entry) has a number of potential clinical applications.

PSYCHOTHERAPY

Definition
Psychotherapy is any process of re-education aimed at helping a

185

troubled person through the use of primarily psychological interventions in contrast to bodily treatments such as the prescribing of drugs.

Example
Psychoanalysis (see entry) is one of several kinds of psychotherapy. Although historically psychoanalysis was the first of the contemporary psychotherapies, the two terms *psychoanalysis* and *psychotherapy* should not be used as synonyms. Psychotherapy is the larger general category, and psychoanalysis is subsumed within it.

Connections
There are many specific kinds of psychotherapy. Nonetheless, it is possible to discern three main trends. The first trend is the *psychoanalytic* one in which it is assumed that there is an unconscious mental life (see *psychoanalysis*). A second trend is the *behavioristic* one in which it is assumed that much maladaptive behavior is due to faulty learning (see *behavior therapy, counterconditioning*, and *desensitization therapy*). A third trend is the *humanistic* one in which it is assumed that the human being has consciousness and will (see *client-centred therapy, humanistic psychology, logotherapy* and *rational-emotive therapy*).

There has been much debate over the effectiveness of psychotherapy. Because there are many kinds of psychotherapies and also many kinds of human problems and mental disorders, it is impossible to give a categorical *yes* or *no* answer to the simple question, 'Is psychotherapy effective?' One has to answer in terms of specific psychotherapies and specific problems. Research indicates that desensitization therapy, for example, is helpful in the treatment of certain phobic disorders. It is not useful, however, in the treatment of a psychotic disorder (see entry).

The ancient and literal meaning of psychotherapy is 'a healing of the soul or mind.' And, broadly speaking, this meaning is still retained.

PSYCHOTIC DISORDERS

Definition
Psychotic disorders are severe mental disorders in which there is

loss of touch with reality as well as gross maladaptive behavior. Some of the symptoms associated with psychotic disorders include personality disorganization, thought disturbance, mood disturbances, delusions, and hallucinations.

Example
Schizophrenic disorders are one of the principal kinds of psychotic disorders. The major distinguishing feature of this set of disorders is substantial impairment of the ability to think clearly. Schizophrenic patients do not process information in normal ways; their ideas seem bizarre and completely illogical.

Connections
Four of the principal types of schizophrenic disorders are: (1) disorganized type, (2) catatonic type, (3) paranoid type, and (4) undifferentiated type. The *disorganized type* is sometimes called *hebephrenic schizophrenia* after Hebe, the Greek goddess of youth. The person with this disorder is often incoherent, inappropriate, and silly, behaving much like a very young child. The *catatonic type* is associated with mutism, stupor, posturing, and useless movements. The *paranoid type* is associated with delusions of persecution, greatness, or unfair treatment. The *undifferentiated type* is a general clinical category for schizophrenic patients who do not fit neatly into one of the first three types. Such patients often display delusions, hallucinations, incoherent speech, and nonfunctional behavior.

Two other important kinds of psychotic disorders are: (1) paranoid disorders and (2) affective disorders. *Paranoid disorders* are characterized by systematic and well-organized delusions. This is what sets them apart from schizophrenic disorders, paranoid type. The delusions of the person suffering from what is basically a schizophrenic disorder are lacking in logic and are, consequently, unconvincing. This is not so with persons suffering from a 'pure' paranoid disorder; their story is often very convincing.

Affective disorders are essentially emotional disturbances. *Bipolar disorder*, sometimes called *manic-depressive disorder*, is one kind of affective disorder. Bipolar disorder is associated with extreme mood swings alternating between euphoria and depression.

The kinds of psychotic disorders described in this entry are all known as *functional psychotic disorders*, ones in which there is no obvious pathology at a biological level. (Compare this with the entry for *organic mental disorders*. Also, see the entries for *behavioral genetics* and *neurotransmitter* for a discussion of the role that subtle biological factors may play in the functional psychotic disorders.)

R

RAPID EYE MOVEMENTS (REMs)

Definition
Rapid eye movements (REMs) are abrupt spontaneous changes
in position made by one's eyes during light sleep. The shifts in
position are in both vertical and horizontal directions, and
approximate what the eyeball does when one is looking at an
actual event.

Example
Assume that Felicia's sleep behavior is being observed in a
research setting. During one particular evening she has seven
REM episodes, lasting between ten to twenty minutes each.
These episodes are readily detected by an observer. Her eyeballs
can actually be seen to be moving about quickly under her
eyelids. If Felicia is awakened during a REM episode, she
reports a dream about eighty percent of the time, which is
typical.

Connections
As noted in the definition, REMs are associated with light sleep.
Light sleep is also known as *Stage 1 sleep*, a stage of sleep in which
electroencephalograms (see entry) show that the cortex of the
brain is very active. In fact, Stage 1 sleep combined with REMs is
sometimes called 'paradoxical sleep' because in a physiological
sense the cortex is active and alert, just as it is in a normal waking
state.

Although REMs are associated with dreams, it would be a
mistake to say that REM sleep *is* dreaming sleep. As the example
indicates, subjects do report a dream with most REM episodes if
they are awakened. But sometimes subjects awakened from a
REM episode do not report a dream. Also, subjects in deep sleep
who are not displaying REMs can be awakened, and they will on
some occasions report a dream.

189

RAPPORT

Definition
Rapport is a quality possessed by a relationship when the two or more individuals involved have a harmony of thought or feelings or a set of common understandings.

Example
More than one psychotherapist has asserted that rapport is a necessary ingredient for effective psychotherapy. The patient and the therapist must have the impression that they 'are on the same wavelength,' that they are 'clicking.' If this is felt by both of the individuals, then rapport is present.

Connections
The hypothesis that rapport is necessary for effective psychotherapy should not be taken as one that every clinical psychologist and psychiatrist accepts. Some suggest that rapport can be present, then be lost, then return again. Another possibility is that rapport is absent at first, but can be acquired. A hostile patient may resist therapy at first, but subsequently be won over. On a simple common-sense basis, however, it does seem correct to say that neither a patient nor a therapist are comfortable when rapport is absent.

We generally prefer rapport in our close relationships. A husband and a wife with rapport tend to perceive their marriage as a happy one. The quality of intimacy (see entry) is very similar to the concept of rapport.

Rapport is derived from the French word *rapporter*, meaning 'to bring back.' Broadly speaking, rapport is that which heals, which brings together persons who are apart.

RATIONAL-EMOTIVE THERAPY

Definition
Rational-emotive therapy is a kind of therapy in which a troubled person learns to manage emotions by replacing irrational ideas with rational ones.

Example
Whenever Cassandra, a college student, is given an assignment by a professor, she thinks, 'I'm going to fail. I can't do it.' These

ideas make her highly anxious, and in general interfere with both her happiness and performance as a student. The ideas can be shown to be irrational because she has yet to fail any assignment she has ever been given. Assume that Cassandra is in rational-emotive therapy. Her therapist points out to her that her ideas are irrational, and convinces her through dialogue that this is so. Then he encourages Cassandra to quite deliberately and voluntarily substitute rational ideas for the irrational ones. The moment she catches herself thinking, 'I'm going to fail,' she is to replace that thought with, 'I've never failed an assignment yet. I'll do it for sure.' In time the new rational thoughts become habitual themselves, and her emotional state improves.

Connections
Troubled persons usually have a set of favorite irrational ideas. And these must be flushed out in the course of therapy. Cassandra's therapy would probably require more than working on the two irrational ideas used in the example. For example, she may also have irrational ideas such as, 'People don't like me. I'm not pretty. I'll never get married.'

The father of rational-emotive therapy is the New York psychologist Albert Ellis. Ellis says that his work is inspired by the philosophy of *stoicism*, the teaching that it is not so much events that cause our woes as our *evaluation* of the events. The troubled person, the 'neurotic' person, tends to evaluate events in a dismal light. He or she is often guilty of what Ellis calls *catastrophic thinking*, the tendency to assume from one small mishap that all will be lost, that one's world is ending.

Ellis insists that because irrational ideas are conscious they can be fought at a conscious level without probing into the unconscious mental life. In taking this position he has put himself at some odds with classical psychoanalysis (see entry).

RATIONALIZATION

Definition
Rationalization is an ego defense mechanism in which a superficially plausible excuse is given for a failure, transgression, loss, or maladaptive behavior.

Example
Gertrude is a middle manager working for an investment corporation. She turns in an important report a week late, primarily

because of simple procrastination. Her supervisor is quite displeased with Gertrude's performance, and says so. To herself, Gertrude thinks, 'It's not my fault I had to turn in the report late. They ask too much of me, give me too much to do. What do they expect when there is so much pressure?' Her thoughts have a rational-sounding quality, but are not rational at all. She is using the defense mechanism of rationalization in order to avoid taking responsibility for her behavior.

Connections
Two important kinds of rationalization are sour grapes and sweet lemons. *Sour grapes* involves thinking that something that was once desired is not in fact desirable because something is wrong with it. If one wishes to have a romantic relationship with another person, and is rejected, one can think, 'Oh, well. She's really not too bright, and I noticed that she's much too bossy.'

Sweet lemons requires that one make the best of a bad situation. A loss or a setback can be met with the thought, 'Oh, I guess it's not so bad. Maybe everything happens for the best.' Or, 'Every cloud has a silver lining.'

REACTION FORMATION

Definition
Reaction formation is an ego defense mechanism in which a repressed motive or idea reappears in the conscious mental life in opposite form.

Example
Veronica has much repressed hostility toward her mother. If this statement is taken seriously in psychoanalytic terms, it means that Veronica is at a conscious level unaware of the hostile feelings, pretending to herself that they don't exist. The reaction formation develops in order to buttress the repression. At the conscious level, Veronica forms the idea that she loves her mother more than most daughters. And she sets out to prove to herself, her mother, and others that this is true. She never forgets a birthday, anniversary, or other special occasion associated with her mother. Veronica always has a card, a gift, and so forth. If she fails in this duty, she feels very anxious and uncomfortable until she makes some sort of atonement.

Connections
Critics of psychoanalysis have pointed out that the concept of
reaction formation allows the observer of another's behavior to
have it both ways. If Veronica is openly hostile to her mother,
she is, of course, hostile to her mother. If Veronica is attentive
and affectionate to her mother, she is still hostile toward her
mother! This puts Veronica in a no-win situation from a psychological point of view, and places the observer in a smug one-up
psychological position.

On the other hand, is the concept of reaction formation just
psychoanalytic doubletalk? In defense of the concept, it could be
pointed out that a reaction formation is indicated when there is
compulsiveness, rigidity, and anxiety associated with the conscious idea and its related behaviors. These conditions were
basically met in the example of Veronica's feeling toward her
mother, and it would seem fair to say that the concept of a
reaction formation probably does help us understand Veronica's
behavior.

REACTIVE INHIBITION

Definition
Reactive inhibition is a discrete quantity of specific fatigue that
accumulates each time an organism makes a given response.

Example
Let's say that Merle is learning to become a touch typist. He
takes five timed trials in a row, without rest periods, and his
word-per-minute scores are: 26, 31, 33, 34, and 33. After a
fifteen minute break, he takes a sixth timed trial, and his score is
37, the best score he has ever had. The tendency of the first set of
scores to flatten toward the end of the series, or to reach a
plateau, can be explained in terms of reactive inhibition. The
muscles in Merle's fingers are accumulating reactive inhibition
with each trial. The spurt in performance after a rest period,
called *reminiscence*, can also be explained in terms of reactive
inhibition. A rest period allows for the spontaneous dissipation
of reactive inhibition, enabling Merle to improve his performance.

Connections
The concept of reactive inhibition was proposed by the learning

theorist Clark L. Hull, a very influential thinker in early behavioristic psychology. Hull used reactive inhibition to explain a number of phenomena in learning such as plateaus in learning curves, reminiscence, the superiority of distributed over massed practice, and spontaneous recovery (see entry).

It is, however, possible to explain the same phenomena with a cognitive concept, the concept of attention. When organisms learn, they must attend to relevant aspects of the stimulus situation. Over-exposure to a stimulus leads to boredom and inattention. A break allows for the relief of boredom and restores some of the momentary novelty of a stimulus situation. This enhances attention and in turn performance. Hull, a behaviorist, was, of course, hostile to the concept of attention. So he sought a behavioristic way to explain behavior that earlier psychologists such as James and Wundt (see entries) would have explained in terms of the conscious mental life.

REGRESSION

Definition
Regression is a going backwards of the organism toward an earlier level of development. In psychoanalysis, regression is conceptualized as an ego defense mechanism when childish or infantile behavior is used to cope in an ineffective way with a problem or stressful situation.

Example
When Gerald was seven years old he had a bit of a reputation as a spoiled child. He used to get his way by yelling and shoving. Now at age twenty-three he is having an argument with his wife, and she is besting him. He begins yelling and shoving her about the kitchen, much to her dismay. This behavior on Gerald's part can be clearly seen to be regressive; he has moved backwards and is bringing forth behaviors he relied on when he was a child.

Connections
When regressive behavior is both severe and chronic it is associated with one particular kind of psychotic disorder (see entry), the disorganized type of schizophrenic disorder.

REINFORCER

Definition
A reinforcer is any stimulus that increases the probability of occurrence of a given class of responses.

Example
A rat is learning to press a lever in an instrumental conditioning apparatus (i.e. a Skinner box) in order to obtain pellets of food. With each lever press a single pellet is obtained. The presentation of the food pellets will have the effect of increasing the probability that the rat will press the lever. After a number of food pellets have been obtained, the rat presses the lever at a rapid rate. Thus it can be said that in this case food pellets act as reinforcers for the behavior of lever pressing.

Connections
Much of the importance of the action of reinforcers on the behavior of organisms was spelled out by B. F. Skinner (see entry). Skinner stresses that a reinforcer should not be confused with the more common and popular concept of a reward. A reinforcer is defined empirically, by its effects. It must actually 'strengthen' behavior in order to be correctly thought of as a reinforcer. A reward, on the other hand, is defined subjectively in terms of its perceived value on the part of the giver. Thus the giver of a reward may find to his or her disappointment that a certain reward has no effect on behavior.

Two important kinds of reinforcers are positive and negative ones. A *positive reinforcer* is one that has beneficial consequences for the organism; it always *follows* an operant response (see *operant conditioning*). A food pellet received after a rat presses a lever is a positive reinforcer. A *negative reinforcer* is one that has adverse consequences for the organism; it always *precedes* an operant response. Avoidance learning (see entry) provides an example of how a negative reinforcer works. To elaborate, assume that a rat is given an electric shock. Then it is provided with an opportunity to avoid the shock on the presentation of a warning signal (e.g. a buzzer). Soon the rat will be regularly avoiding the shock. Note that the sequence is such that shock came *first* before the rat's learned behavior.

Note that a negative reinforcer is *not* punishment. Punishment *follows* an undesirable behavior on the organism's part.

RELIABILITY

Definition
In the theory of psychological testing, reliability is a quality present when a test gives stable, consistent, repeatable results.

Example
Assume that a psychologist is attempting to establish the reliability of a new test of intelligence. Here is one way he or she might go about it. Let's say that the test consists of 200 items. The items on the test are randomly assigned to pools of 100 items each, creating subtest Form A and subtest Form B. Then a group of subjects takes the two forms. Every subject takes both Form A and Form B. Thus there are *two* scores for every subject. A correlation coefficient (see entry) is computed on the entire set of paired scores. If the test is reliable, Form A and Form B should display a strong positive correlation. If the test is unreliable, Form A and Form B will show little or no correlation. In other words, in a reliable test, scores on Form A will predict scores on Form B and vice versa.

Connections
The importance of reliability in a psychological test can hardly be overestimated. Attempting to measure a human attribute with an unreliable test would be something like trying to measure the length of a table with a yardstick made out of taffy.

Standardized psychological tests usually publish reliability coefficients in their associated test manuals. With the aid of computers, it is now practical to publish a reliability coefficient for *every item* on the test. (A reliability coefficient is a correlation coefficient computed to determine the reliability of a test or a test item.)

Reliability should not be confused with validity (see entry).

REPRESSION

Definition
In Freudian theory, repression is an ego defense mechanism characterized by a tendency to banish to an unconscious level of the personality those memories, ideas, and motives that are unacceptable to the conscious self.

Example
The forbidden wish, a common theme in psychoanalysis, provides an example of the way in which repression works. Say that
an individual has sexual desire for another person. This is normal
enough. But assume that the other person is a member of the
family. Now we have an incest wish, and this is forbidden. In
terms of the individual's superego (see entry) the wish is completely unacceptable. The ego (see entry) comes to the aid of the
superego and banishes the wish to an unconscious psychological
netherland. The wish does not cease to exist, of course. It may
find expression in dreams, slips of the tongue, or maladaptive
behavior. However, the individual has no direct conscious
awareness of the wish.

Connections
According to Freud, repression is the master defense mechanism. It creates the whole unconscious mental life. The importance that Freud attached to repression is evident in his famous
statement that the mind is much like an iceberg. The unconscious
realm below the threshold of consciousness (i.e. the waterline) is
larger than the tip of the iceberg that we see.

Freud also used the concept of repression to explain *childhood
amnesia*, the tendency that many of us have to show little
memory of events prior to the age of five. Freud asserted that the
first five years of life are so traumatic and full of emotional
conflict that we blot out the whole memory. Freud's interpretation is debatable. For example, it could be argued that the poor
memory of the first five years is traceable to the poorly formed
cognitive structures, or ideas, of the very young child. (See
cognition and *cognitive development*.)

In spite of criticisms that can be made of the concept of
repression, it has proven itself to be useful for explaining many
behaviors that are otherwise quite baffling. Its main value is for
explaining behaviors that are paradoxical or self-defeating.

RESPONSE

Definition
A response is any behavior elicited by a stimulus.

Example
The telephone rings, and one picks up the receiver. The ringing

of the telephone is a stimulus, and picking up the receiver is a response to it.

Connections
The concept of a response is a very general one in psychology, and sometimes is used in conjunction with any behavior. However, strictly speaking behavior is a response only if it is brought forth by a stimulus. A synonym sometimes used for response in ordinary discourse is *answer*; thus a response is, in a sense, an answer to a stimulus. Some behavior is not elicited, but emitted (see *operant conditioning*). Such behavior, often thought of as voluntary, is best thought of as outside of the category of responses. We can call such behavior emitted, voluntary, spontaneous, or willed depending upon our preferences or theoretical framework.

RETICULAR ACTIVATING SYSTEM (RAS)

Definition
The reticular activating system (RAS) is a nervous system structure located primarily in the brain stem. Its primary functions are to regulate brain processes associated with arousal, sleep, and attention.

Example
Assume that a cat is sleeping. This is an experimental animal with an electrode implanted in its RAS. Now a bit of current is passed through the electrode, stimulating the RAS. The cat very quickly wakes up, suggesting that the RAS is a *waking center*, a kind of master switch. Electrodes implanted in other brain sites do not have similar effects when current is passed through them.

Connections
Although the principal location of the RAS is the brain stem, it accomplishes its purpose by sending forth many nerve fibers to various regions of the cerebral cortex. These nerve fibers are the axons of neurons (see entry) with their cell bodies located in the RAS. This network of fibers associated with the cortex is called the *ascending* system.

The RAS also has connections with the spinal cord, and this is known as the *descending* system.

The RAS appears to have basically the same structure and

function in cats, monkeys, and human beings. Thus when one is asleep and awakens suddenly, this 'all-or-none' change is possible because of the many ascending fibers leading from the RAS to the cortex.

RETROACTIVE INTERFERENCE

Definition
Retroactive interference is a phenomenon of learning in which the learning of a second block of material inhibits or depresses the ability to remember a first block of material.

Example
Priscilla is studying French and memorizes a list of twenty pairs of English and French words. Let's call this List 1. Now she memorizes a second list of twenty pairs, List 2. When she attempts to recall List 1, she will find that the learning of List 2 has adversely affected her memory of List 1. Thus List 2 can be said to be exerting a 'backwards' or retroactive effect on her memory of List 1.

Connections
Retroactive interference is a common effect in learning, and adds to our confusion when we are attempting to learn several blocks of related material. The practical way out of the problem of retroactive interference is simple repetition and overlearning of material. Enough familiarity with information eventually makes memory clear.

To add to our troubles as learners, there is also a phenomenon known as proactive interference. *Proactive interference* takes place when the learning of a first block of material inhibits or depresses the ability to learn a second block of material. Thus when Priscilla is learning List 2 the fact that she has already learned List 1 has a proactive interference effect on the learning of List 2. Again, the practical solution is simply repetition and overlearning.

Both retroactive and proactive interference have been demonstrated many times in experiments on human learning.

RISK-TAKING BEHAVIOR

Definition
Risk-taking behavior is behavior in which the individual exposes himself or herself to the possibility of bodily injury or death. Although risk-taking behavior applies to both necessary and unnecessary risks, it is unnecessary risks that are the focus of this entry.

Example
Sidney is an enthusiastic hot air balloonist. He spends many of his weekends taking flights. Hot air ballooning is a dangerous sport. It has one of the worst general records of any recreational activity. Sidney knows this, and yet continues to be active in the sport. The behavior qualifies as a kind of unnecessary risk-taking.

Connections
Other examples of unnecessary risk-taking behavior include hang-gliding, sky-diving, racing cars and motorcycles, and so forth. On a lesser level, almost any of us at some time will drive too fast or ride a roller-coaster. Thus the taking of unnecessary risks is a common phenomenon.

Why do people take unnecessary risks? Two general explanations are the most common ones offered by psychologists. The first explanation is essentially psychoanalytic. The risk-taker may have a great fear of bodily injury or death. Therefore a reaction formation (see entry) is used in which the individual flirts with death in order to repress or control irrational fears. In this interpretation the risk-taking behavior is seen as a way of managing or regulating an emotional conflict.

A second explanation is in terms of the human need for arousal. Some people are understimulated by everyday life. They may find their vocations, marriages, or social activities boring. One way to add some excitement to life is to take unnecessary risks. Studies of the personality structures of unnecessary risk-takers suggest that this second explanation has much to recommend it.

One does not need to make a choice between the two explanations. Both may be useful, depending upon a particular case.

ROGERS, CARL RANSOM
(1902–   )

Carl Ransom Rogers is a former president of the American Psychological Association, and was for a number of years associated with the University of Chicago both as a professor of psychology and as an active member of its Counseling Center. He is the father of *client-centered therapy*, a therapy that emphasizes the importance of the individual's own capacities for change and personal growth (see entry).

The assumptions of client-centered therapy have spread well beyond the domain of counseling. They have become influences on communication between couples and parent-child relationships. Although specific communication skills can be identified as arising from the inspiration of client-centered therapy, the central theme of these skills is *unconditional positive regard* for the other person. Even if the behavior of another person is distressing, it is the behavior itself that must be judged and perhaps even criticized, not the personality of the other. Thus a mother is advised to say to her child, 'Your room is getting a bit messy. Please pick it up,' in preference to, 'You're such a sloppy person.'

Rogers has been one of the leading figures in humanistic psychology (see entry), and his influence has been largely of an inspirational nature. His writings strongly suggest that people can solve their personal problems, that they are significant agents in their own destinies, and that communication between people can be improved by the application of specific principles.

Among Rogers' books are *Client-Centered Therapy* (1951), *On Becoming a Person* (1961), and *A Way of Being* (1980).

ROLE

Definition
In social psychology, a role is one's public personality, the more or less predictable character that an individual assumes in order to fit in as a member of society.

Example
Dr M. plays the role of physician beautifully. He listens with great compassion to his patients' complaints, expresses concern about their family problems, offers words of hope when

appropriate, and so forth. He manifests these behaviors even on days when he is bored and irritated with his patients. He does not let his private feelings show through to them because of their expectations. When he is alone with other physicians he often expresses negative attitudes about his patients that would be somewhat disturbing to them if they were to hear him speaking.

Connections
Another term for the social role that one plays in life is the *Persona*, a term used by Jung (see entry). According to Jung the Persona arises from an inborn need to provide the self with a buffer between the inner, or psychological, world and the external world. The Persona acts like a mask, and we hide behind it to a certain extent. (Jung's use of Persona is derived directly from the Greek word *persona*, meaning a mask worn by an actor in a play.)

The concept of social roles also enters into transactional analysis (see entry). According to transactional analysis, when people play life games (see *game*) they play them from social roles such as Alcoholic, Victim, Rescuer, Persecuter, Martyr, Lover, Loser, Winner, and so forth. One way out of the trap of self-defeating life games is to develop insight into one's own social roles and the way in which they may be limiting personal growth.

RORSCHACH INKBLOT TEST

Definition
The Rorschach inkblot test is a projective personality test consisting of ten standard cards containing bisymmetrical ambiguous stimuli.

Example
Kyla is a subject taking the Rorschach test. The clinical psychologist giving the test asks her to use her imagination and report what she 'sees' in the cards. The psychologist notices that Kyla gives an above average number of responses in a scoring category called Human Movement. For example, she says she sees people dancing, a person taking a walk, an old man fishing, a child bouncing a ball, and so forth. One interpretation of a high level of perceived Human Movement is that Kyla has a particularly rich imagination and fantasy life. Another interpretation is that

she is an autonomous person, feeling very alive and capable of self-direction.

Connections

The Rorschach test was introduced into clinical psychology by Hermann Rorschach, a psychoanalyst, in 1921. The theory of the test is based on the concept of the ego defense mechanism of projection (see entry), the central idea being that projections from the unconscious level of one's personality determine the way in which one perceives the inkblots. The inkblots in and of themselves are 'nothing'. Thus anything that is said about them comes from one's personality.

The ten cards are divided into subgroups. The first five cards contain no color. The next two cards contain some bright red. The last three cards contain several colors. One of the scoring categories is Color, and the number of responses given to the colors is used to make hypotheses about the subject's emotional life.

Rorschach suggested scoring categories and ways of interpreting the test. Since Rorschach's early work other systems have been presented. Scoring categories include the already mentioned Human Movement and Color. In addition, other categories include Location (i.e. the specific part of the blot being responded to), Content (e.g. human figures, animal figures, inanimate objects, etc.), Popularity (i.e. the evaluation of a response as common or uncommon).

Although it is widely believed that the Rorschach test is the most profound of the personality tests because it probes the unconscious level of the personality, it has the drawback of not being highly reliable. A number of studies of the Rorschach support this statement. Therefore, the Rorschach should be used to evaluate a person's personality only when it forms part of a battery of other tests.

S

SADISM

Definition
Sadism is a tendency to extract pleasure from inflicting pain on another person. The two basic kinds of sadism are *sexual sadism* and *sadistic personality traits*. Sexual sadism is a tendency to experience sexual excitement from a partner's humiliation or suffering. Sadistic personality traits are tendencies such as a desire to persecute or abuse another person.

Example
Carson finds it extremely stimulating to pinch, burn with a cigarette, or make tiny cuts with a knife in, the flesh of his partner during the foreplay leading to sexual intercourse. He also likes to bind a partner and hurl insults at her. Oddly enough, he has sometimes been able to find partners with masochistic tendencies (see *masochism*) who will cooperate with his sexual sadism. When Carson does not have a partner available, he often masturbates with fantasies of cutting, bruising, burning, and binding his partner.

Connections
The word *sadism* is not derived, as common sense might seem to indicate, from the word *sad*. It is derived from the behavior of the Marquis de Sade (1740–1814) who chained, strapped and whipped his partners.

The classical psychoanalytic explanation of sexual sadism is in terms of an overly strict and punitive superego (see entry). The individual thinks of sexual behavior as foul, dirty, and 'nasty.' Thus the person engaging in such activity must be punished, pay a price, before he or she is allowed to engage in the activity. In masochism the price is paid by the subject. However, in sadism the sense of filth is projected onto the partner, and it is the partner who must pay the price. It should be realized that the sense of wrongdoing exists in the unconscious mental life of the subject, but is *perceived* as existing in the partner.

The explanation offered above was an early explanation of sadism, and is certainly not adequate to explain all sadistic behavior. The phenomenon is the result of a set of factors such as strong aggressive tendencies, hostility toward one's partner, and lack of impulse control. ·

SCHOOL OF PSYCHOLOGY

Definition
The term *school of psychology* has two principal meanings, both of them related. First, a school of psychology consists of a group of thinkers and researchers who are followers of a particular system of psychology or its principal teacher. Second, a school of psychology is the system itself, including related assumptions and concepts, shared by the associated thinkers.

Example
Psychoanalysis (see entry) is a major school of psychology. Its father was Sigmund Freud, and some of its principal founders were Alfred Adler, Carl Jung, Otto Rank, and Ernest Jones. The most important single assumption of psychoanalysis is that we have an unconscious mental life. A related assumption is *psychological determinism*, the point of view that all behavior is caused. Some of the concepts employed by psychoanalysis are the death instinct, defense mechanisms, ego, id, latent content, Oedipus complex, and superego (see entries).

Connections
The five major schools significant in the early history of psychology were structuralism, functionalism, psychoanalysis, behaviorism, and Gestalt psychology (see entries). In more recent times a sixth school of psychology has arisen, humanistic psychology (see entry).

The five major schools of psychology exerted their greatest influence from the 1890s to the 1920s. After that time period there was a strong tendency for many psychologists to favor eclecticism (see entry), drawing something of value from more than one school of thought.

SECONDARY DRIVES

Definition
Secondary drives are acquired drives, energizers of behavior learned through their association with biological, or primary, drives.

Example
The motive to earn money is a secondary drive. It derives its power from association with biological drives such as hunger and thirst. With money we can buy food, drink, and other necessities of life.

Connections
Although the original impetus to earn money comes from its association with biological drives, it is possible for an acquired motive to develop in the direction of functional autonomy (see entry). It can, so to speak, acquire a life of its own. Thus many people work for money and hoard it as if it had intrinsic value long after they have more than they need.

Most human motives are complex motives (see entry), consisting of both biological drives and secondary drives.

SELF

Definition
First, the self is the unique individual existing as a being over a span of time. Second, the self is the ego, the 'I' of the personality. Third, the self is one's sense of identity, the perception of being the same human being from week-to-week and year-to-year.

Example
From morning to evening one thinks, feels, and engages in a number of actions. There is a strong thread of continuity running through the day. Subjectively, one feels that it is the same ego, 'I,' or person behaving from moment-to-moment. This is the self as experienced.

Connections
It could be argued that the experience of self is an illusion, that every moment we change and are no longer identical to the organism we were a moment ago. However, the experience of

206

self is so strong that most of us promptly reject this idea. In certain oriental ways of thought such as Zen (see entry), it is asserted that the idea of self or ego is a kind of deception, or part of a screen over reality called *maya.*

The word *self* is often used as a combining form. Thus we may speak of self-abandonment, self-accusation, self-destruction, and so forth.

SELF-ACTUALIZATION

Definition
Self-actualization is hypothesized to be an inborn tendency to maximize one's talents and potentialities.

Example
Paula believes that she has talent as a creative writer. She reads magazines for writers, takes a course in creative writing, is working on a novel, and has made definite plans to submit it to several publishers in the near future. In general, she feels that she is making the most of her life and her opportunities, that she is working toward important goals. The inspiration for the behavior described comes from within Paula, and is not primarily a response to the advice or suggestions of others. It can be said that Paula is demonstrating a strong tendency toward self-actualization.

Connections
The foremost exponent of the concept of self-actualization was Abraham Maslow (see entry). Maslow was inspired in part by the writings and research of Kurt Goldstein (1878–1965) who discovered strong strivings toward wholeness in the behavior of persons with brain damage.

Maslow indicated that self-actualization was very high on the ladder of human motives, above the biological drives, curiosity, the need for safety, and even the need for love. Maslow said that most human motives are *deficiency-needs*, they exist because of a lack. However, self-actualization is said to be a *being-need*, the desire to satisfy a plus, or a positive force, in existence.

Although self-actualization is thought to be an inborn tendency, it is also, Maslow indicated, a weak one. It is like a whispering within or a quiet voice. Therefore it is to a person's advantage to be sensitive to this whispering or quiet voice. Maslow wrote that if the need for self-actualization is inadequately met, it can lead to chronic depression.

SELF-CONCEPT

Definition
A self-concept is a global evaluation made about one's own personality. It is derived from the subjective evaluations we tend to make of our own behavioral traits. As a consequence, a self-concept will either be positive or negative.

Example
Kirsten sees herself as being above average in intelligence, only slightly creative, very responsible, very loving, moderately ambitious, a little too passive in her social relationships, athletic, and slightly more attractive than the average woman. She is not conceited, but does not downgrade herself unnecessarily. The net sum of her subjective ratings is quite definitely on the positive side, and we can say that Kirsten has a 'good' self-concept.

Connections
The terms *self-concept* and *self-esteem* are very similar. Self-esteem refers to how high or low one ranks oneself in terms of subjectively perceived personal status. Therefore a person with a positive self-concept will have high self-esteem, and a person with a negative self-concept will have low self-esteem.

A number of years ago Alfred Adler (see entry) coined the term *inferiority complex* to describe a constellation of ideas and feelings held by an individual who felt incompetent to meet the challenges of life. *Inferiority complex, negative self-concept*, and *low self-esteem* are terms that can be used more or less interchangeably.

SENSATION

Definition
Sensation is a process by which the sense organs (e.g. the eyes, the ears, etc.) convert stimulus energies from the external world into the raw data of experience. It is also possible to speak of *a* sensation as a discrete bit of experience (e.g. a flash of light, a sweet taste).

Example
When light energy enters the eye it causes the breakdown of specific chemicals in the retina called *photopigments*. The breakdown of photopigments releases energy which stimulates neurons (see entry) in the retina to depolarize or 'fire.' It is the firing of these neurons that we experience as light. The process of sensation does not, of course, stop at the level of the retina. The process is completed by relaying visual information through the optic nerve to the *thalamus*, a relay center in the brain. The information is then sent to its final destination, the *visual cortex*, a region at the top and toward the rear of the brain.

Connections
The position of sensation in human experience can best be understood by comparing it with two other related processes, perception and cognition (see entries). Think of the three processes as an ascending stairway. Sensation is on the first step. It is the raw material for experience, but has little meaning or organization. An infant looking at the words on this page would see black marks on white paper, would have about the same visual sensations we have, but the experience would stop there. Perception is on the second step. An older child would perceive wholes, words, but they would have little meaning. Cognition is on the third step. An adult perceives not only words, but ideas. The adult has reached the level of cognition, the highest level of human experience.

SEXUAL RESPONSE CYCLE

Definition
The sexual response cycle is an arousal pattern with the following four stages: (1) excitement, (2) plateau, (3) orgasm, and (4) resolution.

Example
On a particular evening Laura and her husband, Sheldon, are kissing and caressing in their bed. Let us follow Laura through the sexual response cycle. She begins to feel somewhat aroused, and enters the excitement stage. Certain physiological changes take place. Her nipples become more erect, a flush of the skin in both the stomach area and the neck area appears, and her heart rate increases. As both physical and psychological stimulation

continue, Laura enters the plateau stage, essentially an extension of the excitement phase. The areolae of the breasts enlarge, the skin flush spreads over much of the body, and the heart rate becomes even more rapid. Let us assume that the couple is now engaged in sexual intercourse, and that adequate stimulation is being supplied to the clitoris and surrounding nerves. (The *clitoris* is a highly sensitive sexual structure in women located toward the upper part of the vagina. Both the clitoris in women and the penis in men have a sensitive tip called the *glans*.) Laura now enters the third stage of the sexual response cycle, orgasm. A muscle within the vaginal walls called the *pubococcygeus muscle* undergoes several involuntary wavelike contradictions, and Laura experiences this as the peak of pleasure during the cycle. Shortly after the orgasm is over, Laura enters the fourth stage, resolution. She relaxes, her heart rate slows down, and the sexual flush fades. The entire cycle has taken twenty minutes.

Connections
The four stages of the sexual response cycle are quite similar from a physiological point of view for men, with the obvious difference that men ejaculate semen with the aid of bladder muscles during the orgasmic phase.

Much of the first direct evidence on the sexual response cycle was collected by William H. Masters and Virginia E. Johnson in the 1960s. Their research suggests that men tend to go through the cycle at a somewhat faster rate than women. Three to four minutes is not unusual for men if they take no action to extend the cycle. The typical time range for women tends to be ten to twenty minutes. Sexologists often advise a couple to explore ways to induce the female's orgasm prior to the male's.

SEXUAL VARIANCE

Definition
Sexual variance is descriptive of behavior that significantly departs from the sexual norms and standards of a given reference group such as the family, the tribe, the village, or the larger society.

Example
Transsexualism is a kind of sexual variance in which the individual of a given biological gender feels trapped in a body of the

wrong sex, and wishes to lead the physical and emotional life of the opposite sex. Most persons manifesting transsexualism are biological males who want to be females. In certain cases surgery has been performed to give the individual some of the surface anatomical characteristics of the opposite sex.

Connections
Note that the term *variance* is now preferred over more pejorative terms such as *deviance* or *perversion*. There has been a strong effort on the part of mental health workers to be somewhat less judgmental and moralistic concerning the many ways in which people express their sexuality.

Forms of sexual variance defined elsewhere in this book include homosexual behavior, masochism, and sadism (see entries).

There are a number of other types of sexual variance. *Exhibitionism* involves the uninvited display of the genital organs. *Scoptophilia* refers to sexual arousal obtained by watching others engage in sexual activity. *Voyeurism* is obtaining sexual gratification by watching, often secretly (e.g. 'peeping'), the nude body of another person. *Transvestism*, not to be confused with transsexualism, is using cross-dressing as a way of obtaining erotic stimulation. *Oral-genital contact*, once thought to be a kind of perversion, is now so common a practice that sexologists consider it to be a normal and desirable form of sexual activity.

SHYNESS

Definition
Shyness is a tendency to feel uncomfortable, inhibited, awkward, and highly self-conscious in the presence of other people.

Example
Philip hates to go to social gatherings where he must meet a number of people for the first time. He is prone to think thoughts such as, 'They're laughing at me. They're much more sophisticated and poised than I am. I don't have anything to say. I don't know how to make small talk.' In the presence of strangers he has a tendency to get red-faced and even somewhat confused. With family and old friends he has none of these problems. It is quite apt to say that Philip has a problem with shyness.

Connections
Shyness is a common problem. Social psychologist Philip G.
Zimbardo indicates that about 80 percent of subjects he surveyed
suffer from some degree of shyness. However, there are people
who suffer from *chronic shyness*, they are uncomfortable in
almost all social situations that present the slightest amount of
novelty or possibility of being judged. Zimbardo indicates that
about 25 percent of subjects he surveyed suffer from chronic
shyness.

Assertiveness training (see *assertiveness*) can be useful in
helping persons overcome shyness.

SKINNER, B. F.
(1904–   )

B. F. Skinner was long associated with Harvard University, is a
leading behaviorist, and has made substantial contributions to
the study of *operant conditioning* (see entry). (The initials 'B. F.'
stand for Burrhus Frederic, but Skinner seldom uses these
names. His personal friends call him Fred.)

Skinner is also known for a number of inventions in the realm
of psychological technology. These include a controlled environment for infants called an *air crib*, a system of guiding missiles
using pigeons, the operant conditioning apparatus or 'Skinner
box,' and the teaching machine.

The principles of operant conditioning as formulated by Skinner have led to important applications in behavior therapy (see
entry) and child care.

Skinner's way of looking at human beings is distasteful to
many people because he focuses on the mechanical and robotlike
aspects of behavior. In his formal theorizing he has no use for the
common-sense viewpoints that people are conscious and autonomous. In one of his books, *Beyond Freedom and Dignity*
(1971), he argues that the concept of *autonomous man*, meaning
in essence freedom of the will in the human being, is dead. It is an
idea without utility in the prediction and control of behavior.

The great theme in Skinner's works is that behavior is shaped
by its own consequences. We do what pays off. And we stop
doing what does not pay off. (See *reinforcer*.)

Among Skinner's works are *The Behavior of Organisms*
(1938), *Walden II* (1948), and *About Behaviorism* (1974).

SOCIAL BEHAVIOR

Definition
Social behavior is any behavior in which there is an interaction between two or more human beings.

Example
Marriage is one of many kinds of social behavior.

Connections
Other kinds of social behavior include parent-child relationships, friendships, club participation, employer-employee relationships, dating, talking to neighbors, and parties.

Social behavior may be divided into two very large categories: prosocial behavior and antisocial behavior. *Prosocial behavior* is constructive and advances the aims of a given reference group. *Antisocial behavior* is destructive and interferes with the aims of a given reference group. One of our problems as social beings is to find ways to foster prosocial behavior.

Why do we exhibit such a large amount of social behavior? In the nineteenth century it was said that human beings have a *gregariousness instinct*, an inborn tendency to like contact with other people. The rise of behaviorism (see entry) led to a discounting of that point of view. The emphasis was placed on learned aspects of behavior. So the hypothesis that social behavior is acquired won many followers. It is derived from the mutual needs exhibited by human beings existing in groups. And we exist in groups not because of instinctive tendencies, but as a practical means of enhancing survival. More recently the emergence of sociobiology (see entry) has brought back to prominence the possibility of a genetic basis for social behavior.

The smallest unit of social behavior is the *social dyad*, any group consisting of two people.

SOCIAL-LEARNING THEORY

Definition
Social-learning theory is an integrated set of concepts and hypotheses making the general point that much human behavior is learned through our observations of, and interactions with, other people.

213

Example
Billy, age four, has parents and an older sister who all exhibit good table manners. First, he observes other people handling utensils in a certain way, chewing with a closed mouth, and so forth. Second, he is given disapproving looks when he deviates from the standards set by the family. Third, he is given approving looks and sometimes verbal praise when he is particularly correct in his behavior. Through the process of social learning Billy is acquiring the same kind of table manners as those exhibited by his parents and sister.

Connections
Two of the key figures responsible for the rise of social-learning were Albert Bandura and Richard Walters. Together they conducted experiments demonstrating the existence of observational learning. *Observational learning* is learning acquired in part by watching the actions of a model.

Social-learning theory's importance can be understood by contrasting it with radical, or early, behaviorism. Both approaches emphasize the importance of learning. But behaviorism discredited the importance of consciousness. Thus learning by observation was considered to be of little importance because it required such conscious processes as attention and perception. Social-learning is a kind of commonsense protest against the oversimplistic views of early behaviorism. Social-learning theory says in essence, 'Of course human beings are conscious. And of course they learn by observation and the ideas they get from their observations.'

One of the important concepts in social-learning theory is the concept of an *internal reinforcer* (see *reinforcer*). Internal reinforcers exist because human beings have a conscious mental life and an imagination. They praise themselves, take satisfaction in their work, feel a sense of pride, and so forth. These are all kinds of internal reinforcers, or self-rewards, for behavior.

SOCIOBIOLOGY

Definition
Sociobiology is the study of the social behavior of organisms based on the point of view that the underlying sources of such behavior are genetic patterns.

Example

Human beings from time to time display a social behavioral trait known as *altruism*, meaning they will sometimes sacrifice their own welfare, even die, for the sake of other human beings. Sociobiology argues that the aim of such behavior, superficially self-destructive and self-defeating, is essentially the survival of certain genes. This is a principle termed by sociobiologist Richard Dawkins *gene selfishness*. The principle suggests that one would be most likely to engage in altruistic behavior for others who have many genes in common with oneself such as one's children. On the other hand, one would be much less likely to engage in altruistic behavior for a stranger or a member of an outgroup.

Connections

A leading figure in sociobiology is the Harvard zoologist Edward O. Wilson. In his early research Wilson studied the behavior of social insects such as termites and observed that although there isn't much individual intelligence in a single termite there is a substantial group intelligence when they work together. Many other observations of the behavior of social organisms led to the development of sociobiology. One of the principal themes of sociobiology as applied to our own species is simply that there really is something that we can call human nature. There are patterns of behavior determined by innate factors.

If the existence of human nature seems obvious, one should consider that an influential statement in the twentieth century has been the declaration of the existential philosopher Jean-Paul Sartre, 'Existence precedes essence.' Sartre argued that human beings create their own essence, or nature, by their actions and decisions. Wilson's sociobiological formulations directly contradict Sartre's statement.

Of course Wilson is not alone in stressing the importance of inborn factors in human behavior. Plato (see entry) spoke of innate ideas. Jung (see entry) wrote about the archetypes of the collective unconscious. Wilson and the sociobiologists are simply reasserting the importance of nativism (see entry).

SOMATIC THERAPY

Definition

As applied to mental illness, somatic therapy is the administering

215

of any treatment to the body for the purpose of alleviating or curing such an illness.

Example
Electroshock therapy (see entry) is one of several kinds of somatic therapy.

Connections
The principal kinds of somatic therapy include electroshock therapy, chemotherapy, and psychosurgery (see entries). All of these treatments have their advocates and opponents. The advocates of somatic therapy argue that such therapy is essential in the treatment of mental illness, that mental illness often has a basis in a biological disorder. The opponents of somatic therapy argue that it often dehumanizes the patient, that it is overused, and fails to address itself to problems in living the patient may be having.

There is no satisfying definite conclusion that can be drawn from the debate between the advocates and opponents of somatic therapy. A middle-of-the-road position is that somatic therapy has a place in the treatment of mental illness, but it must be used both sparingly and judiciously.

The term *somatic* is derived from the Greek word 'soma,' meaning 'body.'

SPONTANEOUS RECOVERY

Definition
In conditioning theory spontaneous recovery is the reappearance, after a rest period, of a conditioned reflex that had apparently been extinguished.

Example
Assume that a dog has acquired a conditioned reflex such that it salivates upon the presentation of a given tone. Repeated presentations of the tone without food bring about extinction of the conditioned reflex (see *classical conditioning* and *extinction*). Now say that two days of rest are given to the dog and it is again presented with the tone. The conditioned reflex appears again. It is not as strong as it once was, but neither is it completely extinguished.

Connections
Here is one approach to explaining spontaneous recovery. When a conditioned reflex is being extinguished the process can be looked upon as a kind of learning, the *unlearning* of a conditioned reflex. It is possible that a specific fatigue factor (see *reactive inhibition*), or perhaps a lack of attention, depresses the performance of the organism somewhat below the actual amount of unlearning. Thus the rate of extinction looks more rapid than it actually is. A period of rest allows for the dissipation of fatigue or boredom, and the actual learning present manifests itself at full strength.

Spontaneous recovery in the extinction of conditioned reflexes is much like the ability of magic candles to relight themselves after they have been blown out. From a practical point of view a person who is trying to extinguish an unwanted habit should keep in mind the lesson to be learned from conditioning experiments with animals. A 'bad' habit seems to be broken, and then it often reappears. Repeated efforts to break, modify, or extinguish the habit are often required before it is gone once and for all.

SQ3R STUDY METHOD

Definition
The SQ3R study method is a systematic way to learn information from books and prepare for examinations. The designation *SQ3R* stands for survey, question, read, recite, and review.

Example
Duane, a college student, is preparing for an examination on Chapter 4 of a history textbook. He knows how to use the SQ3R method and decides to employ it. First, he *surveys* the chapter. He becomes familiar with its length, headings, subheadings, boldface terms, captions under illustrations, and so forth. Second, he makes up a set of *questions* based on the survey. In this particular case Duane writes thirty-five questions on the chapter. Third, he *reads* for the answer to each question. Note that his reading is not passive. It is oriented toward finding the answer to a specific question. Thus he does not get bored by the textbook and find himself unable to concentrate. He makes a short note next to each question indicating its correct answer. Fourth, he *recites* the answer to each question without looking at the written note. If he cannot answer the question, he refreshes

his memory by looking at the note. If he can answer the question, he verifies his answer by checking the note. This recitation process demands *recall* of the material, and helps Duane prepare for either multiple-choice or essay examinations. Fifth, shortly before the examination Duane *reviews* the question and answers. This is a rapid review, accomplished for Chapter 4 in about twenty minutes. He has avoided cramming, and uses the last study time available to him effectively.

Connections
The SQ3R study method was devised by Francis P. Robinson in 1946 at the Ohio State University. Robinson tested the method extensively and found that it was of real assistance to students with academic problems. It gave them an organized way to approach learning from a textbook, and reduced much of their confusion. A large percentage of students found that the method helped them achieve better grades on examinations.

The method has been tested more than once, and it has stood the test of time. Today it is highly regarded as one of the best ways for students to study.

STANDARD DEVIATION

Definition
The standard deviation is a measure of the dispersion, or scatter, of a set of scores from the mean of the set.

Example
The standard deviation is found by subtracting the mean from each score. This yields a new set of scores called *deviation scores*. Each of these is squared. A sum of these squared scores is taken. This sum is divided by the number of scores in the set in order to obtain an average squared deviation. This figure is known as the *variance*. The square root of the average squared deviation, or variance, is the standard deviation.

Here is a numerical example:

SCORES	DEVIATION SCORES	SQUARED DEVIATION SCORES
9	+3	9
8	+2	4
8	+2	4

6	0	0
5	−1	1
4	−2	4
2	−4	16
—	—	—
42	0	38

Mean = 6   Variance = 5.43
(42 ÷ 7 = 6)   (38 ÷ 7 = 5.43)

$\sqrt{5.43}$ = 2.33 = Standard Deviation

Connections

The computational process presented in the example can be summarized with the formula:

$$SD = \sqrt{\frac{\Sigma x^2}{N}}$$

SD	= Standard deviation
$\sqrt{}$	= Square root
Σ	= Sum (i.e. add)
x^2	= Squared deviation score
N	= Number of scores in the set

The standard deviation is considered to be a highly reliable measure of dispersion. One of its important characteristics is that in the case of a normal curve (see entry) 68.26%, or about two-thirds, of the scores will reside within one standard deviation above and one standard deviation below the mean. Thus the standard deviation can be used to define, on a statistical basis, the concept of 'normal' on intelligence, personality, creativity, aptitude, and interest tests.

STANFORD-BINET INTELLIGENCE SCALE

Definition

The Stanford-Binet intelligence scale is a standardized psychological test. It is an individual intelligence test, requiring administration by a trained examiner on a one-to-one basis with a subject. The physical test itself consists of a case containing toys, blocks, printed card material, and an instruction booklet.

Example
The Stanford-Binet is based on the measurement of intelligence by the *performance method*. In other words, 'Intelligent is as intelligent does.' Children and adults with high levels of intelligence should be able to give more correct answers to thought-provoking questions and problems than less intelligent persons.

Let's say that Kendra, age eight, is asked the following question: 'John went to war and died as a hero in a big battle. After the war was over he came home and married his home town sweetheart. What do you have to say about this story?' If Kendra correctly says, 'That's impossible. You can't come home and get married when you're dead,' then the examiner records a correct response and moves Kendra up the scale to a more difficult item. Allowing for some errors, how far up the intelligence scale Kendra can proceed provides a measure of her mental age, which can be converted to an intelligence quotient (see entry).

Connections
The Stanford-Binet assesses several aspects of intelligence including comprehension, mathematical ability, reasoning, perceptual ability, and so forth.

The test was inspired by the work of Alfred Binet (1857–1910), a French attorney who devised the first practical intelligence tests. The Stanford-Binet is a direct outgrowth of his work. The principal researcher responsible for the Stanford-Binet was Lewis Terman of Stanford who adapted Binet's intelligence scale for use in the United States. Terman published the first English-language version of the Stanford-Binet in 1916, and since that time the scale has undergone several revisions and new editions.

STATISTICAL TEST

Definition
A statistical test is a formal mathematical tool used to evaluate whether or not the differences observed between two or more groups at the conclusion of an experiment are due to chance fluctuations or are the result of the experimental treatment.

Example
Let's say that a psychological experiment is conducted with two groups, a control group and an experimental group (see *experimental method*). Each group has a mean, or arithmetical

average. The mean of the experiment group is larger than the mean of the control group, as was predicted by the experimental hypothesis. However, the difference is small. On the other hand, the groups are large, suggesting that even a small difference between means may be significant, may represent an actual experimental effect.

A statistical test known as the *t* test can be used to resolve the dilemma presented above. The *t* test is used to evaluate the significance of a difference between means. *t* is a *random variable*, a variable distributed according to the laws of chance. It was studied by a mathematician who wrote under the pseudonym of Student, thus it is often referred to as Student's *t*.

The scores from the experiment described above can all be included in a formula for calculating *t*, and a single *t* value will emerge. If the *t* value is small, this suggests that the difference between the two groups is due to chance. If the *t* value is large, this suggests that the difference between the two groups is due to the experimental treatment.

In actual experimental work, the researcher consults a table of *t* values based on the number of subjects within each group. These tables state exact probabilities for *t* values of differing magnitudes.

Connections
Experimental psychologists use a number of statistical tests to evaluate data in addition to Student's *t*. The choice of a test depends first on underlying mathematical assumptions made as part of the measurement process. Second, the choice depends on the number of groups in the experiment. Third, the choice depends on the number of experimental treatments, or factors, being administered in the experiment. Ph.D. candidates in experimental psychology usually take several courses in statistics and experimental design as part of their requirements for the degree. The correct use of statistical tests is an important part of the work activity of psychological researchers.

STEREOTYPE

Definition
In social psychology, a stereotype is a fixed set of attributes imposed by an observer on all members of a given group.

Example
Jack, a plumber with little formal education, has a stereotype about intellectuals. He labels them 'eggheads.' And he believes that they are all snobs, mixed-up, homosexuals, absent-minded, and lazy.

Connections
Stereotypes are often held about minority groups. In a given social setting, people of almost any race and religion have been members of such a group, and stereotypes about them have formed. Stereotypes contribute to racial and religious prejudices (see entry) because they tend to be passed on in the family from parent to child.

One of the principal logical errors associated with stereotypes is *false allness*. Members of a stereotyped group are treated as if they are all the same, without regard to their individuality. Thus even if it is true that individual A has some of the attributes commonly associated with the given group, it might not be at all true about individual B in the group.

STIMULUS

Definition
The concept of a stimulus is one of the most general and broadly conceived ones in psychology. It carries a heavy load and is used in several ways. First, thought of in the most general of terms, a stimulus is any fluctuation in an energy system that produces any kind of a response in an organism. Second, a stimulus is a fluctuation in an external energy source (e.g. light, sound) capable of exciting a receptor organ (e.g. the eye, the inner ear). Third, a stimulus can be *covert*, within the organism; an idea, a concept, or a wish can be a stimulus to action. Fourth, a stimulus can be a prior response; a stimulus can produce a response, that response becomes a stimulus for the next response, and so forth. This often happens in a behavior chain such as when one recites the alphabet.

Example
The level of light intensity in a room suddenly increases and one's pupils involuntarily react by constricting and admitting less light to the retina. This is known as the *pupillary reflex*. The change in the level of light is a stimulus.

Connections
It was the hope of John Watson (see entry) that as psychology became more and more scientific responses would be strictly predictable on the basis of the known properties of stimuli. This led to a way of thinking in behavioristic psychology known as stimulus-response (S–R) psychology in which the organism was looked on somewhat as a learning machine. The early hope of Watson has faded with time. As indicated in the definition, the concept of a stimulus goes well beyond the oversimplified idea of a stimulus as a fluctuation in energy impinging on a receptor organ. With the increasing complexity of the idea of a stimulus it has been of course impossible to draw up simple and clear-cut functional relationships between stimuli and behavior in any broad meaningful sense.

Although the concept *stimulus* has several meanings, this does not mean that the concept is too general to be of use. On the contrary, the concept of a stimulus is a central and powerful one in psychology.

STIMULUS GENERALIZATION

Definition
Stimulus generalization is a tendency for a stimulus similar to an original conditioned stimulus to evoke a conditioned response at a somewhat reduced level.

Example
Assume that a dog has been conditioned to salivate at a tone of 1200 cycles per second (CPS). Now a tone of 1000 cps, a tone of a lower pitch, is sounded. The dog again salivates, but not as much as to the 1200 CPS tone. It can be said that the dog has generalized, has perceived the similarity, between the two tones.

Connections
Staying with the above example, if a tone of 1400 CPS, a tone of a higher pitch, is sounded, the dog will also generalize and salivate. There will be a tendency on the dog's part to produce the conditioned reflex to tones either higher or lower in pitch than the original one. But the more discrepant the tones are from the original one, the more reduced will be the magnitude of the conditioned response. This decline in magnitude on either side of the original conditioned stimulus can be graphed, and the

function on the graph is called the *stimulus generalization gradient*.

Stimulus generalization is more than a laboratory phenomenon, and plays an important part in explaining conditioned emotional reactions and acquired fears. A child has had a painful experience with a dentist and has acquired a fear of the dentist, the dental chair, the associated equipment, the dentist's white smock, etc. Now the child is taken to the barber. Again there is a chair, a white smock, a smiling professional person, tools on a counter, etc. If the child shows fear in the barber shop, it can be understood as a case of stimulus generalization. The child is perceiving the similarity between the first situation and the second one.

STREAM OF CONSCIOUSNESS

Definition
The phrase *stream of consciousness* was coined by William James to convey his assertion that one's conscious mental life constantly flows like a river or a stream. The events of the day follow each other without being boxed or framed in perception. On the contrary, they form a seamless whole.

Example
Let's say that one arises, washes, dresses, eats breakfast, takes a bus to one's place of employment, greets fellow workers, sits at a desk, makes a telephone call, and so forth. Although each of these events is described in discrete terms in the first sentence of this paragraph, they are experienced in a continuous way. One event blends into another without well-defined borders. It is our language that forces us to talk about experience in choppy terms, but this does not reflect the flowing nature of experience.

Connections
William James (see entry) developed the idea of the stream of consciousness in part as a protest against the teachings of Wilhelm Wundt (see entry). Wundt emphasized the structure of consciousness, the association of ideas and the formation of concepts. James felt that Wundt's view of consciousness was too rigid, too stiff, that it lost sight completely of the active and dynamic aspects of human experience.

As part of the concept of the stream of consciousness James

likened attention (see entry) to the movements of a bird. The bird lands here for a moment, takes flight, and then lands there for a moment. And it keeps repeating the process. So it is with human attention. It is restless, constantly on the move, seeking new objects of perception.

STRESS

Definition
Stress is the system of internal forces, organic or psychological, tending to produce wear and tear on the body.

Example
Joanna is a very busy person subjected to much time pressure. She feels that she is always in a hurry and must meet many responsibilities. The time pressure and the burden of responsibilities are *stressors*, sources of stress. The sum total of adverse effects that the stressors may have on her body is *stress*.

Connections
There is ample experimental and clinical evidence to support the hypothesis that excessive and chronic stress can induce illness. (See the *general adaptation syndrome* and *life change units*.)

Stress researcher Hans Selye made a formal distinction between distress and eustress. *Distress* is harmful and destructive. However, *eustress* is desirable and may even be life-enhancing. An interesting challenge, an exciting opportunity, or a rewarding vocation may produce eustress or 'good' stress. Without eustress life would hardly be worth living. So the message of modern stress research is not to avoid all stress, but to seek optimal levels of stress.

STRUCTURALISM

Definition
Structuralism is a school of psychology based on the assumption that the primary aim of psychology should be to study associations of sensations, perceptions, simple ideas, and complex ideas that compose the content of human consciousness.

Example
The word *storm* represents a relatively complex idea. The simpler

ideas that make it up include associations of *rain, wind, lightning, thunder*, and so forth. These ideas arise from perceptions such as the sight of rain falling, hearing thunder, and so forth. And in turn these perceptions themselves arise from simple sensations (see entry). In brief, a complex idea is a kind of structure made up of the elements already described.

Connections
The father of structuralism was Wilhelm Wundt (see entry). His approach to the study of consciousness was inspired by the teachings of such philosophers as John Locke (see entry) who asserted that all knowledge comes from experience (i.e. from things that are seen, heard, touched, etc.).

Structuralism is of substantial historical importance. It has the status of being the first formal school of psychology, and is associated with the founding by Wundt in 1879 of the first psychological laboratory. Structuralism was a major force in psychology for about thirty years, but its authority was greatly undermined eventually by functionalism and Gestalt psychology (see entries) in particular. Both of these schools of psychology agreed that the study of consciousness was important. However, they felt that structuralism went at it the wrong way.

Functionalism argued that structuralism was too static. Consciousness is more like a flowing stream than a structure (see *stream of consciousness*). Gestalt psychology insisted that sensations did not create organized wholes. On the contrary, sensations are abstractions *from* organized wholes. The complex wholes come first *before* the sensations.

By 1920 structuralism was considered to be a dead school of psychology. However, the structural approach to the study of consciousness has enjoyed a bit of a resurrection in modern times. For example, Piaget's approach to cognitive development (see entry) is structural in nature.

SUBCONSCIOUS MIND

Definition
The subconscious mind is the level of mental life assumed to exist just below the threshold of consciousness.

Example
Kristina is a creative writer. When she has a half-formed idea for

a story she sets it aside and 'forgets' about it for a few days. When she returns to the idea she often finds that the plot and characters seem to be ready-made. It can be argued that the story incubated, or developed, at a subconscious level.

Connections
The term *subconscious mind* was coined by a group of French psychologists, such as Pierre Janet (1859–1947), who through the use of hypnosis found evidence for mental events below the conscious level.

Freud also accepted the existence of a subconscious mental life. His term, however, is the *preconscious level*. Freud argued that there was a level lower than the subconscious (i.e. preconscious) level. He termed this the *unconscious level*, a level of mental life created by repression (see entry).

The subconscious level, unlike the unconscious level, does not contain repressed material, and is accessible by an act of will. Thus ordinary memories are said to reside in the subconscious mind.

The word *subliminal* is also associated with the subconscious mind. The *limen* is another word for the threshold of consciousness. Thus a *subliminal perception*, for example, is a perception taking place at a subconscious level. It is believed to have an effect on the person; but the person is not aware of the effect. The extent and power of subliminal perceptions is a subject for debate.

SUBLIMATION

Definition
Sublimation, a psychoanalytic term, is a defense mechanism in which *libido*, or psychosexual energy, is displaced from its original target onto a secondary one.

Example
Dunton is a very shy and inhibited young man. Although he is very attracted to young women, he has not yet developed the self-confidence and social maturity required to have satisfying relationships with the opposite sex. His avocation is oil painting. One of his recent canvases is a lush one of ripe fruit. A possible psychoanalytic interpretation of his painting activity is that he finds it a partial outlet for blocked sexual desire. It is not too

far-fetched, perhaps, to suggest that the painting's ripe fruit symbolizes his own sexual ripeness. Sublimation thus acts for Dunton as a kind of safety valve helping him to maintain ego integrity as he moves toward being able eventually to express his sexual drive more directly.

Connections

Freud felt that modern civilization produces a certain amount of sexual restraint in all of us. Even in marriage there are often frustrations and limits on the way in which libido can be expressed. And perhaps there are people who crave multiple partners from an unconscious level who at the same time observe a strict moral prohibition against philandering. So in more ways than one it seems reasonable to hypothesize that sexual energy finds outlets other than the obvious one. Freud felt that much of the beehive of activity that we call the industrialized world stems from rechanneled sexual energy.

SUICIDE

Definition

Suicide is the voluntary taking of one's own life.

Example

Peyton, an aging novelist, blows his own brains out with one of several guns he owns. He leaves a suicide note in which he speaks of the unfairness of literary critics, the lack of love in his life, and the boredom of his existence. Members of his family at the funeral note that he has been depressed for a long time. He has not written a successful novel for twenty years. Others speak of his three divorces. Still others speak of his alienation from his daughter.

Connections

The word *suicide* is derived from two latin roots: *sui*, meaning 'oneself,' and *caedere*, meaning 'to kill.' Note the similarity to *homicide*, which is derived form the latin root *homo*, meaning 'man.'

According to the World Health Organization about 500,000 people per year commit suicide. In the United States suicide is the tenth most common cause of death for all ages. However, it is the third most common cause of death for individuals in the second half of the adolescent period. Thus it is clear that suicide is a problem of substantial proportions.

Not all suicide is direct. The psychiatrist Karl Menninger spoke of *chronic suicide*, a pattern of self-destructive behavior exhibited by some persons. These individuals destroy themselves slowly with addictive behaviours associated with obesity, alcoholism, and drug addiction. The number of people who commit chronic suicide is much larger than those who are direct about the act. Only blatant suicide is recorded in the suicide statistics.

The causes of direct suicide and self-destructive behavior cover a spectrum of human motives including depression, boredom, loss of meaning in life, and the fantasy that one's death will punish another person.

SUPEREGO

Definition
The superego is, according to psychoanalytic theory, the side of the personality that is morality-oriented. It is the self's perception of right and wrong.

Example
Lon, a married man, is tempted to seek sexual relations outside of his marriage. His id (see entry) in essence tells him, 'Go do it! Have some fun! You only live once!' His superego, derived from a strict moral training as a child, says in essence, 'Stop! Think of the consequences. You can't insult your wife like this. What you want to do is wrong.' Lon happens to have a well-developed superego, and he obeys its injunctions.

Connections
The concept of the superego originated with Freud. He hypothesized that people with an overdeveloped superego are prone to neurotic reactions. The constant conflict between the wishes of the id and the prohibitions of the superego produces a chronic state of anxiety and tension. People who on the other hand have an underdeveloped superego are prone to personality disorders. They are irresponsible and impulsive.

According to Freud the superego has two sides. These are the conscience and the ego ideal. The *conscience* is the side of the superego that issues warnings and informs the self that certain wishes are forbidden. The activity of the conscience produces guilt feelings. The *ego ideal* is the side of the superego that sets forth goals, goals often derived from a child's perception of parental ambitions.

SYMBOL

Definition
A symbol is any stimulus that stands for an idea or object other than itself.

Example
The word *chair* is a symbol for the actual chair-in-the-world, the thing we see, sit on, and point at.

Connections
The concept of a symbol plays an important part in dream interpretation. Various theories of what dreams mean, including the Freudian and Jungian ones, assign a symbolical value to the superficial aspects of the dream (see entry).

Thinking is largely possible because of the human ability to manipulate symbols. It is evident that much thinking can be conceptualized as the mental arranging and rearranging of words according to rules of logic and grammar.

It is possible to confuse symbols and objects. Alfred Korzybski (1879–1950) was the father of *general semantics*, an approach to the study of mental life and emotional reactions based on the way in which people react to symbols. Because the symbol and what it refers to are easily confused certain problems can be created. For example, say that one member of a couple often says to the other member in a convincing way, 'I love you.' But the speaker seldom does loving things. The person being assured of love may be baffled for a long time, confusing the word love with love itself. Korzybski was fond of reminding people, 'The word is not the thing.'

SYMPTOM REMOVAL

Definition
Symptom removal is the process of inhibiting or extinguishing a

maladaptive behavior pattern without regard for its underlying psychodynamics.

Example
Anne suffers from *agoraphobia*, a neurotic condition that makes it difficult for her to leave home or travel with comfort. She seeks therapy for the problem and is treated by a behavior therapist. The therapist uses desensitization therapy (see entry) and pays very little attention to the experiences in Anne's past that may have caused the agoraphobic reaction to form. He works directly on the symptom and its severity diminishes substantially.

Connections
The two most common methods of direct symptom removal are hypnosis and desensitization therapy (see entry). Freud was dissatisfied with hypnosis, noting that symptoms removed in this way often return. This is probably because when a symptom is removed quickly by direct suggestion it is only temporarily repressed, not extinguished.

However, when a symptom is removed by desentization therapy it is extinguished by a counterconditioning procedure. The research of Joseph Wolpe on behavior therapy (see entry) suggests that symptoms removed in this way tend not to return later. Also, they appear to be removed without adverse side-effects.

Hypnosis can be combined with desensitization therapy in order to induce relaxation or enhance a guided fantasy. One should not think of hypnosis and desensitization therapy as mutually exclusive techniques.

SYNAPSE

Definition
A synapse is the point of functional connection between adjacent neurons.

Example
The foot of neuron A's axon ends near one of neuron B's dendrites. The tiny gap between the axon and the dendrite is called the *synaptic cleft*. It is made into a point of functional contact, or a synapse, between the two neurons by the ability of neuron A to release neurotransmitters from its foot and the

SYNAPSE

ability of neuron B to be excited by these same neurotransmitters. (See *neuron* and *neurotransmitter*.)

Connections

The word *synapse* was introduced into the literature of psychiological psychology by Sir Charles Sherrington (1861–1952), recipient of a Nobel Prize in 1932 for his research on the nervous system. Derived from Greek roots, a synapse is literally a 'joining together.'

In the example the synaptic cleft is referred to as 'tiny.' The actual size of the synaptic cleft is about twenty millimicrons. (A millimicron is one millionth of a meter.)

T

TEMPERAMENT

Definition
One's temperament is one's reactive make-up, the spontaneous side of one's personality. It is a combination of characteristic dispositions arising from the emotions, appetites, and moods.

Example
Gloria's friends know her to be optimistic, energetic, enthusiastic, and slow to anger. She has a great zest for life and fights off dark moods easily. This combination of dispositions describes in large part her temperament.

Connections
Hippocrates would have described Gloria's temperament with the single word *sanguine* (see *personality*).

A perennial question of interest to psychology is this one: Is temperament primarily inborn or acquired? More than one study has shown that even infants show individual differences in temperament. Also longitudinal studies of children suggest that temperament is quite consistent over a number of years. Thus there is evidence suggesting that constitutional traits (see entry) are primary determinants of temperament. Temperament does in fact in large part appear to be inborn.

Having said this it is essential to add that learning can impose substantial modifications on temperament. A basically shy child who receives reinforcement for self-expression may lose much of his or her shyness with development. It is probably best to adopt a two-factor model of temperament in which the first factor is the inborn one and the second factor is the learned one. One's inborn nature can be thought of as the foundation of one's temperamental house, and learned behavior can be thought of as its superstructure.

THANATOLOGY

Definition
Thanatology is the study of death and the dying process.

Example
The research of the psychiatrist and thanatologist Elisabeth Kübler-Ross suggests that people with a terminal illness often go through five states before they reach death itself. These stages are (1) denial and isolation, (2) anger, (3) bargaining (e.g. with God), (4) depression, and (5) acceptance.

Connections
Although death was once considered a taboo subject for psychology, in recent times it has become quite respectable to study it. This only makes good sense in view of the fact that all of us die. A therapist or a counselor working with a very ill person will be more effective if he or she has some understanding of the dying process. And when one faces one's own death it is helpful to have the kind of information being made available by thenatology.

Freud believed that death is an instinct, an instinct that plays a role in destructiveness toward others and eventually in one's own death (see *death instinct*).

THEMATIC APPERCEPTION TEST (TAT)

Definition
The Thematic Apperception Test is a projective personality test in which the subject is asked to tell stories about somewhat ambiguous pictures featuring drawings of human beings.

Example
Maxwell is a patient in psychotherapy and as part of his overall clinical evaluation a psychologist is giving him the Thematic Apperception Test (TAT). The TAT consists of nineteen cards with pictures and a single blank card (for a fantasy projection). Maxwell looks at the cards one at a time and is asked to make up .a story for each card. He is told that the story should have a beginning, a middle, and an end. Also, he is instructed to relate what the characters in the story are thinking and feeling.

Connections
The interpretation of the TAT stories related by the subject are based on the general concept of unconscious motives (see entry). The drama and conflict seen in the cards are created by the defense mechanism of projection (see entry). A pattern of an individual's dominant psychological needs emerges from an analysis of the TAT responses.

The TAT was developed by the Harvard psychologist and personality theorist Henry A. Murray who first published the test in 1938. The theory of the test is identical to the theory residing behind an earlier personality test, the Rorschach inkblot test (see entry). They are both projective tests. However, the TAT provides more structure and facilitates projections having to do with human interactions. The TAT has been extensively used as a tool for personality research and as an instrument for the clinical evaluation of troubled persons.

The word *apperception* means perception at a subconscious level. It is an old term drawn from the writings of philosophers such as Gottfried Wilhelm Leibnitz (1646–1716) and Immanuel Kant (1724–1804).

THINKING

Definition
Thinking is a mental activity, a form of cognitive information processing, utilizing perceptions, concepts, symbols, and images. Some of thinking's purposes are to solve problems, make decisions, and represent external reality.

Example
Let's say that one has been recently insulted by someone else. After the incident is over one ruminates about it. One thinks, 'She shouldn't have said that. It was unfair. If I get a chance, next time I'll tell her a thing or two.' And so forth. One of the several ways in which we think is to consciously run sentences through our minds. The word *ruminate* used above means to meditate or reflect upon, and is a common aspect of the thinking process.

Connections
The early founders of psychology such as Wilhelm Wundt and William James (see entries) took it for granted that we should study thinking. Then John Watson (see entry) and the radical

behaviorists discredited the importance of the study of thinking. In more recent years there has been a great rebirth of interest in the thinking process, and a great deal of work has been done on concept formation, cognitive development, and so forth.

Thinking is usually thought of as a conscious process. However, Freud introduced the hypothesis that unconscious thought is possible. His evidence for this hypothesis came from slips of the tongue, the interpretation of dreams, and so forth. Freud's hypothesis has a number of supporters, and therefore what we call thinking may be said to refer to more than the conscious domain.

THORNDIKE, EDWARD L.
(1874–1949)

Edward L. Thorndike was a professor of psychology associated for more than thirty years with Teachers College of Columbia in the United States. His principal interest was learning theory, and he is an important forerunner of behaviorism. Watson (see entry) drew heavily from the work of both Thorndike and Pavlov. Thorndike's interest in psychology was sparked by a course he took from William James at Harvard, and Thorndike's first learning experiments were conducted in the basement of James' home using baby chickens as subjects. It is reported that the experiments were a source of delight to James' children.

Thorndike was unimpressed by the many wonderful tales of animal intelligence. He said that no one writes about animal stupidity. For every dog that finds its way home there are perhaps one hundred lost ones who cannot. It was Thorndike's contention that animals do not reason or move ahead in solving problems by bursts of insight. Instead, they learn on a more or less mechanical basis using a trial-and-error approach. Successful behaviors are satisfying and 'stamped into' the nervous system. (See the *law of effect*.)

Thorndike saw learning as a set of connections, connections between a stimulus and a response. Each connection is strengthened when it leads to a satisfying state of affairs. This whole line of theorizing about learning provides the assumptive foundation upon which Skinner (see entry) built his edifice of work with operant conditioning.

Thorndike eventually applied his animal training methods to children and young adults with a substantial measure of success, and he became influential in the arena of educational psychology. His book *Educational Psychology* was published in 1903, and Thorndike was awarded the rank of full professor the following year. Another influential book by Thorndike was *Introduction to the Theory of Mental and Social Measurements* (1904), and Thorndike is today recognized as a leading figure in the early mental testing movement.

TIP-OF-THE-TONGUE PHENOMENON

Definition
The tip-of-the-tongue phenomenon is the inability to voluntarily recall a bit of information that one is sure is in one's memory.

Example
One is trying to think of the name of a motion picture star, a star who is quite familiar. In frustration one tells a friend, 'You know. He starred in *Destination Tokyo* and *Mr. Lucky* years ago. One of the all time greats. Don't tell me! His name is on the tip of my tongue!' An hour later the name pops into consciousness. It is Cary Grant.

Connections
The tip-of-the-tongue phenomenon provides a particularly clear distinction between the concepts of recall and recognition. *Recall* is a process by which we can retrieve a given item of memory by an act of will. *Recognition* is a much less demanding task. It only requires that we pick out the correct item of memory from a set of items presented to one or more of the senses. Let's say the friend in the above example had said, 'Allow me to give you four names. One of them will be the correct name.' Under these circumstances the recognition would have been swift.

The temporarily lost bit of information associated with the tip-of-the-tongue phenomenon is not generally considered to be repressed to an unconscious level. The usual interpretation is that the information is at a subconscious level (see *subconscious mind*), and that it is difficult to recall because of interference effects from competing bits of information.

TOUGH-MINDED

Definition
When a person has a tough-minded character or temperament he or she is thought to be practical, oriented toward facts, and unsentimental.

Example
John Watson (see entry) was tough-minded in his approach to psychology. He wanted it to be a field of study dominated by experiments, an absence of subjectivity, and rigorous data analysis.

Connections
William James (see entry) made a distinction between thinkers in fields of study such as philosophy and psychology with tough-minded and tender-minded temperaments. He said that the *tough-minded* thinkers displayed traits such as these: empiricist (going by facts), sensationalistic, materialistic, pessimistic, irreligious, and hardheaded. He said that the *tender-minded* thinkers displayed traits such as these: rationalist (going by principles), intellectualistic, idealistic, optimistic, religious, and emotional. Abraham Maslow (see entry) provides an example of a tender-minded thinker.

James noted that the two kinds of thinkers seldom have much respect for each other.

TRAIT

Definition
A trait is a tendency to behave in a predictable or reliable manner. It is an outstanding feature of one's personality, and thus it is common to speak of personality traits.

Example
One of Upton's traits is cleanliness. He takes a shower every morning and evening, brushes his teeth three times a day, puts on fresh underclothes after every shower, vacuums and dusts his bedroom twice a week, and so forth.

Connections
The existence of traits is one of the things that convinces many

observers that psychology has some basis for claiming that it is a science. A science requires stable and repeatable phenomena. In the case of human behavior there is a popular conception that this condition cannot be met. The unanalyzed view is, 'Anybody can do anything any time they want to because people have free will.' Traits suggest just the opposite point of view. People are creatures of habit. They become set in their ways. And behavior *is* predictable to some degree.

TYPE A BEHAVIOR

Definition
Type A behavior is a behavior pattern dominated by aggressiveness, impatience, self-absorption, and an inability to relax.

Example
Paxton, age thirty-seven, is described by a close friend in Type A terms. His friend says, 'Paxton is a very ambitious individual. He really wants to set the world on fire. His ambition makes him restless and perpetually angry. He is prone to snap at people for little or nothing, and he's always trying to do two things at once. I tell him that he ought to slow down and enjoy the scenery as he travels through life. But he just scoffs and brushes me off. Maybe you wonder why I like him. He's basically a very interesting and likeable guy. He's just running too fast.'

Connections
The Type A pattern was first identified as a clinical syndrome by the cardiologists Meyer Friedman and Ray H. Rosenman in the 1970s. They stated that persons with the Type A pattern are somewhat more prone to heart disease. The Type A pattern is just one risk factor among others such as eating a high fat diet, obesity, lack of exercise, smoking, and so forth. Nonetheless, there is good evidence that it is a very real risk factor in heart disease. Essentially, it seems that the person exhibiting Type A behavior induces much of his or her own stress (see entry).

Friedman and Rosenman contrasted Type A behavior with Type B behavior. The Type B pattern is characterized by assertiveness in contrast to aggressiveness, moderate goals, patience, concern for the welfare of others, and the ability to relax at appropriate times. Persons with the Type B pattern are much less prone to heart disease.

U

UNCONSCIOUS MOTIVE

Definition
According to psychoanalytic theory, an unconscious motive is
one that is forbidden by the superego, and in turn not acknow-
ledged by the conscious self. It is a drive, impulse, wish, or desire
that has been banished by the defense mechanism of repression
to the unconscious level of the personality.

Example
Colin has a desire for sexual intercourse with his sister, but he has
converted the desire into an unconscious motive. This means
that although the desire does in fact exist, he has no conscious
awareness of it. In fact if he was told that he had an incest wish,
he would deny it with anger. Evidence in favor of the existence of
the wish is given to the astute observer in the form of slips of the
tongue, dreams, and in Colin's conscious attitudes toward his
sister.

   He often uses his sister's name when he intends to make a
reference to his girlfriend. He recently had a dream in which a
prince from an enchanted land married his own sister, but in no
way identified the dream with himself. He hates to kiss his sister
hello or goodbye, arguing that this sentimental display is repug-
nant to him. Psychoanalytic theory suggests that his distaste for
kissing his sister is a reaction formation (see entry) helping Colin
defend against his unconscious wish.

Connections
The concept of unconscious motivation plays an integral part in
psychoanalytic theory. Freud felt that the moral censorship
imposed by the superego in a highly socialized setting tended to
create many forbidden wishes. These forbidden wishes are primarily in the areas of sex and aggression. And so it is not

surprising that incest wishes, a desire for sexual experimentation, and hostile impulses constitute the bulk of unconscious motives.

The critic of the theory of unconscious motivation points out that the psychoanalysts have it both ways. If Colin embraces his sister and tries to kiss her in an erotic manner, he clearly has an incest wish. If he is distant and conservative, this is taken as evidence in favor of the existence of a reaction formation, and he still has an incest wish!

The defender of psychoanalysis points out that there is a happy medium. The brother without an incest wish would be quite willing to give his sister a hello or goodbye kiss, but there would be no erotic overtones.

V

VALIDITY

Definition
In the context of psychology, the concept of validity applies primarily to standardized psychological tests. A test is said to be valid when it measures what it is supposed to measure.

Example
Are standardized intelligence tests such as the Stanford-Binet and the Wechsler Adult Intelligence Scale (WAIS) valid? They correlate highly with an independent criterion such as grades in school. There is a strong tendency for students with high IQ scores to have a high grade point average. Conversely, students with low IQ scores tend to have a low grade point average. (There are, of course, individual exceptions to the tendency.) Therefore, the tests cited above are taken to be basically valid. If IQ scores on standardized tests had no predictive value at all, the tests would be considered invalid.

Connections
It is extremely important that the author of a psychological test go to some extremes to establish its validity. An invalid test is worse than worthless. It can be misleading. Unfortunately, two kinds of validity are often confused, face validity and predictive validity. *Face validity* refers to the superficial characteristics of the test. For example, a would-be test author might draw up a set of true-false items having to do with a personality trait such as assertiveness. The questions might on a common-sense basis seem to be valid. If so, the test would have face validity.

But face validity can be misleading. A test can have face validity and be completely useless in terms of making predictions. *Predictive validity*, on the other hand, is established by correlating the test with independent standards of behavior. For example, to find out if the assertiveness test has predictive validity, it would be necessary to evaluate it against either actual life situations or another test of assertiveness already known to be valid.

VARIABLE

Definition
A variable is a trait, attribute, dimension, or property capable of taking on more than one value or magnitude.

Example
Intelligence quotient (IQ) is a variable because IQ scores can range over quite a wide spectrum of values. John's IQ score is 83, Mary's IQ score is 102, Harry's IQ score is 123, and so forth.

Connections
Two variables of particular interest in experimental psychology are the independent variable and the dependent variable. The *independent variable* is the variable in an experiment under the control of the experimenter. It is presumed to affect the behavior of the subjects in the experiment. For example, rats might be run through a maze under different conditions of food deprivation. In such an experiment the independent variable would simply be: *number of hours of food deprivation*.

The *dependent variable* is the variable in an experiment that measures the behavior of subjects. Rats in the above experiment might be scored on blind alleys entered on their way to a goal box baited with food. In this case the dependent variable would simply be: *number of errors*.

When the results of an experiment are convincing, it is possible to state a functional relationship between the independent variable and the dependent variable. In the rat experiment cited the experimenter might find that an increase in number of hours of food deprivation tends to bring about a decrease in number of maze errors made by the rats. In common-sense terms, the results suggest that more motivated rats tend to make fewer mistakes when running mazes for food than less motivated rats.

Although the above result is both trivial and obvious, it shows how functional relationships, or 'laws' of behavior, can be studied. Advanced research on motivation, perception, and learning making use of both independent and dependent variables has led to findings that are neither trivial nor obvious.

VERBAL LEARNING

Definition
Verbal learning is the kind of learning that takes place when the content acquired by the subject consists of words, nonsense syllables, or concepts.

Example
Raymond is a student in a university psychology course. He studies Chapter 5 in the textbook and takes an examination on its content, a block of information covering physiological psychology. He has learned a number of terms and their associated concepts, and these are the focus points of the examination. His activity falls in the category of verbal learning. Most academic learning is of this kind.

Connections
Verbal learning is contrasted with *motor learning*, the kind of learning that takes place when the content acquired by the subject consists of a skill such as swimming, throwing a ball, riding a bicycle, and so forth. Although verbal learning is on a presumably higher cognitive level, this in no way downgrades the importance of motor learning. For example, a great deal of motor learning is involved in playing a musical instrument such as the violin.

A device that has been useful in the experimental study of verbal learning is the nonsense syllable (see entry).

Although distribution of practice (see entry) appears to be of some importance in all types of learning, it does not appear to be as important for verbal learning as it is for motor learning.

VERIDICAL PERCEPTION

Definition
Veridical perception is perception that is truthful, or correct.

Example
One sees an old friend by chance in a department store, greets

the friend, and the friend acknowledges the greeting in a cheerful manner. Neither person has seen the other for several years. One's perception in this instance is regarded as veridical because the friend's reaction supports it. The positive reaction says in essence, 'Yes, you are right in recognizing me as John S.' Ordinary life would be impossible without many veridical perceptions.

Connections
It is, of course, quite possible for perception to be nonveridical, or incorrect. For example, it is not at all unusual to recognize an old friend in a public place, begin a greeting, and realize with a start that this is a stranger!

There are many other examples of nonveridical perception. The delusions and hallucinations of mental patients with psychotic disorders (see entry) are nonveridical perceptions. Also, various kinds of optical illusions induce us to make incorrect evaluations.

There are two principal kinds of nonveridical perception, false positives and false negatives. *False positives* take place when one assigns to an object of perception a quality that is not objectively present. Perceiving a stranger as a friend, delusions, and hallucinations are all examples of false positives. *False negatives* take place when one fails to assign to an object of perception a quality that is in fact objectively present. Perceiving a friend as a stranger, not recognizing one's own name when it is called, and failure to detect important signals and cues in one's environment are all examples of false negatives.

W

WATSON, JOHN BROADUS
(1878–1958)

John Broadus Watson was the father of behaviorism, and was elected to the presidency of the American Psychological Association in 1915. He was a lifelong foe of sloppy research and vague ideas. He considered Freud's theories a hodgepodge of foolish notions. And he had very little use for the other major schools of psychology.

The way out of the murky roads of speculative philosophy and subjective psychology could be found by following the avenue of *behaviorism* (see entry), a school of psychology holding that the concept of consciousness is neither necessary nor useful in the description, explanation, prediction, and control of behavior.

Watson advocated for psychology an ambitious program of research stressing the gathering of data through well-designed experiments. The purpose of psychology is to be able to predict an organism's response in terms of a given stimulus. This is sometimes known as S–R psychology (i.e. Stimulus-Response psychology), and such a psychology pays little attention to thoughts, feelings, or what is generally called 'mind.'

Watson was particularly influenced by Ivan Pavlov and Edward L. Thorndike. As a result of their research, he stressed the importance of the general concept of learning. Behavior does not arise from instincts or any other innate given. Instead, it is acquired through conditioning. Watson's prestige gave major impetus to the study of learning, and it has become a major area of interest in contemporary psychology.

Watson also made his influence known in the area of child rearing. He recommended that infants and toddlers be raised in a systematic and organized way, that they be conditioned according to a plan in the direction desired by the parents. He also indicated that children should not receive too many sentimental expressions. Such expressions do not build character. Watson's views on human development were very influential throughout the 1920s and the 1930s, but they are no longer taken as seriously as they once were.

Among Watson's books are *Psychology From the Standpoint of a Behaviorist* (1919), *Behaviorism* (1925), and *Psychological Care of the Infant and Child* (1928).

WECHSLER ADULT INTELLIGENCE SCALE (WAIS)

Definition
The Wechsler Adult Intelligence Scale (WAIS) is a standardized psychological test consisting of a Verbal Scale and a Performance Scale. Each of these scales contains a number of subtests capable of assessing different dimensions of intelligence. The scoring of the test yields an overall intelligence quotient (IQ) as well as a Verbal IQ and a Performance IQ.

Example
Odell, age twenty-five, is having his intelligence tested with the WAIS. One subtest of the Verbal Scale is called *Similarities*. Odell is asked a question from this subtest. The question is, 'In what way are the sun and the moon similar?' (Note: This question is not actually on the test, and is intended only as an illustration. Items on the test are kept confidential to insure its validity.) Odell answers, 'The sun and the moon are astronomical objects.' This answer is scored as correct. Every item on the test is scored as correct or incorrect. A grand total is arrived at, and this is converted to an IQ score based on Odell's age of twenty-five. Odell's overall IQ turns out to be 112, suggesting he is in the Bright Normal classification (see intelligence quotient).

Connections
One of the chief advantages of the WAIS is its ability to yield both a Verbal IQ and a Performance IQ. The author of the WAIS, clinical psychologist David Wechsler, recognized that there is more than one kind of intelligence. Some people are very good with concepts and ideas, but they cannot easily build or construct things. Others are good with their hands, but have little use for abstractions and the world of thought. Still others are

comfortable in either domain, and these people may have both a high verbal and a high performance IQ.

Subtests associated with the Verbal Scale are titled Information, Comprehension, Arithmetic, Similarities, Digit Span, and Vocabulary. Subtests associated with the Performance Scale are titled Digit Symbol, Picture Completion, Block Design, Picture Arrangement, and Object Assembly. The titles of the subtests are roughly descriptive of the kinds of tasks demanded of the subject being tested.

There is also a test developed by David Wechsler for children called the Wechsler Intelligence Scale for Children (WISC). Like the adult scale, it also yields a Verbal IQ and a Performance IQ.

The Wechsler Scales are popular intelligence tests, and are used in many settings including mental hospitals, schools, and clinics.

WERTHEIMER, MAX
(1880–1943)

Max Wertheimer was a German psychologist and the father of Gestalt psychology (see entry). It was while he was teaching at the University of Frankfurt that Gestalt psychology was born. Using Wolfgang Köhler (see entry) and Kurt Koffka as subjects, the first experiment in Gestalt psychology was conducted on the phenomenon of apparent movement, named by Wertheimer the *phi phenomenon*. The *phi* phenomenon takes place every time one sees a motion picture. What is essentially a set of still slides is perceived, if presented in a certain way, as movement. Wertheimer was able to show, using a tachistoscope to produce the effect, that the *phi* phenomenon depended on critical time intervals. More importantly, he argued that the phenomenon could not be explained in terms of discrete sensory elements or any other set of psychological elements. It was an irreducible experience in which the Gestalt, or organized whole, *preceded* psychological parts. In so arguing, Wertheimer flew in the face of the then prestigious school of *structuralism* and the teachings of Wilhelm Wundt (see entries).

After Köhler and Koffka served as subjects in the first Gestalt psychology experiment, Wertheimer explained the experiment to them. (They did not know the experiment's purpose while they were serving as subjects.) After Köhler and Koffka understood the experiment, they became enthusiastic supporters of Gestalt psychology and did much to advance its position. All three men emigrated to the United States eventually, and established Gestalt psychology as a school in that country.

During the time he lived in Germany Wertheimer became a personal friend of Albert Einstein, and studied his creative processes, with Einstein's cooperation, from the Gestalt psychology point of view. He was able to show that Einstein's inspiration often began with a grand idea, essentially a Gestalt, and details such as a specific formula were derived from the idea. Wertheimer's discussion of Einstein's creative processes can be found in Wertheimer's book *Productive Thinking* (1959).

Wertheimer formulated a number of laws of perceptual organization such as *closure* and the *figure-ground relationship* (see entries). A basic assumption of these laws is that they are inborn. Our tendency to see objects of perception as organized wholes is a given of the way in which the human nervous system processes data. Thus Gestalt psychology is essentially based on the doctrine of *nativism* (see entry).

Wertheimer applied his ideas to educational psychology. He argued that children need to be taught global concepts that help them attain an overall insight before they are introduced to particulars. If particulars are taught first, the student is often confused and fails to understand the meaning of what is being learned.

Although Wertheimer was influential, he was not a prolific author. Köhler's writings did more to advance Gestalt psychology than did Wertheimer's. Two of Wertheimer's important publications are the seminal article 'Experimental Studies of the Perception of Movement' published in Germany in 1912 and his book *Productive Thinking* (1959).

WILL

Definition
The will is thought of as a mental faculty enabling the individual to make conscious choices. Deciding between alternatives, taking positive action, or inhibiting action are all powers traditionally associated with the will.

Example
Mary has been trying to stop smoking with very little success. At

one point she tells a friend, 'I guess I just don't have much willpower.' This statement implies the acceptance of the existence of the will on Mary's part. It also implies that the capacity of her will to inhibit action – resisting cigarettes – is weak.

Connections
The value of the concept of the will has been much debated in psychology. Behavioral psychologists, for example, think that the concept of the will has been overworked. They say the concept is largely circular. If Mary doesn't stop smoking, it is because she has no willpower. But why do we say she has no willpower? Because she doesn't stop smoking. Behavioral psychologists argue it would be better to examine Mary's specific smoking habits with an eye to how they might be modified.

Another perennial debate in both philosophy and psychology has revolved around the question, 'Is the will free?' One set of thinkers argue in favor of a doctrine called *voluntarism*, meaning that human beings are conscious and can make real choices for which they must be held fully responsible. Another set of thinkers argue in favor of *determinism*, suggesting that all behavior is caused.

WILL TO MEANING

Definition
According to the psychiatrist Viktor Frankl, the will to meaning is an inborn impulse to find purpose and significance in life.

Example
Frankl says that the will to meaning is satisfied by discovering positive values. Bramwell, age forty-two, is the father of three children. He believes that it is important that he be the best father he can be because he cares deeply about the well-being of his children. This is an example of a positive value. If Bramwell has a number of similar values such as believing that it is important to love his wife, being concerned about the health of his aging parents, and striving for excellence in his vocation, then his life will be filled with meaning.

Connections
Frankl along with advocates of humanistic psychology (see entry) has taken note of the fact that an increasing number of

troubled persons are complaining of loss of meaning in life. They may not put it in precisely this way. Instead, they may complain vaguely that life makes no sense, nothing adds up, everything's silly, there's no point in doing anything, and so forth. Such individuals, says Frankl, are suffering from an *existential vacuum*, a feeling that life has a hole or empty spot in it. The existential vacuum exists in such persons because they have lost sight of positive values. They may have developed the idea that it is pointless to raise children, that a loving relationship with a member of the opposite sex is a myth, that the human race is on a fast road to nowhere, and so forth.

The only cure for the existential vacuum is the rediscovery of lost values. Frankl helps troubled persons do this by means of an approach known as logotherapy. *Logotherapy* is a kind of psychotherapy (see entry) consisting of a set of discussions about the meaning of life. The logotherapist uses logic, persuasion, and any other means at his or her disposal to point the suffering individual in the direction of positive values. Often there is a rebirth of meaning in the person's life.

WUNDT, WILHELM
(1832–1920)

Wilhelm Wundt was a philosopher, a physiologist, a psychologist, and the father of structuralism (see entry). He founded the world's first psychological laboratory at the University of Leipzig in 1879, and this date is taken to be a turning point in the history of psychology. Before 1879 psychology had the status of a subfield of philosophy. After 1879 psychology was recognized at the university level as a major field of study in its own right.

Wundt was greatly influenced by John Locke (see entry) and British empiricism in general. Wundt believed that the primary purpose of psychology is to study how associations of sensations and simple ideas form complex ideas. The tool for studying association was termed *introspection*, a process requiring trained subjects to look into their own consciousness and report their discoveries.

Wundt's approach to psychology was the earliest one, and in consequence it had high status and great prestige for about thirty years. However, it was eventually attacked from many sides, and was considered to be a dead school of psychology by the time Wundt was an old man (see *structuralism*).

251

WUNDT, WILHELM

Wundt's interests were wide-ranging. For example, between 1900 and 1920 he published ten volumes of a work titled *Folk Psychology*. In this work he explores the psychological development of humankind. Other publications by Wundt include *Physiological Psychology* (1880) and *Outlines of Psychology* (1896).

Y

YOGA

Definition
Yoga is a mental and physical discipline aiming to attain mystical union of the individual with the All, the Universe, the Great Myself, Cosmic Consciousness, or the Godhead.

Example
The mystical union spoken of in the definition is called in yoga *samadhi*. In the book *Autobiography of a Yogi* the Swami Paramahansa Yogananda describes *samadhi* with ecstatic phrases such as *torrential bliss* and *blessed experience*. In reading Yogananda's account one receives an impression of great joy and meaning. *Samadhi* is by its very nature a relatively brief experience, and the yogi must 'return to Earth.' Nonetheless, it is possible to repeat *samadhi* for renewed inspiration.

Connections
Yoga is of interest to Western psychologists for at least two reasons. First, practitioners of a system known as *raja yoga*, or royal yoga, are often adept at altering consciousness through meditation. Their methods have been explored in connection with biofeedback training (see entry). Second, yogis claim to have paranormal experiences such as telepathy and extrasensory perception. So their ideas have been studied by psychologists interested in researching psi abilities (see entry).

Yoga originated in India, and has historical roots going back more than two thousand years.

YOUNG-HELMHOLTZ THEORY

Definition
The Young-Helmholtz theory of color vision postulates that color vision is made possible by the existence of three kinds of neurons in the retina. These neurons are differentially sensitive to the wavelengths of light associated with the sensations of red, green, and blue.

Example
Let's say that one is looking at a red object. How does one see the color? According to the Young-Helmoltz theory the impression of red arises from wavelengths of light approximately 700 nanometers in length. (Wavelengths of light are associated with the electromagnetic spectrum, and constitute a narrow band of that spectrum ranging from 400 to 700 nanometers. A *nanometer* is one billionth of a meter.) Cones, specialized neurons in the retina, particularly sensitive to light of 700 nanometers depolarize or 'fire,' and this is experienced as red.

Connections
The Young-Helmholtz theory was independently postulated by physicists Thomas Young (1773–1824) and Hermann Ludwig Ferdinand von Helmholtz (1821–1894). It is the first great physiological theory of color vision.

According to the Young-Helmholtz theory, color experiences other than red, green, and blue are explained in terms of the well-known laws of light mixing. Thus if the retina is stimulated by all of the wavelengths at one time, one sees white. If the retina is stimulated by light of approximately 600 nanometers, it simultaneously excites neurons maximally sensitive to light of 700 nanometers and also light of 400 nanometers. Either excitation alone would produce either a red or a green sensation. However, working together the sensation produced is yellow.

At this point the theory runs into a major snag. Persons who are red-green blind see yellow perfectly well! And yet the theory does not predict this. On the contrary, the theory assumes that something is defective or lacking in the cones of persons with red-green blindness. And therefore they should also have trouble seeing yellow if yellow arises from the simultaneous firings of two kinds of cones.

Because of problems in the Young-Helmholtz theory other theories of color vision have arisen. For example, the Ladd-

254

Franklin theory postulates the existence of a fourth kind of cone, one that is sensitive to light of 600 nanometers, a cone producing a sensation of yellow. Thus there may be four, or even more, primary sensations involved in color vision.

Although there are a number of color theories, the important point is that most of them assume the existence of specialized cones with differential sensitivity to specific wavelengths of light. Contemporary physiological research supports this general view. Thus the most important basic concept in the Young-Helmholtz theory continues to receive wide support.

Z

ZEN·

Definition

Zen is a form of meditative Buddhism aiming to help the individual achieve a state of enlightenment characterized by the direct experience of the true nature of reality without the intermediaries of abstractions, words, beliefs, concepts, or dualisms. (Although it is conventional to use the word *Zen* as a complete term, the more formal and complete usage is *Zen Buddhism*.)

Example

Wade J., a professor of philosophy at a university in the United States, has been granted a one-year sabbatical leave in order to study Zen under the auspices of a *roshi*, or Zen master, in a temple in Japan. Each day Wade sits and meditates with a group of young monks. He also has regular brief private interviews with the Zen master in order to help Wade evaluate his progress toward *satori*, or enlightenment.

After one year of work the Zen master is unable to verify for Wade that he has even once reached *satori*. Wade's descriptions of his experiences and altered states of consciousness during meditation fall far short of what the *roshi* would be willing to call *satori*. He tells Wade that he is too intense, that he has been trying too hard. He is like a teacup that is filled to the brim. More tea cannot be added. The cup must be emptied. Wade is so full of Zen, so interested in it, that no Zen can be added. The Zen master advises Wade to continue meditating on a less regular basis with a *roshi* in the United States.

Wade continues working toward *satori* when he returns to the United States, but in a less intense manner. After two more years of meditation he suddenly has an unexpected change of perception in which he is unable to discriminate himself from the external world. Everything is Self; or everything exists but Self. He is not sure. He seems to be conscious, but he is not conscious that he is conscious. *He literally cannot think.* He feels as confused and helpless as an infant. When he comes out of this state and describes it to the Zen master in the United States, he is told that he has attained *satori.*

The experience leaves him a very changed person. It is as if a flash of lightning has illuminated a previously dark landscape. Now that the lightning is gone, the landscape is still remembered. Wade still recalls what it is like to be unable to perceive the world in categories. *Dualisms* such as I-You, Success-Failure, Life-Death, Good-Bad, and so forth are seen by Wade as mental constructions, not ultimate realities. He develops a much more relaxed and less striving attitude toward life. For years he wanted to be a famous philosopher. Now he is much more content to live each day on its own terms, taking satisfaction in small events unpreoccupied with lofty goals.

He even gives up meditation and never again strives for a second *satori.* Like a voyager who has arrived home at last by the use of a certain bridge, he can burn the bridge behind him. He no longer needs it.

Connections

The Japanese word *Zen* is derived from the Chinese word *ch'an,* meaning meditation. There are two principal schools of Zen in Japan, the Rinzai school and the Soto school. The *Rinzai school* uses the *koan,* or paradoxical question, as a device to bring about a rapid or sudden *satori.* The novice meditates upon seemingly meaningless questions such as, 'What is the sound of one hand clapping?' The *Soto* school emphasizes *zazen,* or just sitting quietly in meditation. (Wade's two Zen masters were members of the Soto school. Perhaps this is why Wade's *satori* was so long in coming.)

Zen is of interest to Western psychologists for at least two reasons. First, it is clear that Zen meditators can alter their states of consciousness. *Roshis* have been studied by physiological psychologists, and are able to produce above average amounts of the alpha rhythm in electroencephalograms (see entry) taken during meditation. The alpha rhythm is the rhythm associated with relaxation. Thus the study of Zen has implications for biofeedback training (see entry).

Second, Zen teaches a philosophy of life, a way of liberation from unnecessary suffering. Although *roshis* often deny that there is any explicit teaching in Zen, more than one Western observer has detected in Zen a general theme of non-striving, of accepting things as they come. This is only reasonable in view of the fact that Zen is actually a kind of Buddhism, and the same general theme is found in Buddhism. Consequently, the teachings of Zen have been of interest to students of psychotherapy and personality (see entries).

Bibliography

This is a selective bibliography. A complete listing of all of the books and articles consulted in preparing *A Dictionary of Key Words in Psychology* would number more than five hundred. The sources listed here are either primary ones or particularly useful ones. The majority of them have the additional advantage of being readily obtainable.

Ackerman, E., Ellis, L. B., and Williams, L. E. *Biophysical Science* (2nd ed.). Englewood Cliffs, N. J.: Prentice-Hall, 1979.

Adler, A. *What Life Should Mean to You*. New York: Blue Ribbon Books, 1937.

American Psychiatric Association. *A Psychiatric Glossary* (5th ed.). Washington, D. C.: American Psychiatric Association, 1980.

American Psychiatric Association. *Diagnostic and Statistical Manual of Mental Disorders* (3rd ed.). Washington, D. C.: American Psychiatric Association, 1980.

Anastasi, A. *Psychological Testing* (5th ed.). New York: Macmillan, 1982.

Aquinas, T. *Basic Writings of Saint Thomas Aquinas*. Edited by Anton C. Pegis. New York: Random House, 1945.

Aristotle. *Works*. Translated under the editorship of W. D. Ross. Oxford: Clarendon Press, 1952.

Aronson, E. *The Social Animal*. San Francisco: W. H. Freeman, 1976.

Bateson, G. 'Breaking Out of the Double Bind.' As interviewed in *Psychology Today* by D. Goleman, 12 (1978), 42–51.

Berne, E. *Games People Play*. New York: Grove Press, 1964.

Binder, V., Binder, A., and Rimland, B. (Eds.). *Modern Therapies*. Englewood Cliffs, N. J.: Prentice-Hall, 1976.

Binet, A. and Simon, T. *A Method of Measuring the Development of Intelligence of Young Children*. Translated by Clara H. Town. Chicago: Chicago Medical Book Co., 1915.

Boring, E. G. *A History of Experimental Psychology* (2nd ed.). New York: Appleton-Century-Crofts, 1950.

Coopersmith, S. *The Antecedents of Self-Esteem*. San Francisco: W. H. Freeman, 1967.

BIBLIOGRAPHY

Corsini, R. (Ed.). *Current Psychotherapies*. Itasca, Ill.: F. E. Peacock, 1973.

Craighead, W. E., Kazdin, A. E., and Mahoney, M. J. *Behavior Modification: Principles, Issues, and Applications*. Boston: Houghton Mifflin, 1976.

Delgado, J. M. R. *Physical Control of the Mind: Toward a Psychocivilized Society*. New York: Harper & Row, 1969.

Descartes, R. *Discourse on the Method of Rightly Conducting the Reason*. Translated by Elizabeth S. Haldane and G. R. T. Ross. Cambridge: The University Press, 1912.

Eccles, J. 'The Synapse.' In *Progress in Psychobiology*. R. F. Thompson (Ed.). San Francisco: W. H. Freeman, 1976.

Ellis, A.. and Harper, R. A. *A New Guide to Rational Living*. Hollywood, Calif.: Wilshire Book Co., 1976.

Erikson, E. H. *Childhood and Society* (2nd ed.) New York: Norton, 1963.

Eysenck, H. J. (Ed.). *A Model for Intelligence*. New York: Springer-Verlan, 1982.

Feshbach, S. and Weiner, B. *Personality*. Lexington, Mass.: D. C. Heath, 1982.

Fine, R. *A History of Psychoanalysis*. New York: Columbia University Press, 1979.

Fischer, K. W. and Lazerson, A. *Human Development*. San Francisco: W. H. Freeman, 1984.

Frankl, V. E. *Man's Search for Meaning*. Boston: Beacon Press, 1962.

Freud, S. *The Interpretation of Dreams*. London: Hogarth Press, 1900.

Freud, S. *The Ego and the Id*. London: Hogarth Press, 1923.

Freud, S. *An Outline of Psychoanalysis*. New York: Norton, 1949.

Gregory, R. *Eye and Brain: The Psychology of Seeing*. New York: McGraw-Hill, 1973.

Hall, C. S. and Lindzey, G. *Theories of Personality* (3rd ed.). New York: Wiley, 1978.

Harlow, H. F. 'The Formation of Learning Sets.' *Psychological Review*, 56 (1949), 51–65.

Hilgard, E. R. and Hilgard, J. R. *Hypnosis and the Relief of Pain*. Los Altos, CA.: William Kaufmann, 1983.

Horney, K. *Our Inner Conflicts*. New York: W. W. Norton, 1945.

Hunt, M. *The Universe Within*. New York: Simon & Schuster, 1982.

James, W. *The Principles of Psychology*. New York: Henry Holt, 1890.

Jung, C. *Modern Man in Search of a Soul*. New York: Harcourt, 1933.

Jung, C. *Memories, Dreams, and Reflections*. New York: Holt, Rinehart & Winston, 1972.

Kant, I. *The Critique of Pure Reason*. Translated by J. M. D. Meiklejohn. London: Bohn, 1855.

Köhler, W. *Gestalt Psychology*. New York: Liveright, 1947.

Lazarus, A. A. *The Practice of Multi-Modal Therapy*. New York: McGraw-Hill, 1981.

McClelland, D. D. *Studies in Motivation*. New York: Appleton-Century-Crofts, 1955.

Maccoby, E. E. and Jacklin, C. N. *The Psychology of Sex Differences*. Stanford, CA.: Stanford University Press, 1974.

Maslow, A. H. *Towards a Psychology of Being*. Princeton, N.J.: D. Van Nostrand, 1962.

Masters, W. H. and Johnson, V. E. *Human Sexual Response*. Boston: Little, Brown and Company, 1966.

Murray, H. A. *Explorations in Personality*. New York: Oxford University Press, 1938.

Myers, D. G. *Social Psychology*. New York: McGraw-Hill, 1983.

Neher, A. *The Psychology of Transcendence*. Englewood Cliffs, N. J.: Prentice-Hall, 1980.

Pavlov, I. P. *Selected Works*. K. S. Kostoyants (Ed.). Moscow: Foreign Language Publishing House, 1955.

Piaget, J. *The Language and Thought of the Child*. New York: Harcourt, Brace, 1926.

Piaget, J. *The Child's Conception of the World*. London: Routledge and Kegan Paul, 1951.

Rahe, R. H. and Holmes, T. H. 'Life Crisis and Major Health Change.' *Psychosomatic Medicine*, 28 (1966), 774.

Restak, R. M. *The Brain*. New York: Doubleday, 1979.

Rogers, C. *On Becoming a Person*. Boston: Houghton Mifflin, 1961.

Rosenhan, D. L. and Seligman, M. E. *Abnormal Psychology*. New York: Norton, 1984.

Selye, H. *The Stress of Life*. New York: McGraw-Hill, 1956.

Skinner, B. F. *The Behavior of Organisms*. New York: Appleton-Century-Crofts, 1938.

Skinner, B.F. *About Behaviorism*. New York: Alfred A. Knopf, 1974.

Storr, A. *The Essential Jung*. Princeton, N. J.: Princeton University Press, 1983.

Sperry, R. W. 'The Great Cerebral Commisure.' In *Psychobiology: The Biological Bases of Behavior*. J. L. McGaugh, N. W. Weinberger, and R. E. Whalen (Eds.). San Francisco: W. H. Freeman, 1967.

Suzuki, D. T. *What Is Zen?* New York: Harper & Row, 1972.

Thompson, R. F. *An Introduction to Physiological Psychology*. New York: Harper & Row, 1976.

Watson, J. B. *Behaviorism* (2nd ed.). New York: Norton, 1930,

Watson, R. I. *The Great Psychologists* (3rd ed.). Philadelphia: J. B. Lippincott, 1971.

Wender, P. H. and Klein, D. F. *Mind, Mood, and Medicine*. New York: Farrar, Straus, and Giroux, 1981.

Wertheimer, M. *Productive Thinking*. New York: Harper & Row, 1959.

Wilson, E. O. *Sociobiology: The New Synthesis*. Cambridge, Mass.: The Belknap Press of Harvard University Press, 1975.

Yalom, I. D. *Existential Psychotherapy*. New York: Basic Books, 1980.

Yogananda, P. *Autobiography of a Yogi*. Los Angeles: Self-Realization Fellowship, 1974.

Topical index

TOPICAL INDEX

Name index

Subject index

SUBJECT INDEX

SUBJECT INDEX